S. N. Haskell
Man of Action

S. N. Haskell
Man of Action

by
Ella M. Robinson

TEACH Services, Inc.
PUBLISHING
www.TEACHServices.com • (800) 367-1844

World rights reserved. This book or any portion thereof may not be copied or reproduced in any form or manner whatever, except as provided by law, without the written permission of the publisher, except by a reviewer who may quote brief passages in a review.

The author assumes full responsibility for the accuracy of all facts and quotations as cited in this book. The opinions expressed in this book are the author's personal views and interpretations, and do not necessarily reflect those of the publisher.

This book is provided with the understanding that the publisher is not engaged in giving spiritual, legal, medical, or other professional advice. If authoritative advice is needed, the reader should seek the counsel of a competent professional.

Facsimile Reproduction

As this book played a formative role in the development of Christian thought and the publisher feels that this book, with its candor and depth, still holds significance for the church today. Therefore the publisher has chosen to reproduce this historical classic from an original copy. Frequent variations in the quality of the print are unavoidable due to the condition of the original. Thus the print may look darker or lighter or appear to be missing detail, more in some places than in others.

Copyright © 2004 TEACH Services, Inc.
ISBN-13: 978-1-57258-282-8(Paperback)
Library of Congress Control Number: 2004105704

www.TEACHServices.com • (800) 367-1844

Preface

Among the most colorful of the early Seventh-day Adventist church workers was Stephen Nelson Haskell. A self-made man, fearless, and endowed with ingenuity, courage, and vision, Haskell led in a number of enterprises that were accepted and established by the denomination. He was the first to make an around-the-world trip in the interest of Adventist missions, taking almost two years. He was a leader in city mission work, and we think of him as the father of the tract and missionary societies from which developed the Book and Bible Houses and two departments of the church—the Publishing and the Home Missionary (now the Department of Lay Activities).

Mrs. Ella M. Robinson, granddaughter of James and Ellen White, is well qualified to write the story of Stephen Haskell. In her early teens she was in his Bible class during the first year of the Avondale Training School, in New South Wales, Australia; also, she met him often as he made frequent visits to Sunnyside, Ellen G. White's home in Australia, and later to Elmshaven, in California. But Mrs. Robinson did not rest alone on memory for this account. She was given access to the White-Haskell correspondence, comprising nearly three hundred letters written by Mrs. White to the Haskells and many hundreds of letters by the Haskells to James and Ellen White and their son, William C. White, the author's father. These letters are now housed in the White Estate vault. Published reports in the *Review and Herald* and other denominational journals also furnished rich contemporary data for the story.

We are admonished that as a people "we have nothing to fear for the future, except as we shall forget the way the Lord has led us, and His teaching in our past history" (*Life Sketches,* p. 196). Mrs. Robinson is to be commended for this volume, the result of two years' painstaking work in research and writing.

ARTHUR L. WHITE, Secretary
The Ellen G. White Estate

Washington, D.C.
January 1, 1967

Contents

Why Elder Haskell?	7
Preaching and Peddling	13
Layman Leader	24
The "Child of His Hope"	36
That New England School	48
Across the Waters and Back	57
Pioneering in Australia	69
In New Zealand	79
Again in Europe	89
Scouting for Missions	95
An Adventurous Journey	103
Calcutta and Beyond	110
Alone, Yet Not Alone	121
With the Pioneers in Africa	130
Teaching at Avondale	143
The Sure Foundation	160
Meeting the Holy Flesh Fanaticism	168
The New York City Mission	177
The Crisis in New York	189
Traveling Teacher	196
At Loma Linda	211
Leading California	217
The Temperance Campaign	225
Workers Together With God	235
Finishing the Course	246

Why Elder Haskell?

A Word From the Author

GENEVIEVE MELENDY closed the door of the telephone switchboard office in the General Conference building. Her day's work was finished. On her way down the hall she glanced into the lighted room where I was still at work. "What are you doing with all those old files of letters?" she asked.

"I'm scanning one or two thousand pages of correspondence and some hundreds of articles and reports, gathering items from which to piece together a story of Stephen N. Haskell's life."

"I'm glad somebody's doing that," she said, adding, "Did you know that he was responsible for my being a Seventh-day Adventist?" Then she told me the story of her grandfather's conversion.

In the early days of his preaching, Haskell held a series of tent meetings in Amherst, New Hampshire. Crowds came to listen as, night after night, he presented the message. One young man, Bryant Melendy, attended faithfully. On the closing night, when the call was made for any who were willing to render full allegiance to Christ by keeping all His commandments to come forward, Bryant walked to the front of the tent. He walked alone. Every eye was upon this shy young man, but not one person joined him.

The next morning at breakfast Bryant's father remarked, "Those meetings surely gave us something to think about, but I don't believe the Lord is too particular about which day we keep holy. Do what you think is right, Bryant, but if you keep the seventh day as the Sabbath you will be out of step with the whole community."

"It doesn't concern me what others think about my decision," the young man spoke firmly, "but I must obey God at all costs."

Doubtless Haskell, the young preacher, thought that his long and earnest effort at Amherst was a near failure. Could he have looked into the future and realized that his one lone convert would become the progenitor of a whole band of gospel workers, his discouragement would have turned to rejoicing. Could he have known that ten or more denominational workers would trace their lineage back to Bryant Melendy, he would have counted all his effort as nought, in contrast with the reward gained from that one small-town effort in New Hampshire.

The sturdy threads of Haskell's influence were interwoven with many lives. I once asked the well-known radio preacher H. M. S. Richards if he had known Stephen Haskell.

"Yes, indeed," he replied, and related the following incident. "At a camp meeting held in Waterloo, Quebec, in the year 1921, I mentioned that I needed more songbooks for an evangelistic effort I was conducting. S. N. Haskell, almost ninety years old, was present. He met me outside the tent, pulled out his pocketbook, and emptied it, pouring its entire contents into my hands. It amounted to a little more than seven dollars, and paid for several copies of *Christ in Song*.

"I remember Stephen Haskell as a deep and constant student of the Word of God," continued Elder Richards. "He hardly dared take out his Bible while waiting at a station for a train, for fear he would become so absorbed in studying some line of truth that he would lose all contact with time. His train could come and go and he be left sitting there in the station still studying his Bible."

At the Review and Herald, D. E. Mansell, one of the book editors, asked, "In your book, will you tell about the 'haskell'?"

"The Haskell? The entire book is about Haskell! What do you mean?"

Brother Mansell then told me about the "haskell," said to have been invented by S. N. Haskell. "It's a little device," he explained, "for pulling up tent stakes. It is still in use, I believe, on the New England campgrounds. It consists of a lever on wheels with a chain attached to the end of the shorter arm. With the chain wrapped around the stake, and with the axle acting as a fulcrum, the operator pulls down on the handle and quickly and easily draws the stake out of the ground." It seems that Elder Haskell was a handyman as well as a great preacher.

That remark about the handyman brought to my mind a scene I once witnessed on the Avondale school estate in Australia. The elder, in overalls and rubber boots, was working with a group of students building a wooden bridge. He was a favorite leader of the work teams. No matter what the job, whether plowing or planting, building fences or draining land, he always found the best and easiest way of accomplishing it. Then, too, he was ever ready to enter into individual experiences and problems of students in an understanding and helpful manner.

Many people cherish memories regarding Elder Haskell. When Eugene Farnsworth was a lad in Washington, New Hampshire, some seventy miles northwest of South Lancaster, Haskell, then in the prime of life, visited churches in that area. On one occasion, Farnsworth recalled, snow was deep and the weather extremely cold. "I remember seeing him pushing his way with his horse through the deep snowdrifts, visiting all the members. . . . This was characteristic of his life and labors throughout the long years of his ministry."[1]

A story is related demonstrating Elder Haskell's faith in God's personal guidance. While on a preaching tour in Georgia, Haskell felt impressed to leave the train unexpectedly at a deserted-looking station, explaining briefly to his secretary, a young man traveling with him, "Someone here needs help." The two were soon standing on the station platform with baggage piled beside them. There was not a soul in sight. They waited, praying silently.

Soon a car appeared. The driver greeted them. "Are you expecting someone to meet you?" he asked. "No," replied the elder, "but perhaps you can tell us if there are any Seventh-day Adventists in this part of the country?"

"Yes," replied the man. "An Adventist family lives about six miles from here. They operate a little school. I'll be glad to take you there."

The story continues: "Away they went with grateful hearts. Upon arriving, Elder Haskell remarked that he would go alone to the door of the house. After repeatedly knocking at the door he heard a faint voice inviting him in. As he entered he knew there was sickness in the home. The mother and her two daughters were ill, and the mother was quite discouraged. After a few kindly remarks and inquiries, Elder Haskell picked up the family Bible from the nearby table and read some of our heavenly Father's choice promises to the poor mother and daughters. Then came his warm and tender prayer for the sick ones, and heaven seemed nearer.

"He learned that the family conducted a self-supporting school for the neighborhood. Soon he saw children coming to the little schoolhouse close by and begin playing in their schoolyard, doubtless hoping their good teacher would be able that morning to teach. Elder Haskell gently advised the mother to let him send the children home, and tell them not to return for two weeks. This was done. The mother recovered quickly, also the girls, and after they had had a good rest, the school work was taken up again. Years later the mother told me that Elder Haskell's visit put new life into their hearts and into their work, and that they were never again discouraged over it." [2]

When as a girl I sat under Elder Haskell's tutelage at Avondale, I had no idea that at some time, then in the distant future, I would be asked to write the story of his life. Had I known it, I might have given more careful attention to his reminiscences of pioneer days in the Advent Movement. I would also have plied him with many questions. My memory yet retains some of his favorite and oft-repeated stories. Other incidents have been gathered from Haskell reports and articles—miles and miles of them—printed in the *Review* and other denominational journals, and from his voluminous personal correspondence.

Incidents from these sources have been drawn together into a narrative, giving a partial portrayal of what God accomplished through one individual wholly dedicated to His service.

Many titles have been accorded Stephen Haskell. He is "Father of the Tract and Missionary Societies," "Prince of Pioneers," and the "Apostle of Personal Evangelism." He was an early and staunch supporter of health and temperance reform, of true education, and of God's leadership through the Spirit of Prophecy writings.

An unusual measure of practical common sense illuminated his counsels. And in his character were blended the qualities of faith, humility, and love—faith that never hesitated to advance at God's command, however great the difficulties before him; humility that often necessitated the laying aside of his own cherished plans that he might accept divine guidance; and love that seemed to embrace with a heavenly influence every soul it touched.

A word of appreciation is due to Mrs. Alta Robinson for her efficient assistance in the preparation of this manuscript; also to Arthur L. White for his help in preparing this work and for writing the chapter "Meeting the Holy Flesh Fanaticism" (pages 168-176).

ELLA M. ROBINSON

[1] *Review and Herald,* Dec. 14, 1922, p. 17.
[2] *Ibid.,* Dec. 6, 1962.

The "haskell," a lever on wheels used for pulling up tent stakes, said to have been invented by S. N. Haskell.

S. N. Haskell in his prime.

Preaching and Peddling

YOUNG STEPHEN HASKELL stood by Mr. How's bedside—so the story goes—and listened to his employer's dying words:

"You've been faithful, Stephen. I appreciate your help. Now I'm leaving you, for I can't live long. The farm and everything on it will be left in your hands. I know you'll do your best." With difficulty the man continued, "But Stephen, I'm worried about what will happen to Mary. For years I've been both father and mother to her. Now, with her so helpless and dependent, I don't know what to do." Tears glistened on his pale cheeks as he concluded, "This is a lot to ask of a young man like you—but when I'm gone, could you look after her, Stephen? She has no one else in all the world!"

The young man hesitated. These were heavy responsibilities to be placed on the shoulders of a hired boy seventeen years of age. For several years Mary had been partially paralyzed, and he had helped the father when she needed to be lifted and carried in and out of the house. He had become fond of her. Solemnly he promised Mr. How that he would fulfill every obligation, then left the room.

After Mr. How's funeral, Stephen spoke words of comfort to Mary. Then he sat thinking for a long time—wondering and praying. How could he fulfill his promise except to marry the lonely invalid? He was not yet eighteen, and Mary was about forty years old! In spite of her age and her helplessness, Stephen kept his promise. He proposed. Mary accepted and said that she loved him. They were married! He felt at the time and ever afterward that the difference in their ages was minimized by the cultural and educational advantages she contributed. She had been a teacher. Her tastes were literary; she enjoyed writing poetry. Also she had collected a library of choice books, which they often read together.

Mary's nature was deeply spiritual and at the same time thoroughly practical. Always patient and contented, never complaining under depressing circumstances or physical suffering, she cultivated sunny thoughts and had cheering words for those around her. More than forty years later, shortly after her death in 1894, Stephen wrote to Ellen G. White, in typewritten capital letters, "I LOVED HER AND SHE LOVED ME."

The youthful bridegroom was born in the town of Oakham, Massachusetts, April 22, 1833, "the year the stars fell." From early childhood he possessed the faculties of clear reasoning, prompt and independent action, and firm adherence to his decisions. Two stories he told of his boyhood days illustrate these characteristics.

The first related to an experience when he was eight years old. A temperance lecturer came to the town and gave a number of lectures. He presented the matter to the Sunday school. Stephen felt a desire to sign the pledge when he saw a number of others about his age, including his two sisters, go forward. But he was fond of sweet cider, and thought that his signing the pledge would prohibit his drinking it. So he began to wonder what serious thing would happen if he should not always keep his pledge.

When he asked, "What if the pledge is broken?" someone said that the names of the signers would be sent to Washington; and if the pledge was broken the name would be crossed from the roll. The thought of such dishonor settled the question with Stephen. "If I sign," he said to himself, "I will never break the pledge."

Someone asked whether drinking sweet cider would be a violation of the pledge.

"No," said the speaker; "sweet cider is the juice of worms and rotten apples; it is not breaking the pledge to eat rotten apples or drink the juice of worms."

Then Stephen signed the pledge, his appetite for sweet cider being considerably lessened.

By signing he became a member of the Cold Water Army, and received a silk badge inscribed with these words:

"So here we pledge perpetual hate
To all that can intoxicate."

The other incident occurred four years later. The teacher told the children that they must not play on the ice during the noon hour, and that he would punish anyone who did. So the boys talked it over.

Finally Stephen said, "He dare not kill us. If he should lick us it wouldn't last long; and if he only scolded us, that wouldn't amount to anything."

This settled the question. It is to be hoped that their pleasure exceeded the punishment they must have received!

At the age of fifteen Stephen was converted and joined the Congregational Church, of which his parents were members.

A little later, probably at the time of his marriage, he paid his father one hundred and fifty dollars for his time, which, he said, "was more than I was worth to him." In harmony with the then-existing custom, a son's time and earnings belonged to his father until he was twenty-one years of age.

At the time Stephen and Mary were married they were both Methodists. They knew God, and each strengthened the faith of the other as they prayed for Mary's healing. Within two years Mary's health was so far restored that she was able to resume many of her former activities. Of these activities we get a glimpse from one recorded statement that she "could manage spirited horses as few men could." In a letter written at the age of sixty-one Stephen speaks of always having from one to three horses on the place.

When Stephen was nineteen he heard a sermon on the Second Advent that thrilled and inspired him. This was his introduction to Adventists—not Sabbathkeeping Adventists, but others who had also been in the Miller movement of 1844. He began at once to share with others the good news of the imminent return of the Lord Jesus, which he ever afterward referred to as the "blessed hope." He talked of it whenever opportunity offered. One day while visiting an acquaintance, he was showing how the Scriptures are proved true by fulfilled prophecies.

"Stephen, why don't you preach?" the friend suggested. "You ought to hire a hall and preach."

"Well, I will," the young fellow answered half jokingly. "If you'll hire the hall, I'll preach."

A few days later his friend came to him: "We have the hall, now we want you to preach to us." Stephen was completely taken aback. Not willing to back down, however, he gathered up courage and met the appointment. He repeated to a full house the sermon that had set him on fire and which he remembered almost word for word, "sweating all the time," as he said afterward. His hearers were surprised with his message; more than this, they were thrilled. Soon a small company of earnest Christians gathered around Stephen, and he served them unofficially as religious leader.

Whenever he spoke of the coming of Jesus, gladness filled his heart, brightened his face, and animated his voice. The words, "You ought to preach! You ought to preach!" repeatedly sounded in his inner being. Was this the voice of God? What should he do? Or could this be the echo of his own desires, or, perhaps, of the undue persuasion of his friends?

Stephen also considered the fact that he had to earn a living for himself and Mary. A soapmaker who sold his own product, he was often on the road. "In those soap-selling days he often let his horse take its own time while he worked algebra problems and eventually mastered the subject. Perhaps it was the schoolteacher instinct in Mary, who, realizing that he needed the logical thinking in his sermons that the subject might give him, suggested the idea."[1]

The young man decided to put the problem to the test. He would preach. Yet he hesitated, fearful of embarrassment and failure.

He went to a little town on the shores of Lake Consecon, Ontario, on business. Asked to preach to the people there the same things he had been telling his friends, he accepted the challenge. Here was his opportunity to make a trial of preaching. If he failed, he would be among strangers, where it would not be so embarrassing to him. But if his preaching resulted in the conversion and baptism of some person or family, he would accept that as a sign that the inner voice he had heard was God's call to the ministry. Here is the story, gathered from several accounts which he wrote later:

At a certain house a woman welcomed him. After he had announced his mission, she invited him to hold a meeting in her home that evening. There was a houseful of eager listeners. After the meeting she told him that she had dreamed about him the evening before.

When he came, she noticed the peculiar color of his trousers and how short they were, and recognized him as the young man from the States whom she had seen in her dream. Arrangements were made for meetings to be held in a schoolhouse about four miles from her home.

Success attended his efforts. Evening after evening the schoolhouse was crowded, with people standing outside at the open windows. The blessing of God was so evident that Haskell began to wonder whether he should give his life to preaching. Still he had not received the definite answer for which he had prayed—that someone would ask for baptism. So he decided to close the lectures and return to the States. Yet how could he learn whether there was anyone under conviction? His days were so fully occupied preparing the evening sermons that he had no time to talk with people personally and to inquire into their religious experience.

After preaching in the schoolhouse for about ten days, he was invited to another neighborhood. He started to the second appointment on foot but was given a ride by a man driving a two-horse farm wagon. He learned that the farmer and his wife had been attending the meetings and that they both had experienced conversion and wanted to be baptized. The next time Haskell visited them he found not only the man and his wife but twenty-five persons desiring baptism. Accepting this as the asked-for sign, he decided to devote his life to preaching. Fired with zeal and unabashed by the fact that he was unordained, the young preacher baptized them all. One old man had threatened that if anyone should undertake to baptize his wife, he would go into the water and take her away. Haskell assured her that the Lord had said, "Believe, and be baptized," and that He would take care of her husband. As the old man watched the baptism from the shore, the Holy Spirit so rested upon him that he gave his heart to the Lord right there at the water's edge, and requested baptism himself.

In 1853, before his twenty-first birthday, Stephen attended an Adventist camp meeting in Winsted, Connecticut, in company with two or three other young men who were beginning to preach. Before returning home, Haskell decided to visit the Adventist group in Canada that had formed as a result of his preaching the year before. At

Haskell as a young preacher.

the Springfield, Massachusetts, railway station he surrendered his baggage check to the agent, then wondered what to do with his trunk. He did not wish the inconvenience of taking it on a journey that would have to be made partly by land and partly by water. The young men accompanying Stephen helped him solve his problem. They found William Saxby, a tinsmith for the railway company, who had a shop near the station. As Haskell himself relates:

"He kindly offered to take my trunk, and keep it for me as long as I wished. He was a Sabbath-keeper, and the first one whom I had ever met.

"At once the conversation turned, among those men who were with me, on the Sabbath question. I listened, and readily saw they had nothing from the Bible with which to vindicate themselves for the observance of the first day, and I knew I had nothing. It appeared to me, at the time, very strange that I could think of no scripture upon that point, but so it was. I soon made up my mind I would never be found in that condition again. After some conversation, William Saxby turned to me, and began to talk to me, when I abruptly replied, 'If you want to keep that old Jewish Sabbath, you can do so, but I never shall.' This ended all conversation at the time.

"That evening proved to be the evening for a meeting of the Sabbath-keepers, and we all were invited to go to meeting; but concluding from the conversation I had heard at the railway station, that we might have a hard time to defend the Sunday, I did not wish to go, and replied that I was not feeling very well, and thought I would not attend. Brother Saxby took in the situation at once, and said he did not feel very well, either, and he was not going to attend. So he took me home with him, and hung up a chart illustrating the three messages [of Revelation 14], the sanctuary, etc., . . . and gave me, in short, a synopsis of present truth.

"Although I did not at all believe in the explanation which he gave, I then and there fully made up my mind that I would examine the subject, and be prepared for him or any one else who ever in the future should present such views to me. . . .

"I remained with him until I left the town [on a preaching tour to Canada], and he very wisely avoided all conversation with me on the subject entirely new to me, upon which I was wholly unprepared to converse, and of which I did not wish to hear until I had investigated it, and could prove it to be false. Upon my leaving, he furnished me with a few small tracts. One was 'Elihu on the Sabbath.'

"I read and re-read the Sabbath tract, and I could see nothing but Scripture in it. Then I read my Bible, and became convinced of the truthfulness of the statements and position of the tract. I was then on a boat going to what was known as the 'Carrying Place,' to hold some meetings at the head of Consecon Lake, Canada.

"Sabbath morning the boat stopped about five miles from the landing I was booked for. . . . I got off at Trent, and went to the woods, and thus spent the day in reading my Bible and praying on the subject. Finally, before night, I came to the conclusion that, according to the best light I had, the seventh day was the Sabbath, and I would keep it until I could get further light. So I have kept it ever since." [2]

Stephen was not preaching for money. He had learned that there was little money in preaching unless the audience proved unusually generous; so he kept on with his soapmaking and selling, ingeniously combining his method of earning a living with his zeal and desire to work for the Lord.

During the following summer he attended an Adventist conference at Worcester, Massachusetts, with the intention of laying the Sabbath question before the people. It seemed so clear to him that he had no doubt of being able to convince every member present that it was the duty of man to keep the whole law of God. But he was greatly disappointed; he was not permitted to preach one sermon during the entire conference, and few would even discuss the subject.

However, at the close of the conference Thomas Hale, a friendly soul, out of sympathy (so Stephen thought) invited the young seventh-day keeper to his home in Hubbardston, Massachusetts. The Haskells rented rooms in the Hale house and remained with them that winter. Here he found a company of Adventists who were happy to have this ardent young man preach for them every Sunday. Soon the Hales and a number of others embraced the Sabbath and the third angel's message. They held meetings on Sabbaths, Sundays, and two evenings each week. They organized themselves into a church and celebrated the ordinance of foot washing, which was new to the Haskells.

About this time Haskell learned that there were people who refused to eat swine's flesh because, according to the Bible, it was unclean meat. He at once discontinued its use.

It was not long until S. G. Mathewson, pastor of this company of Adventist believers, came to Hubbardston to look after his flock. He labored to convince them that they had taken a wrong position regarding the seventh-day Sabbath; and as a result of his reasoning, several of them became confused. They said to Haskell, "When you talk to us it appears plain enough that the seventh day is the Sabbath; but when Mathewson talks to us, it appears that the law is abolished. Now will you have some conversation with him on this subject, so we can see who has the truth?"

Relating this experience years later, Haskell commented, "Of course I said 'yes,' but I was frightened almost out of my wits at the thought of it.

"At the close of an evening meeting, the brethren introduced the subject, and Elder Mathewson and I sat down at a long table, one at each end, and these friends stood on each side to listen. He first spoke rather impatiently, and said, 'Now, what is your strongest proof that the seventh day is the Sabbath?'

"After thinking a moment, I tremblingly said, 'The fourth commandment. That says the seventh day is the Sabbath, and I do not know anything to prove God ever contradicted it.' " [3]

Mathewson then quoted several texts in such a way as to make it appear that they sustained his position that the law had been abolished and that no one was under obligation to keep it. After he had quoted a text, placing his meaning upon it, Haskell would suggest reading it from the Bible. Then, as he read the scripture, he would place particular emphasis upon the words that showed up the error of his opponent's arguments. They spent an hour or more in this way. Haskell was sure that the Spirit of the Lord was helping him in his lack of experience; for the young men present failed to see any force in Mathewson's reasoning, and Mathewson himself seemed to see that Haskell was correct.

"Finally," wrote Haskell, "he quoted Acts 20:7, giving the text as evidence that the disciples did meet for worship on the first day. . . . Not knowing how it did read, [I] said, I did not think it read so. . . . In a fit of anger [he] closed his Bible, and threw it down upon the table, saying as he arose, 'I have heard enough about that old Sabbath question. I do not want to hear any more.' . . .

"When I went to my room, I turned to the text, and found that it *did* read as he had quoted; and it was evident that he had done the same, for in the morning he said to me, 'That scripture did read as I quoted last night.' The only reply I made was, 'Yes, I found it did.' This was my first experience in Sabbath-keeping, and the manner of embracing it."⁴ Perhaps Mathewson was as sincere as Haskell had been when he told William Saxby that he would "never keep that old Jewish Sabbath." But Mathewson was not sufficiently interested in the question to give it further study.

Only a few months previous to this experience Mary Haskell had met Saxby for the first time and had become convinced that the observance of the Bible Sabbath was a matter of importance. Although she had been scrupulously trained from early childhood in Sunday observance, she wrote in a letter to the *Review* that she was so deeply impressed by the Christian spirit in which Saxby presented the importance of keeping the commandments of God that she was convinced he had the truth, and joined him in Sabbathkeeping.

After this, when passing through Springfield, the Haskells were often guests at the home of their friends, the Saxbys. When apart, the two men continued their friendship through correspondence.

One wintry day when Haskell answered a knock on his door, he was greeted by a pleasant-faced man a little past middle age, who introduced himself as an Adventist preacher and an observer of the seventh day. He said, "I understand that you are a friend of William Saxby, and that you have recently begun keeping the Sabbath of the commandment. He has written and requested that I spend a little time with you, instructing you more fully in Bible truth."

Needless to say the stranger, who introduced himself as Joseph

Bates, was warmly welcomed, and soon was deep in Bible study with the Haskells. Bates also addressed the members of the little church. The Hales and others became interested, and united to form a Bible study group. On cold winter evenings they met around the long table in the Hale family's ample kitchen. For ten days the visitor remained in Hubbardston, studying the Bible with the Haskells and these new Sabbathkeepers.

Joseph Bates traced down the lines of Bible prophecy, covering the earth's history from earliest times to the consummation of the great controversy between good and evil. He dwelt long on his favorite theme, the three angels' messages of Revelation 14, which according to the prophecy were even now being proclaimed "to every nation, and kindred, and tongue, and people." The startling announcement of the first angel that the hour of God's judgment had come, with its clarion call to "worship him that made heaven and earth," laid fresh emphasis on the creatorship of God and upon the significance of the Sabbath as His memorial.

Elder Bates next took up progressively the important doctrines of salvation. His students followed closely, turning from text to text and making notes for further study. As they compared scripture with scripture, new light dawned upon their understanding. Traditional beliefs which had troubled them because of their inconsistency, and which had made religion seem mysterious and incomprehensible, were relinquished; and the beautiful facts of faith as taught by Christ and His apostles and prophets stood out in their glorious simplicity.

Wrote Haskell, "He preached to us from breakfast till noon, and from dinner till night, and in the evening we had a general meeting. At that time I subscribed for the *Review* and have taken it ever since."[5] When Elder Bates left, he took back with him an order from the Haskells for a copy of each tract and paper published by the *Review and Herald* office. These he received through the mail a few days later, all enclosed in one small package.

---
[1] Rowena Elizabeth Purdon, *That New England School*, p. 21.
[2] *Review and Herald*, April 7, 1896, p. 217.
[3] *Ibid.*
[4] *Ibid.*
[5] Letter to W. W. Prescott, Aug. 23, 1907.

Layman Leader

IN 1864 THE HASKELLS moved from Hubbardston to South Lancaster, Massachusetts, and joined the small company of Seventh-day Adventists there. Soon after their arrival Elder J. N. Loughborough met with the group, and in the nearby home of Lewis Priest he organized them into a church. The little band were drawn close as they celebrated the ordinance of foot washing and partook of the Lord's Supper. That Sabbath day only eight persons signed their names as charter members, covenanting to "keep the commandments of God and the faith of Jesus." Brave souls they were, fearing not to stand alone, daring to be different, willing to bear ostracism and ridicule for the cause of truth. Stephen Haskell was chosen leader, and Lewis Priest, Jr., was the local elder.

It was not long before the Priests' front room became too small to accommodate their increasing numbers; Stephen Haskell then fitted up a large room in an old Odd Fellows Hall, which he had purchased for a dwelling house. For five years this room in the Haskell home served as a chapel for the little church. Only occasionally was this new group of believers privileged to hear a discourse by an ordained minister, for in those days they were few, and the out-of-way places were not often visited.

But Stephen Haskell was a good organizer and a diligent student of the Word. His personal business affairs, whatever they might be at the time, were kept in the background, always subordinate to the interests of the gospel work. To proclaim God's message had been his principal interest in life since his first youthful experience in evangelism, when God's signal blessing confirmed his call to the ministry. He gave his time unstintingly to the interests of the South Lancaster church and to other small congregations springing up in the vicinity. Nor did he confine his labors to the small-church circle.

Wherever he was able to awaken an interest among his customers or associates, he took time from his regular business to instruct them in Bible truth. The company of believers in South Lancaster was warm in its first love, and most of those who joined in fellowship shared the same spirit of devotion.

One day four sisters in the church who felt a burden for their own children met for a season of prayer. They formed a prayer band. Others joined them, and once a week they came together for prayer and an exchange of experiences. Prayer led to activity. Soon they were writing to absent members and laboring with backsliders; they were calling on neighbors, sharing with them the blessed hope of Christ's return, lending them papers, tracts, and books, and ministering to those in need.

In December of 1868 a general meeting was held in South Lancaster to consider the developing work in New England. At this time, it seems, the Haskells became personally acquainted with Elder and Mrs. James White. Stephen Haskell knew so little about Seventh-day Adventist forms of organization that he did not even realize there were report blanks to be filled out; so he "got up one" himself, giving the number of churches and Sabbath schools in New England with their membership, listing the number of members in each church who were making regular payments to the Systematic Benevolence fund, and mentioning other items.

He wrote: "I was not at this time even licensed. I well remember when Brother White read the blank [that I had prepared], he passed it around to J. H. Waggoner and J. N. Andrews, and smiled with one of his knowing smiles. I suppose at the present day under such circumstance I would be reprimanded. But a committee was appointed and they brought in a recommendation, in substance as follows: We recommend this conference of four States to be organized, and S. N. Haskell be ordained to the ministry, and be its president. If I had been nominated as pres. of the U.S. it would not have surprised me more." [1] But the actual organization was not to come until 1870.

In Haskell's personal correspondence we are given a glimpse into those rugged beginning years when denominational organization was in its infancy and when many God-inspired, God-impelled men at their own expense invested labor, time, and money—sometimes health and life itself—in the cause that was so dear to their hearts.

He wrote of his activities in organization, beginning in the late 1850's: "I preached, organized churches and Sabbath Schools, ordained elders, paying my own expenses, etc., but I was not even licensed. Did not know it was necessary to have a license to preach. At that time, in the East, many of the Sabbath keepers were much as Brother White described them, like an old bag of buttons, of all shapes and sizes. There were more different beliefs among them than heads or horns on any of the beasts in the Bible. But I was good to them all, so all were friends to me."[2] During these early days, the territory where he worked was known as the New England mission field.

At the meeting in December, 1868, in South Lancaster, just three months after the gathering at Wright, Michigan, which launched the camp meeting program of Seventh-day Adventists, a unanimous vote had been taken to hold a camp meeting in New England the following summer "either before or immediately after haying." The Whites invited Haskell to spend a little time with them in Battle Creek. This he did, and was so inspired by the earnest, consecrated work of the brethren at headquarters that he determined to devote his best strength and energies to proclaiming the special message God had committed to the remnant church.

He was particularly impressed by the urgent appeals of Elder and Mrs. White for the believers to scatter truth-filled tracts everywhere, "like the leaves of autumn." Haskell had always favored the free use of tracts; he would never forget that it was a tract that had focused his attention on the vital Sabbath message, previously overlooked in his personal study of the Scriptures. He now returned to New England resolved to push the literature ministry even more vigorously than before.

Back in South Lancaster, he found the group of women meeting every week in his home, faithfully carrying on their church and neighborhood ministry. He encouraged them to organize themselves into a missionary society. On June 8, 1869, he met with them for that purpose. They took the name Vigilant Missionary Society. They were only about ten in number; most of them were busy housewives with

Mrs. Mary Priest (left) and Mrs. Roxie Rice, first secretary and first president, respectively, of the original Vigilant Missionary Society at South Lancaster, Massachusetts.

little schooling and no special training in methods of soul winning. But their hearts burned with the urge to share their blessings with friends and neighbors. Mrs. Roxie Rice was appointed president; Mrs. Mary Haskell, vice-president; Mrs. Mary Priest, secretary; and Rhoda Wheeler, treasurer.

At three o'clock every Wednesday afternoon they met to pray and plan. Each member was assigned a portion of the neighborhood to visit during the week. They found joy in ministering to the sick, in sharing their temporal blessings with destitute families, and in bringing good cheer to the aged, the lonely, and discouraged. Whenever opportunity was favorable, they offered prayer, and they distributed many printed messages. The society also carried on an extensive missionary correspondence. Guided by Stephen Haskell's counsel and stimulated by his enthusiasm, they gathered from various sources, far and near, hundreds of names of persons to whom they mailed papers accompanied by letters which often prompted their recipients to much prayerful thought.

The following year Maria Huntley and her mother moved to South Lancaster from Washington, New Hampshire, and joined the society. Maria was elected president; and under her energetic and efficient leadership its activities expanded to include overseas correspondence. It is reported that Maria studied French for the sole purpose of communicating with persons of that nationality, and that another member, Mary Martin, mastered sufficient German to enable her to write intelligent letters in that language.

Early in July of 1869, M. E. Cornell, called to work in New England, ordered a large tent from Boston at a cost of $500. He handed Stephen Haskell a list of pledges amounting to $220, and turned over to him the responsibility of raising the remainder of the $500, at the same time bestowing on him the title, "Treasurer of the Tent Fund." Evidently this commission was carried out with Haskell's usual promptness, for a few weeks later there appeared in the *Review* a notice of evangelistic meetings being held by Brethren Cornell and Rodman in "the New England tent."

When Haskell expressed his regrets that the brethren did not see their way clear to invest in a second tent, Evangelist P. C. Rodman came to his assistance and shared with him personally the expense of another tent. These two tents both served their purpose in the first New England camp meeting, which opened on September 5, 1869, and continued for a week. The camp meeting was held in a beautiful pine grove in the rural village of South Lancaster. This was the meeting planned for in December, 1868, when the Whites were in South Lancaster.

No statistics seem to have been preserved, but it is recorded that a goodly number camped on the ground; and also that many persons were entertained in the vicinity in the homes of church members. A fair representation was present from each of the New England States and from New York. A. C. Bourdeau attended with about forty from Bordoville, Vermont. The two large tents had been erected in which to hold meetings should it rain, and they proved serviceable during several showers. They also afforded sleeping quarters for some who had no other provision for the night.

Haskell, on the camp meeting committee, had spared neither time nor labor in perfecting arrangements for the meeting. On Sunday special trains from Worcester and Nashua brought at least four thousand visitors to the campground. In the forenoon, Elder Waggoner delivered a timely message in a tent crowded with attentive listeners.

In the afternoon the crowd was even larger. Every seat in the tent was filled and crowds stood around on the outside, quietly listening while Mrs. White gave a portrayal of the first and second advents of Christ. Nearly the entire audience was moved to tears, including many who had come out of curiosity to hear a woman preach.

Two thousand tracts, most of them *The Sufferings of Christ,* by Mrs. White, were freely handed out.

At the second South Lancaster camp meeting, held in August of 1870, the organization of the New England Conference was effected. At first it included only the four States of Massachusetts, New Hampshire, Rhode Island, and Connecticut. The independent preacher who had so faithfully served as church leader, evangelist, camp meeting organizer, financial adviser, and promoter of tract and missionary work in the New England mission field was duly elected conference president. He proved worthy of the responsibility placed upon him, and from that day held important offices in the denomination until near the time of his death.

Whether he was paid anything for those early years of service, he has not taken the trouble to mention. But this we do know, that the property that Stephen and Mary inherited from her father was rapidly being invested in the cause of truth.

When on August 24, 1871, the newly organized conference met in annual session at Amherst, New Hampshire, there were not more than sixteen churches, with a total membership of less than three hundred, in all the four States that constituted the New England Conference. Only two ordained ministers and two licentiates were working in the field. But those few delegates refused to be discouraged. True, the members were few, but they were multiplying. The churches were small but growing. The scarcity of ministerial help proved a challenge to the entire membership, and to meet this challenge the united forces of the church were called into action.

Elder Haskell had closely observed the progress of the Vigilant Missionary Society. As he witnessed the fruitage of its activities in the vigorous growth of the South Lancaster church, he thought of what a wider application of its principles could accomplish. He extended its organization as rapidly as possible to the whole conference by establishing the Tract and Missionary Society of the New England Conference of Seventh-day Adventists (November 6, 1870). He divided the entire territory into districts and appointed a director for each district in the conference.

Each director was to see that every church in his district selected a "librarian," who would order supplies of literature, receive donations for the literature fund, and forward them to the district director. Also, in connection with the church quarterly meetings, the librarian would conduct a special session for the purpose of considering the interests and work of the society. Every three months all cash receipts were to be forwarded to the Tract Society office, which had been set up in the home of Lewis Priest, Jr., at South Lancaster. The name Vigilant Missionary Society was retained for the women's auxiliary to the New England Tract and Missionary Society. (Later the Vigilant Missionary Societies sometimes included men.)

Over in Battle Creek James White heard about this New England Tract and Missionary Society. Ever alert and watchful for new methods of advancing the Advent message, he and his wife made a trip to South Lancaster. They spent a week in the Haskell home, investigating plans and methods. In the *Review* Elder White expressed himself as being "happily disappointed at finding the New England Conference in so prosperous a condition." He commended its president, stating that Brother Haskell was "an excellent manager," who had "good brethren to second his efforts."

"A few years since, this was missionary ground, and a discouraging field," he wrote. "Ministers from other States who then labored here as missionaries, were largely sustained from the treasury of the General Conference. Now this Conference [New England] fully supports its own ministers, meets the expenses of those who labor

Headquarters of the first Tract and Missionary Society, in the home of Lewis Priest, Jr., at South Lancaster, Massachusetts.

among them from other States; and besides this, puts annually, several hundreds into the treasury of the General Conference. . . .

"They also have missionary and tract societies which are efficient in looking after the wants of worthy widows and orphans, in corresponding with scattered and distant friends who need instruction and encouragement in the things of the Spirit of God, and in the circulation of tracts, pamphlets, and books. They are placing three of our bound volumes in all the best [public] libraries within the Conference. . . . And this small Conference alone has raised, the past season, for the Publishing Association, and the Health Institute, the sum of three thousand dollars."[3]

He also described the systematic manner in which they obtained new subscriptions and renewed old ones, collected dues, and settled accounts of the worthy poor, all by appointing certain church members who, through visiting and correspondence, prevented the accumulation of indebtedness to the publishing house.

A vision of a denomination-wide enterprise, built on the same plan as the New England Tract and Missionary Society, loomed large in the mind of James White. He was convinced that the one who had brought the societies to their present state of efficiency was the one to promote the project on a wider scale. He persuaded Stephen Haskell to return with him to Battle Creek and assist in laying the foundation for a broader work. After the brethren had counseled together, Elder White, early in 1872, published a pamphlet suggesting that the other conferences follow the pattern set by the New England Tract and Missionary Society.

In March, a few weeks after Elder Haskell's return from Michigan, he assisted in forming the New York Tract and Missionary Society. He had written in the *Review* urging the different State conferences to take hold of the matter, select proper persons, and unitedly make one general rally in order to spread the message into every nook and corner of the land.

During the next two years frequent notices appeared in the *Review*, stating that at such and such a quarterly meeting the organization of a Tract and Missionary Society would be considered, or that the first, second, or third meeting of the society would convene, often ending with the promise, "Elder Haskell is expected to be present." Societies began to spring up here and there; and wherever there was a lively Tract and Missionary Society there was sure to be a growing, thriving church.

While the few ministers in the field were working for the joy of service, supported by desultory and precarious contributions, and at times sustaining themselves by part-time work at odd jobs, many laymen were working for souls as if they really believed that they, too, had a commission from on high; and the Vigilant Missionaries were watching over the new converts, corresponding with absent members, and searching out and reclaiming backsliders.

One Friday afternoon a young man, employed away from home, came into the house where he was boarding, his week's work finished. He had recently accepted the seventh-day Sabbath and by special arrangement was exempt from duty on that day. But there was to be a party in the home that evening. He was battling with the problem—Should he violate his conscience and attend, just that once? Or should he risk the displeasure of the family, and especially of the daughter, by absenting himself? As he entered his bedroom that afternoon to change from his work clothes, he saw a letter lying on the dresser. He tore open the envelope and hastily read its contents, then sat down on the bed and read it through again—slowly, noting every word. Why were tears chasing one another down his cheeks?

The letter was from one of the Vigilant Missionary members—just a brief friendly note to let him know that he was missed. They hoped that he was not too lonely. They were praying for him, that he might be true to his convictions and have strength to stand for the right amid worldly associates. He read the letter a third time, then dropped to his knees. His decision was made.

That evening, instead of dancing with the beautiful young lady, for whom he felt no small attraction, he followed his usual Friday evening practice and spent the time in Bible study and prayer. That night there came a change in his feelings; the alluring but world-loving young woman lost her attraction for him. Their ways parted. A few years later this young man, Asa Robinson, married Loretta Farnsworth, daughter of William Farnsworth, of Washington, New Hampshire, the man whose name has been handed down as the first among Sabbathkeeping Adventists. Asa entered the ministry, and together they engaged in city mission work.

The influence of the efforts of these united, praying women is seen in another experience a few years later—in the spring of 1876—when word was sent out that there would be no New England camp meeting that year. Ministerial help was scarce. James White had written that he and his wife could not be with them. But the Vigilant Missionary sisters did not see it that way. A group of them engaged in special prayer that God would give them a camp meeting. When Elder Haskell heard of this, his faith rose to the occasion and he said, "Their prayers must be answered; we shall have a camp meeting this year."

For a campground a pleasant grove of oak and pine, with the Boston and Maine railroad running along one side, was selected at

Groveland, Massachusetts, about forty miles northeast of South Lancaster. As the time for opening drew near, Haskell made out a list of special favors that he wanted the railroad company to grant, and with young Asa Robinson he went to see Mr. Ferber, its president.

The list filled two large sheets of foolscap paper. Haskell wanted, without charge, two carloads of freight transferred from the storage rooms at South Lancaster to the campground and returned at the close of the meetings. He wanted free passes for the conference and committee men, and half-fare permits for campers coming from a distance. Trains should be run on Sundays as well as weekdays, with extra trains during the week. A platform needed to be built beside the track, and water piped to the grounds.

Mr. Ferber glanced at the list and frowned, but a few pleasantries put him in a happier mood. He tapped a bell, and an office boy appeared. "Take these men to the manager's office," he ordered.

The manager read over the list, then looked up and said, "Gentlemen, why don't you ask for the world?"

"Oh, we thought we would be a little modest," said Haskell.

"We got everything we asked for," Robinson stated, "except the platform was not to be so long."

Volunteer workers soon had the underbrush cleared away and the ground ready for tents. Campers came in, more and more of them, until the camping area had to be enlarged twice. Since Elder Haskell had made sure that leading New England newspapers carried advance notices of the meeting, curious residents of nearby cities flocked in every morning and home again when the evening meetings were finished. Especially over the weekend the people crowded the regular trains. Extra trains had to be run. According to report, one conductor who could not squeeze his way through the coaches was compelled to "take to the roof in order to signal the engineer."

One reporter commented, "Happy were they who brought their own lunch baskets." "The throng swept down on the eatables like an army of grasshoppers. . . . The provision stand was repeatedly replenished from the Winter Street Bakery of Haverhill, till that obliging firm were utterly cleared of eatables, yet the demands were unsupplied."⁴ Contrary to expectations, Elder and Mrs. White were present.

The following report appeared in the Haverhill *Publisher* of August 29:

"Sunday was a great day at the meeting in the woods at Bradford, by the Seventh-day Adventists, bringing together the largest assembly of people ever convened in this region for a similar purpose.... The railroads were taxed beyond the utmost capacity of all their preparations for the occasion, and large numbers were prevented from attendance by not finding means of conveyance at the time the trains started....

"Two steam yachts were very busy, and omnibuses and barges were constantly running, while private carriages without number thronged in the way.... As it was, it was thought that fully 20,000 visited the grounds during the day."⁵

Elder and Mrs. White each spoke twice, he on doctrines and she on her favorite theme, "Christian temperance." She was invited to speak the following day at Haverhill City Hall under the auspices of the Reform Club. Her audience filled the hall to its capacity of 1,100.

The camp meeting was a triumph. A number who attended were baptized and joined the church. D. A. Robinson, Asa's older brother, was ordained to the ministry there; later he went to Africa and India as a missionary. And to think that there might have been no Groveland camp meeting at all, except for a consecrated group of women who believed that "Prayer changes things"!

---
¹ Letter to W. W. Prescott, Aug. 23, 1907.
² *Ibid.*
³ *Review and Herald*, Nov. 14, 1871, p. 172.
⁴ *Signs of the Times*, Sept. 14, 1876, p. 308.
⁵ Quoted in M. E. Olsen, *Origin and Progress of Seventh-day Adventists*, pp. 284, 285.

The "Child of His Hope"

AT THE ELEVENTH session of the General Conference, which opened in Battle Creek, March 11, 1873, Stephen Haskell was one of the delegates, representing the New England Conference. He was one of the first to render his report. After the reports were given, several resolutions pertaining to the general work were considered, with emphasis on the Health Institute, the Publishing Association, and the projected denominational school. The work of the tract and missionary societies was then given attention, and a vote of approval was passed. Elder Haskell was asked to visit churches throughout the conferences in the interest of the societies. No other assignment could have given him greater satisfaction. Now he had full authorization to push this branch of the work rapidly forward.

From this time on his letter headings indicate somewhat the extent of his travels. He spent a few days, sometimes a week, at one church, then went on to another, holding institutes, conferences, and classes in missionary correspondence and house-to-house visitation. He organized new tract societies and reorganized old ones. Each society was established on a sound basis of operation, with the territory districted, officers appointed, their duties outlined, and an adequate system of reporting installed. No loose ends were left to dangle, not if Stephen Haskell could prevent it. This was God's work, and it must be executed with vigor and skill. It is doubtful that anyone ever questioned his right to the title, Father of the Tract and Missionary Societies.

For sixteen years, while engaged in this organizational work, he carried the responsibility of the New England Conference—and for part of that time the presidency of California and Maine as well! He had the oversight of their various branches of activity—evangelistic, Sabbath school, health and temperance, religious liberty, and anything else. He was at the same time a member of the General Conference Committee, the Publishing Association, and the Health Institute board.

With so many enterprises demanding his attention, it may not seem surprising that we find him occasionally adding to his usual letter ending, "Yours in hope," the two significant words "and haste." Even while traveling he was writing letters, reports, and articles promoting the great object ever uppermost in his endeavors—the tract and missionary work.

The persistence with which he weaves this theme into nearly all his writings is illustrated by an article setting forth the proper observance of Thanksgiving Day. He tells of a brother who prepared a wholesome and tasty dinner and "invited the poor, the lame, and I know not but the blind, to partake of the same, and then spent a season of prayer and praise and in recounting the mercies of the past year and the deliverances God had wrought for them. And so full of gratitude to the Author of every good and perfect gift did the heart of this brother become, that he made a thank-offering of twenty-five dollars to the tract society, which will purchase 80,000 pages of tracts . . . for free distribution."[1]

In his promotional work Haskell repeatedly urged that the children be given an opportunity to participate. He wrote about certain of his little friends aged six and seven who refused to spend their pennies for candy and knickknacks, but were eager to earn and save money to invest in the missionary cause.

In his reports he mentions that all the churches seem willing to work if they can find some way to pay for the required literature; and he tells of various plans being devised, such as taking subscriptions for the *Health Reformer* and using the profit to pay for literature to distribute personally or by mail.

He warned against the danger of working in a legalistic spirit without depending upon God; and he promised that, "with our hearts warm with the love of God, other hearts will become electrified and be aglow with the same spirit." He assured farmers that they need not be excluded from this soul-saving enterprise, and offered them some rather straight advice: If their large farms kept them at home, then let them sell off forty acres or so, and reduce their cares. He then made this stirring comment, "If the cause in which we are engaged means anything, it means everything; and to dabble with it at our fingers' ends, . . . look out first for ourselves and then give a little of our surplus time and means for the cause, is solemn mockery." [2]

Following the March, 1873, General Conference Haskell organized State societies in Illinois, Minnesota, Iowa, Nebraska, and Ohio. He spent two or three weeks in each place, then a few weeks strengthening the Michigan societies. By July he was back in New England, catching up on important work that had accumulated during his absence. Time had to be given to the establishment of the Vermont and Rhode Island societies and to arranging for the South Lancaster camp meeting, which would come in August. Those duties accomplished, he left his carefully organized conference affairs in other hands, though still retaining the presidency, and started out again on his broader mission.

Let us picture him on a warm September day sitting in the coach of a noisy, slow-moving train of the year 1873—young folks chattering around him, children running up and down the narrow aisle, people eating from lunch baskets. He has reversed one of the car seats so that two seats face each other. His luggage is piled on the rack overhead and beside him. He opens his satchel, finds writing pad and pencil, and scribbles a note to his "dear Mary." If only she could be with him on this trip! How they would enjoy a leisurely visit together, a luxury for which they seldom found time at home! But of late Mary's health has been failing. Even short trips exhaust her. Stephen wonders how she will endure weeks of loneliness and pain without even once hearing his cheering voice. He recalls her standing in the doorway of their South Lancaster home blinking back the tears at their parting. "I'll be all right, Stephen; you go right on and do God's work." She had smiled as she said it.

A man sitting across the aisle from him opens a window, then closes it quickly as he feels the wilting heat reflected from the ground outside. Stephen stamps and addresses his letter to Mary. He thinks about the work he has left behind. Yes, there are a few matters he forgot to mention in his careful and detailed instructions. Pulling out his pocketknife, he sharpens a pencil and applies himself again. For hours he bends his broad shoulders over his writing, stopping only to wipe the perspiration from his face and a cinder from his eye, or to walk to the far end of the car for a drink of tepid water. The lamps are lighted, but he works on.

The lights are dimmed. He feels around in the semidarkness for his lunch box, takes out a few crackers and an apple—he has forgotten about supper! Finally he closes his eyes, thanks God for the blessings of the day and for the privilege of service. He prays for Mary and himself, for James and Ellen White, for Elder Butler, the General Conference president; he does not forget his associates in New England and the workers in the far-scattered fields. Then he lays his head back and sleeps.

Elder Haskell was on his way to Illinois, Iowa, Minnesota, Wisconsin, and Michigan. He planned to attend the twelfth annual session of the General Conference at Battle Creek, the second session to be held that year (Nov. 14, 1873). There it was voted that a General Tract and Missionary Society, designed to unify the State and local societies, should be organized. This was organized the next year, at the 1874 General Conference in August. James White was elected president and S. N. Haskell business agent. Subsequently Maria Huntley was appointed secretary and Jennie Thayer, assistant.

During 1874 a monthly journal, *The True Missionary,* was published. (After one year of publication *The True Missionary* was merged with the *Review and Herald.*) It contained reports and letters from individuals, gave helpful instruction to the societies, and related experiences illustrating various methods of approach and the results attained.

The paper announced that the Vigilant Missionary Societies' chief objective was the promoting of pure religion through visiting and praying with families, distributing and mailing tracts and papers, and missionary correspondence. In its pages Haskell wrote of the good to be accomplished by placing our health and religious journals and best bound books in college reading rooms and public libraries throughout the country, which would raise the standard of truth in every town and city. Other duties were enumerated, such as writing to absent members, caring for the worthy poor, and finding homes for orphan children.

Both district and conference quarterly meetings of the Tract and Missionary Societies were to be held. These were weekend gatherings to acquaint all with the constitution and rules of the organization; to select officers and outline their duties; to bring in financial and statistical reports; and, most important, to pray and counsel together and exchange experiences.

Haskell was a strong believer in reporting. He maintained that a good reporting system tends to unify action by enabling the various societies to work in close collaboration with one another. He believed that the recounting of battles fought and victories won would stimulate sister societies and members to persevere in the work. As an added benefit, he wrote, "A visiting spirit, . . . which is so much needed, will be encouraged, not to chit-chat upon nothing in particular, but to inquire after one another's spiritual welfare." [3]

From time to time reports appeared in the journal, missionary letters were printed, suitable programs were suggested, and important matters to be dealt with at the quarterly meetings were presented. Responsible leaders were installed, and their numerous duties outlined, among which was the rather large assignment of seeing that every member had an interest in every department of the work.

Each society had its president, vice-president, secretary, treasurer, and corresponding agents. These agents distributed literature and contributed names of interested persons who might desire to read further on some particular subject. The plan was effective, if somewhat intricate, as Mrs. White commented in a letter to Haskell. A person in a distant country, on receiving a journal from "nobody knew where" and often in an unfamiliar language would, from mere curiosity if nothing else, seek out someone who could read and interpret it for him. Thus new centers of interest and fresh opportunities for correspondence were constantly being created. In time the societies had members acting as corresponding agents in many parts of the world.

Haskell's inspirational articles were sprinkled with his favorite slogans of courage and faith, such as these written in 1874 in the one volume of the short-lived journal *The True Missionary:*

"Facts, experience, and the word of God, justify our believing that success will attend every judicious effort to spread this truth" (p. 58).

"It is when sacrifices that cost something are called for that the heart is tested" (p. 87).

"We should ask for great things and expect them" (p. 58).

"God is at work; and, work as fast as we may, his providence will keep ahead of us" (p. 68).

"The times call for action. . . . We have something else to attend to besides our farms and merchandise" (p. 37).

"The efforts we have made . . . [are] only a little field drill, testing the strength of our system, and learning how we can work together. Soon we shall be called upon to do something besides skirmish and drill" (p. 29).

"Love is an active principle, and cannot live without works. . . . The soil in which it grows is not the natural heart; but love is a heavenly plant, and flourishes only in a heart renewed by the grace of God" (p. 28).

In an effort to boost the courage of his fellow workers, he bade them take a backward look, to go back about twenty-five years earlier, when the whole edition of our publications printed every two weeks was carried to the post office in a carpetbag, whereas now, in *one week, seven cartloads* of reading matter, allowing thirty bushels to a cartload, were sent from the publishing house at Battle Creek to different parts of the world.

In October, 1874, Elder Haskell presented in *The True Missionary* a report of the Tract and Missionary Societies, covering the four years since their first unit was organized in New England. A rather complete report it was for those days when statistical records were scarce, for the early workers seem to have been too busy making history to spend much time recording it.

The report includes 15,000 subscriptions obtained for our periodicals, which was estimated at 260,000 visits of the *Review* and 60,000 visits of the *Instructor* and *Health Reformer;* between three and four million pages of reading matter distributed, mostly free; thousands of our books placed in public libraries; nearly 10,000 families visited and prayed with—an impressive report indeed, coming from only 1,800 reporting members in seven State conferences.

He further stated that ten new "cotton churches" (tents) were then operated successfully west of Michigan. And at all the camp meetings that season he had had calls for publications in German, French, Swedish, and Danish.

The report closed with an appeal for deeper consecration.

Two years later Elder Haskell was able to report that the fruits of visiting from house to house were being seen in different parts of the country, where individuals and small companies were embracing the message.

Haskell was a man of courage, endurance, and unbounded optimism. Neither weariness nor pain, bad roads nor poor transportation facilities, summer heat nor winter wind and snow—nothing!—dampened his spirits or abated his efforts. His persistent endeavors to meet all appointments, even under the most adverse conditions, were contagious. He wrote that at meetings where he expected only a small attendance or none at all, the brethren came in from different places, traveling all the way from ten to thirty-five miles. He tells of one brother who walked twenty-five miles so that his family might ride.

While he was visiting in New York State in January of 1876, when it was "neither sleighing nor wheeling," one brother, living fifty miles away, started for the meeting on a stoneboat (a heavy sled used on the farm), came twenty-five miles, where he obtained a wagon, and brought another brother with him. Then he returned home and brought his family to Randolph, a distance of twenty-five miles, where another meeting was held. Twenty-five miles was quite a journey without automobiles and along unpaved country roads where horses' feet and wagon wheels would sometimes sink deep in the mud.

The missionary chief was prompted to report encouraging experiences through the pages of the *Review* as a means of stirring others to action. He wrote about one sister who gave a few tracts and copies of the *Signs of the Times* to a man traveling to Washington, D.C. Some months afterward she received a letter from a Sunday school teacher who had begun to keep the Sabbath. The writer said that she had been troubled because she could not harmonize the Word of God with the views taught by her pastor. The man who had received the Adventist literature was attending her Sunday school class, and he was able to answer some of her questions to her satisfaction. He had found the answers in the papers handed him by the Adventist sister and had passed them on to his Sunday school teacher. She read them, then gave them to her neighbors. This resulted in thirteen converts.

Haskell was elected president of the General Tract and Missionary Society in 1876. There were difficulties which might have discouraged a leader possessed of less cheerful perseverance. In some churches he found the early enthusiasm of its members dead or dying. Much earnest work was required to arouse them to feel their responsibility. If he was prevented by other appointments from remaining with a certain church long enough to accomplish his purpose, he would arrange to return later. He might plan a field day of house-to-house visitation and follow it with an hour or two of consultation with the workers, reviewing the experiences of the day, answering their questions, and giving instruction as to the best methods of approach. Nor would he give up until the entire church was at work again.

Some societies became discouraged because they had fallen behind in their payments for publications. With characteristic energy Haskell then launched into the task of soliciting contributions, squaring up old accounts, and establishing a new literature fund with which to carry on a strictly cash business with the office. Otherwise, how could the *Review* and the *Signs* publishing houses continue operating? The members usually saw the point and were willing to sacrifice to raise the funds required.

As Elder Haskell's work increased rapidly in the Central States, he decided to move his home. This was easily done. It simply meant moving Mary; for he always said, "Home is wherever Mary is." So he brought her to Battle Creek and arranged for her to board with an Adventist family, the Chinnocks. She would be happier there because she could see him oftener, and he would be spared anxiety over her possible loneliness. Mary Haskell was glad to be relieved of the "uphill work of cooking." She spoke of Mary Chinnock as one of the best of cooks.

And lest someone misjudge Mrs. Haskell, it might be mentioned that nearly a century ago cooking with its attendant housekeeping *was* "uphill work." Electric stoves, refrigerators, and modern heating and cooling systems were unknown. Baking was done in the oven of an iron cookstove, which must be stoked from a wood box or coal hod—the bread, cake, pie, or roast constantly watched and dampers manipulated to preserve even temperatures. Perishable foods were usually kept in a cool cellar underneath the house, and when needed must be carried up a narrow flight of stairs to the living apartments.

There were few prepared foods, and of course nothing frozen. Canning was a new and rarely used art. Beans, peas, lentils, dried fruits, and raisins were not packaged, and had to be picked over by hand and washed, and the small bits of gravel removed before cooking. Usually all water for household purposes was carried into the house in a bucket from the back-yard pump, and with a long-handled tin dipper ladled out for drinking or cooking. Kerosene lamps had to be cleaned daily and filled, then wicks trimmed, and the globes polished. Water pitchers on bedroom washstands must be filled for use the next morning, for there were seldom bathroom or toilet facilities in the house.

Once a week or oftener the entire house was swept with a dampened broom, the kitchen floor scrubbed, and rugs hung on the clothesline and beaten with a stick or broom to remove the dust. Family washings were soaped, soaked, and rubbed clean by hand on a washboard, rinsed, then run through a hand wringer or wrung by hand. When the clothes were hung on the line to dry, the weary housewife would empty the tubs and hang them on their respective nails on the back porch, ready for use again on bath day. She would then look wistfully at the clock, hoping for a fifteen-minute breathing spell before stoking the kitchen stove and preparing supper.

Stephen provided the two Marys (Mary Haskell and Mary Chinnock) with a horse and buggy in which they might ride out together and go shopping or visiting. We wonder whether he rode with them when he was at home on those occasional surprise visits that his wife told her friends about. When away he faithfully wrote to her every week, and she returned the favor.

Soon after its organization the General Tract Society established a literature fund, sustained largely by gifts from the various State conferences. To this fund all Adventists were invited to contribute. Through the years it paid for thousands of packages of tracts and the required freight on all that were not carried to their destination free of charge by the obliging railroad companies. At seaports ministers and laymen formed friendships with officers and sailors, who then permitted packages of tracts and journals to be placed aboard ships bound for distant lands. The captains, though seldom interested in the contents of the packages, were usually willing to carry them free of charge, then toss them onto some wharf where their ship might anchor; there they lay until the foreign corresponding agent of the society or some other interested person picked them up and distributed them.

While the vessels bearing these messengers of truth were weathering wind and tempest the vigilant missionaries who had sent them forth were praying that angels would guide them to truth-hungry souls. Thus the printed pages often preceded the missionary.

Every page was precious. Even outdated periodicals were bound in volumes and sent abroad. Haskell wrote to James and Ellen White encouraging them with his own forecast that their writings would someday be read in many languages.

He told of a captain on the Baltic Sea who was rejoicing in present truth through literature sent from America. He wrote, "All labor, such as loading and unloading his ship, is laid aside on the Sabbath; and, although the doctrines seem strange at the ports where he stops, he gathers the natives about him and gives them the reasons for his new-found faith." [4]

Back in the 1860's, when Elder Matteson was preaching among the Scandinavian people in the United States, he felt so keenly the need of literature in their own languages that he went into the *Review* office and himself set type for our first Swedish tracts.

As soon as the earliest of these were off the press they were welcomed by the new Scandinavian believers in the States, then sent to friends and relatives in the homeland, thus acquainting them with the new truths they had acquired through Bible study. As fast as literature could be produced in French, German, Italian, Swedish, and other foreign languages it was sent to the various countries of Europe. The Italian Mission became a distributing center for the islands of the Mediterranean. With a club of *Signs of the Times* sent from America, a British Tract and Missionary Society was organized in January, 1880, and immediately began systematic distribution.

Meanwhile, the South Lancaster society was still active and growing. The following notice, typical of those times, appeared in the *Review:* "The general quarterly meeting for the New England Tract Society, also its annual meeting, will be held in So. Lancaster, Mass., commencing Nov. 21, and continuing over the Monday following. Bring your straw ticks, buffalo robes, and bedding, and accommodations will be made for three hundred." [5]

From 1874 Haskell urged society members to sell periodical subscriptions, with small books as a side line or as premiums. George King, among others, worked thus several years before he persuaded the brethren to issue our first large doctrinal book, *Daniel and the Revelation*, especially for the colporteurs.

Eight years after the first General Tract Society was organized its field of operation had so greatly expanded that it was given a larger name. From 1882 on, its letterheads bore the title: *"International Tract and Missionary Society."* From time to time, during the '80's, they carried the motto, "Our Mission is the World," or "Christ died for all," and in smaller type, "Publications in Danish, Swedish, German, French, Spanish and English"; and listed publishing houses at Battle Creek, Michigan; Oakland, California; Grimsby, England; Basel, Switzerland; Christiania, Norway; and Melbourne, Australia. The name of Maria Huntley appears on the stationery as secretary and S. N. Haskell as president.

Since its birth in 1874 the Tract Society, through its many

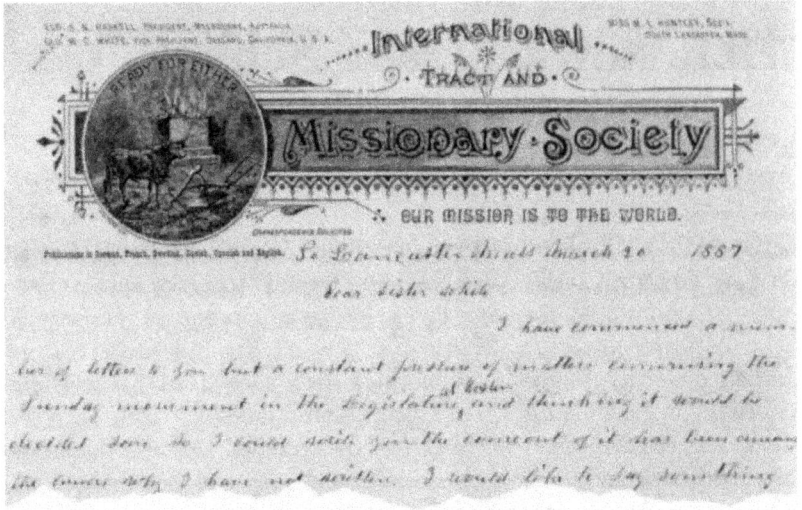

A letter from Haskell to Ellen G. White, showing a typical letterhead of the International Tract and Missionary Society.

branches, had sent out enormous quantities of truth-laden books, tracts, and pamphlets to lands far and near. In 1884, soon after its enlargement, the International Tract and Missionary Society placed 10,000 standard Seventh-day Adventist books in public libraries throughout the United States, at a cost averaging more than a dollar a volume, besides sending many bound books to English and Australian libraries.

At the age of ten years Haskell's "Child of Hope"—the Tract Society—had reached a strong and vigorous maturity.

[1] *Review and Herald*, Jan. 7, 1873, p. 30.
[2] *Ibid.*, Nov. 4, 1873, p. 164.
[3] *Ibid.*, April 1, 1880, p. 218.
[4] Letter to James White, July 28, 1878.
[5] *Review and Herald*, Nov. 7, 1878, p. 152.

That New England School

THE BEGINNING of 1875 found Elder Haskell in Battle Creek. For days Battle Creek's West End had been a scene of unusual activity. A ministerial institute was in progress, closing on January 3. The dedicatory exercises of the first Seventh-day Adventist college building were held the next morning, and several special evening meetings were held. But the blessing usually attending such an occasion seemed dampened by a spirit of criticism. As the ministers tramped back and forth between their lodgings and the Bible Institute classes, there was whispering: "Why this expensive outlay in building, when all available funds are needed for the support of ministers who are proclaiming the message? Is this the time to launch a great educational program? Should young men be encouraged to spend time gaining a formal education when without further training, they can put their talents to immediate use for the Master?" And so grew the spirit of dissatisfaction with "the leaders."

In one of the evening meetings during this time Mrs. White addressed the assembly. She spoke emphatically regarding the necessity of the workers' taking broader views of their God-given task. She dwelt upon the importance of laying much broader plans for the education of workers for evangelism both at home and abroad. She said that progress in sending workers to other lands was altogether too slow and inadequate. She told of a vision in which she had seen individuals and groups in various places searching their Bibles and praying for light, finding there the promise of Christ's return to redeem His people, and also discovering the truth regarding the sacredness of the seventh-day Sabbath. She saw small companies keeping the Sabbath of the Lord without knowing that there were any other Sabbathkeepers in the world. And she stated that as the brethren heard of such companies it would be their duty to send experienced ministers to labor among them and teach them the way of truth more fully. The publishing work was to be enlarged.

She had been shown printing presses in other countries, she said, and if she should ever see them, she would recognize them.

Elder Haskell was deeply moved by her words, and long afterward related how vividly he remembered that meeting. He was sitting up front, next to James White, when White stood and interrupted her to ask a question, and he remembered her replying, " 'I am telling you what I have seen, and I have seen that there are fields all ready for the truth that we have not entered, and that have not been thought of, and that there will be papers published in those fields. . . .' Again Brother White interrupted her. He said 'To what fields do you refer?' She said she could remember but one, that the angel had mentioned, which was Australia."[1]

Now Haskell's immediate duty lay in the preparation of missionaries for the broadening work. For their education and training, schools were needed. Public schools were succeeding admirably in preparing children and youth for citizenship in this world, but Adventist young people needed special training to prepare them for the work committed to them. During the following year Haskell continued trying to interest students in attending Battle Creek College. All the while a conviction was steadily deepening in his mind that the young people of the New England Conference should have their own training school where, nearer their homes and at less expense, they could prepare for mission service. The thought was continually with him and was often expressed to his fellow workers. But there were difficulties. Where would the money come from? Could competent teachers be found?

Such questions posed no obstacle to the man of faith. Were not all God's commands backed by His promises? His counsel was to step out by faith, trusting God to prosper His word.

As the months went by he continued talking, praying, and planning. He searched for competent teachers who would staff the school. And when he found two who he felt confident would adhere to the pattern of true education which God had given His church, he made the bold statement that the school would soon be opened.

Without waiting for the erection of a building, Haskell rapidly completed plans for temporary quarters, and the opening day was set. Surprised readers saw this notice in the *Review:* "The school at South Lancaster opened to-day, April 19, with fair attendance." [2]

With characteristic optimism the elder remarked that the number present was larger than expected and that others would doubtless join them later.

In spite of that small beginning, April 19, 1882, was a banner day in the New England Conference; it marked the birthday of the South Lancaster Academy, now Atlantic Union College, an institution which, under the hand of God, has educated and trained hundreds of Seventh-day Adventist youth for Christian service, including some of the earliest pioneer missionaries to foreign lands.

And now, on this opening morning of school, young people present look around the room. They are in the little wagon repair shop that has served the church family four years as a chapel. Now that they have a newly erected church building the shop is ready to be put to another use. It is rather small, only 18 by 24 feet, according to Elder Haskell's measuring stick. It has undergone a transformation and is already taking on the appearance of a schoolroom. A few charts and maps and two or three pictures hang on the walls. Fifteen or twenty desks have been gathered from here and there, including one larger than the others, which will be shared by the two teachers. On the teachers' desk lie a few reference books which, judging by their appearance, have already done good service in the field of education and are now waiting to be of further use.

What is it that lends such an atmosphere of dignity and charm to the occasion? There is nothing imposing about the room or its furnishings. Rather, it lies in the group of founders assembled there. Seated in front, facing the happy students, are five people: Elder Haskell; D. A. Robinson, pastor of the South Lancaster church and newly elected chairman of the school board; G. H. Bell, the recently appointed school principal; Maria Huntley; and Edith Sprague. Miss Sprague is a graduate of Battle Creek College and will assist Professor Bell in teaching.

The clatter and chatter in the schoolroom dies down as Elder

Haskell rises deliberately and begins speaking in his kind, fatherly way. He tells the young people that he knows they will appreciate the privilege of receiving instruction from experienced Christian teachers. "You are fortunate," he says, "in attending the school while it is yet small, because you will receive more individual attention than will be possible later, when a larger number of students will claim their teachers' time. You are greatly blessed in having Prof. Goodloe Harper Bell as your principal. Professor Bell is recognized as one of the foremost educators in the State of Michigan. He gave up a lucrative teaching position to join the Seventh-day Adventists because he loves God and His special message for this time and wants to see our young people receive the kind of education that will fit them to be good missionaries.

"It was Professor Bell," he continues, "who started the little primary school in the outgrown Review and Herald office building—the school that, with the blessing of God, has grown into our dear Battle Creek College. For several years he has been head of the English department of the college. Now he has come here to help us get our new school started in the right way. He knows how to teach. He can make any subject interesting, especially that jaw breaker, grammar; and he loves young people." Haskell takes his seat and calls on Professor Bell to speak.

The principal from Michigan shows himself to be truly great; he talks to those young people earnestly and carefully, as though he were addressing a university audience. He says to them, in substance: "The education given in this school we hope will be of a more practical nature than that given in most schools of the land, because it will combine the development of physical, mental, and spiritual powers." He adds that any education which merely fills the student's mind with a mass of facts and hurries him through a course of study that he may obtain a diploma does not meet his mind as true education. "True education not only trains the mind," he continues, "it strengthens the character and reveals itself throughout life in the accomplishment of grand and noble work for the world.

"The aim of this school will be to train Christian workers. The Bible will be its foundation, and agriculture its A B C. In our study of science we shall learn how the *word* of God helps us better to understand the *works* of God. We shall bring into our literature classes only that which conforms to Christian principles. Physical labor will be combined with the study of books."

Pastor Robinson then speaks a few words, followed by the two young women. Elder Haskell asks the students to make their own decision in regard to the plan of combined mental and physical labor, and to make suggestions.

By the end of this first school day they are ready with a hearty response in a meeting called by the students themselves. Orville Farnsworth, one of the older boys, acts as chairman and presents to the students a few resolutions which he and his younger friends have drawn up:

"Whereas, A school has been opened in South Lancaster among S.D. Adventists; and—

"Whereas, It has required sacrifice on the part of its founders to start the enterprise, and will require still more to carry it on successfully; therefore—

"Resolved, 1. That we, as students, desire to show our appreciation of the efforts put forth in our behalf, by doing all we can to build up this institution.

"2. That we, the young men and boys of this school, request the School Committee to provide us one acre of land for cultivation.

"3. That we donate to the school the proceeds of all that shall be raised on said land."

The girls have also been in consultation, and are now given a chance to present their resolutions:

"Resolved, That we, the young ladies of the South Lancaster school, feeling anxious to do our part in sustaining the same, will be responsible for the laundry work, and for all necessary repairs in the clothing of the young men who donate their time in cultivating land for the benefit of the school; and that we will be glad to help in any other way whenever opportunities present themselves."[3]

These resolutions are unanimously adopted, and an acre of land is at once reserved for cultivation by the young men.

There had been a little pleasant rivalry between Elder Haskell and Elder William White as to which school—one in Massachusetts, the other in California—would be first to open. When Stephen Haskell read of the opening of Healdsburg College just eight days in advance of his own little school in South Lancaster, he wrote his friend Willie, remarking gamely, "I had to build mine; yours was already built."

For over four months Elder Haskell had been preparing to fulfill an assignment given him at the General Conference session in December of the previous year. He had been asked to visit the various missions in Europe. G. I. Butler, General Conference president, felt that it was important to have one of the leading brethren become acquainted with conditions in Europe, in order to cooperate to the best advantage with the fellow workers overseas.

Elder Haskell left for his mission tour as soon as he was satisfied that the school was well started and that provision had been made for its successful continuance. Before sailing he had the satisfaction of seeing the student enrollment more than doubled; and when he returned after an absence of six months he found that the school had outgrown its shop-chapel schoolhouse and had been moved into the two-room unfinished basement of the church building.

Rowena Purdon, a pioneer Lancastrian, described these quarters: "The stones of the foundation formed the side walls, the ceilings were the timbers of the floor above, and Mother Earth made a silent floor for noisy feet. A wood furnace stood in one corner, and kerosene lamps supplied light." [4]

On his return from overseas Haskell wrote: "We found the school at this place prospering finely. Everything seemed to be moving like clock-work, and perfect harmony prevailed among the students. A woody-yard has been opened in the interests of the school. The students labor three hours per day, and by this means they have in some instances been enabled to nearly pay their board. There has been an outside sale of wood during the last two weeks of over $100 worth. . . . The land cultivated by them last term has yielded a profit of about $60 which had been contributed to the school. The housework is performed by the lady students. . . . A good religious interest already exists among the students and nine have been baptized." [5]

Above, left: The first school building erected for the South Lancaster Academy (1884) after two years in temporary quarters. Above, right: The 1884/85 faculty of the academy, headed by D. A. Robinson. Below: Haskell Hall, the administration building of the present Atlantic Union College, named for S. N. Haskell.

Thanksgiving Day, November 29, 1883, was a memorable day in the South Lancaster church. Mrs. White was present and gave an earnest address in which she reminded her hearers that the real purpose of Thanksgiving Day was to recall God's mercies and favors with thankful hearts. She was followed by Haskell, Robinson, and other faculty members with appeals for gifts of money with which to purchase land and erect school buildings. To these appeals she added her own stirring words: "When I remember how forward our brethren in New England have been to respond to every appeal for means for our missions and the various enterprises connected with present truth, even calls coming from the Pacific Coast, I feel very anxious that now, when the cause in New England is in great need, the brethren in other sections may reciprocate their liberality."[8] Many testimonies were offered, each one accompanied by the reading of thanksgiving scriptures. Within a little more than thirty minutes the amount of $12,500 was raised, and soon afterward the school experienced a second expansion.

Mrs. White wrote that the brethren agreed that this day was the best Thanksgiving Day they had ever experienced. The meeting closed about two o'clock. "We then took ample refreshments," she said.

The first building was erected the next year, 1884.

As the school grew, South Lancaster's industrial departments were enlarged and strengthened. New industries were added. These included tentmaking, printing, harness and broommaking, cobbling, carpentry, dressmaking, and the household arts. An eight-page monthly, *The True Educator,* was run off the school press. It was devoted largely to methods of education, emphasizing particularly the importance of combining physical and mental labor. Elder Haskell, Mrs. White, Professor Bell, and D. A. Robinson were its chief contributors, though typesetting, proofreading, and presswork were done by students.

Now that the school was well established, Professor Bell resumed his position of special responsibility in Battle Creek College —but apparently not until he had secured the services of Mrs. Sara J. Hall, a young teacher whom he personally had trained, to head the English department at South Lancaster. D. A. Robinson was appointed principal and the faculty was enlarged.

The third denominational school to be established had outgrown its infancy and was considered worthy of a name—"South Lancaster Academy." Later its alumni would speak proudly of Atlantic Union College.

---
[1] *General Conference Bulletin,* April 15, 1901, p. 223. Cf. W. C. White, Document File 105 J.
[2] *Review and Herald,* April 25, 1882, p. 265. Some say there were only eight, but Rowena E. Purdon (*That New England School,* p. 32) lists nineteen names.
[3] *Review and Herald,* April 25, 1882, p. 265.
[4] Purdon, *op. cit.,* p. 35.
[5] *Review and Herald,* Nov. 14, 1882, p. 720.
[6] *Ibid.,* Jan. 15, 1884, p. 34.

Across the Waters and Back

ELDER HASKELL sailed for England from New York on May 7, 1882, on the *Persian Monarch,* a cargo vessel that also carried a few passengers. Awaiting his arrival in Southampton was an Adventist, J. W. Gardner, who had been appointed as his European guide and interpreter. Gardner had traveled in Northern and Central Europe and was somewhat familiar with the customs and languages in the areas.

In England the mission family gave Elder Haskell a warm welcome. After a satisfying meal and a look around, he was ready to sit down and listen as the workers related experiences connected with the beginning of the proclamation of the message in Britain. The first Seventh-day Adventist worker there was William Ings, a Britisher who had lived in the United States and had gone to help in our infant publishing work in Switzerland, then had returned to his homeland in 1878. He began house-to-house work in Southampton, talking and praying with the people and taking subscriptions for periodicals. God blessed his efforts. At the end of the first sixteen weeks he reported ten persons keeping the Sabbath of the Lord. He also visited many ships anchored in the harbor, talked with the sailors and passengers, and handed them literature.

Late that year the General Conference sent J. N. Loughborough to begin public evangelism. His first address in Southampton was delivered on January 5, 1879, in Shirley Hall, to an audience of 150 people. That spring a tent was erected in a suburb of the city, and another series of Bible lectures was given. Maude Sisley soon arrived from America to assist him. She was already successful as a colporteur and a house-to-house evangelistic worker of the type that later came to be called a Bible worker, now a Bible instructor. Loughborough gave seventy-four discourses before the weather became so foggy and rainy that the tent had to be abandoned. A large dwelling, Ravenswood, was leased to serve as headquarters. By 1882 many lights were kindled in other cities. Reinforcements had come from America. At that time A. A. John was conducting a series of lectures in the Hall of Science in Grimsby, Lincolnshire, and also holding open-air meetings and distributing literature in and about the city.

The missionary family in England were of good courage as they talked with Haskell about the new Sabbathkeepers who were so

A workers' council at Ravenswood, the mission headquarters at Southampton, England, during Haskell's visit, in 1882. At the far left are William Ings and his wife; next Jennie Thayer; then R. W. Gardner and his wife; Haskell, with the Loughboroughs' son and daughter behind him; J. N. Loughborough and his wife; a friend.

earnest in their efforts to interest relatives and friends in the grand Bible truths they had recently discovered. These new converts were busy selling journals and lending tracts. Others by their godly lives and Christian ministry were bearing witness to the truth in a quiet way. There were businessmen who merely by closing their shops on Sabbath were awakening a spirit of inquiry into the Adventist teachings. Some churches were suffering persecution, but this served only to increase interest in the message.

The Father of the Tract and Missionary Societies was thrilled when told of the large amount of literature being distributed since the organization of the National Tract Society of England, and more thrilled when he held in his hand a sheet printed on their own press. That small paper was being sent out as a supplement to the *Signs,* but would soon be known as *Present Truth.* In the editorial office he met Jennie Thayer, whom he had known in South Lancaster. He learned that hundreds of packages of tracts were placed by ship missionaries on vessels leaving England for distant ports. Missionaries crossing the Atlantic talked with ship captains and officers and won their cooperation in carrying literature free of charge to various ports.

Many tracts were being distributed among the thousands of Scandinavian and other emigrants aboard ships en route to new homes in the New World. As far as possible this literature was given them in their own language that they might be able to read it during their long voyage and talk with one another regarding the truths presented in its pages.

Haskell wrote home to the *Review:* "The judgment alone will reveal the full results of the ship work. Vessels leaving Southampton have carried our publications to all parts of the world. Many packages have been taken to ports in Africa and other countries, and have been sent to the interior by those who are interested in missionary work."[1] He stated that he believed God was raising up men and women who did not yet have full knowledge of Bible truth to scatter the message.

Haskell and Gardner were planning to attend a conference in Tramelan, Switzerland, in September. Desiring to visit Seventh-day Adventist churches on the Continent, they left England in June. On the way to Switzerland they spent a little time in Paris. Haskell writes: "Some of these [places] were of particular interest to us, since they called to mind scenes in the French Revolution, as well as in connection with the impious worship of the goddess of reason. . . . There is scarcely anything in or about the city of Paris which is not a reminder of the influence which has been so strongly exerted against God and religion."[2]

At Basel the travelers were saddened to find J. N. Andrews rapidly failing in health. He was so weak that he could speak but briefly, and often this would bring on a siege of coughing. Though in the late stages of tuberculosis, he was using his remaining fragment of strength in writing articles and tracts and in editing the French paper, *Les Signes des Temps*. He was able to write by dictation.

Late in June they visited Tramelan, where was the oldest Seventh-day Adventist church in Europe. It had originated through the work of a converted Catholic priest named Czechowski, who, while living in America, had joined the Seventh-day Adventist Church. Burning with zeal to spread the knowledge of the heavenly truth that had inspired his soul, he asked to be sent to the Old Country. But the church leaders felt that he should not be sent, at least at that time. He then persuaded another Adventist denomination to send him. He preached the Sabbath anyway and won converts in northern Italy and Switzerland, then he traveled on to Romania, but he did not tell them of his denominational connection. After he had gone some of his Swiss converts in the group at Tramelan found among some papers he had left behind a copy of the *Review*, which bore a Battle Creek, Michigan, postmark.

They were overjoyed to learn that there was a group of people in America who held the same Bible beliefs they had been taught by the converted priest. Albert Vuilleumier opened correspondence with the publishing house, which eventuated in the Swiss believers' sending a representative to America requesting that a minister come and instruct them further.

James Erzberger, a young evangelist who had joined the Tramelan church, was selected to make the journey and transmit the request. It is related that, not being conversant with the English language, he carried with him an envelope addressed to "James White, General Conference, Battle Creek, Mich." This he showed to steamship officers and railroad men along the way; they, in turn, directed him to Battle Creek and the Review and Herald office. For about fifteen months Erzberger remained in the States learning English and becoming versed in Seventh-day Adventist doctrines. Adémar Vuilleumier, also from Switzerland, joined him, having come to America for the same purpose. Adémar worked at the Review office, where he became familiar with publishing methods. During the summer he acted as tent master for evangelistic meetings. At the end of two years he returned to Switzerland. Erzberger had returned home in 1870, ordained as a Seventh-day Adventist minister. Thus the Tramelan group became the nucleus of our work in Europe.

Haskell and his party arrived on July 6 at Christiania (now Oslo), Norway, where they witnessed the baptism of eleven persons; after which seventy-eight brethren and sisters celebrated the Lord's Supper. Then on the next Sabbath and Sunday Haskell held meetings.

On July 12 he went with J. G. Matteson, director of the Scandinavian mission, for a visit to Sweden. At Grythyttehed he preached several times, endeavoring to strengthen the brethren in the tenets of the faith and in tithing, and helped organize a tract society.

Thence he went to the Netherlands, and spent a weekend in Germany before returning to Switzerland.

In August, before the conference, Elder Haskell visited a few Sabbathkeepers at Torre Pellice, in Italy, the fruit of the work of Czechowski. Gardner translated Haskell's English into French, then some members of the group rendered it in the local idiom. With their English, French, and Italian Bibles, the believers gathered around a large table in some home and enjoyed a spiritual feast. As they studied together under the instruction of one thoroughly versed in the Scriptures, they gathered clearer understanding of Bible teachings, their faith in the "sure word of prophecy" was strengthened, their zeal quickened, and their determination deepened to exemplify these truths in their lives.

These people seemed to sense a close connection with the Source of love—that love which "endureth all things." When in the late

Above: A Waldensian valley, in northern Italy. Below: The town of Torre Pellice, a principal Waldensian center.

hours of the night their gatherings broke up, the hearty handshake, the radiant smile, the unrestrained tears, spoke their fellowship of joy better than words could have expressed.

While at Torre Pellice the traveling brethren visited nearby caves in which the Vaudois—the Waldensians—had hidden during times of persecution. At one of these caves the climbers laid aside their coats and heavy garments, and as they continued the exploration they removed their shoes and socks to enable them to cling more firmly to rocks along the narrow passageways. Elder Haskell took one brief look at the entrance, then, with a vigorous shake of his head, he refused to subject his large proportions to the risk of being trapped within. Gardner, a smaller man, took the risk and went inside.

In that dark, tortuous cavern the forefathers of their guide had hidden from their persecutors. The local people told of the days when their ancestors had been hunted like wild beasts, put to the sword, burned at the stake, tortured, and confined in loathsome dungeons for no greater crime than owning and reading a book containing the teachings of Jesus and His apostles and prophets. Experiences related under these circumstances took on new reality and vividness; their present inconveniences seemed by comparison to shrink into nothingness.

The three-day conference at Tramelan, September 8-11, was fully occupied by reports of progress from the widely scattered missions and by consideration of plans for the advancement of the message. A few of the brief interludes between meetings were filled with recitals of experiences in connection with the entrance of the message into Central Europe. The two American brethren enjoyed hearing the story of the first Seventh-day Adventist church in Europe, of their search for light, and of their joy on learning that there was an organized body of Christians on the other side of the world who believed and practiced the Bible truths they had accepted. Elder Haskell doubtless told them of Mrs. White's vision almost eight years before at Battle Creek, Michigan, in which she had seen small groups of people scattered over the earth searching the Scriptures, then looking wistfully to heaven and praying for light.

At this conference Elder Haskell's earnest appeals for all lay members to take an active part in tract and missionary work and to sustain it with their means brought a quick response. The experiences he told awakened firm confidence in the literature ministry as a fruitful means of missionary endeavor.

At the close of the conference a larger gathering of workers was convened at Basel for the purpose of unifying the scattered European missions and discussing methods of evangelism. This gathering was afterward known as the first session of the European Council of Seventh-day Adventists.

In his travels Haskell noted the substantial progress made in the printing and circulation of publications in several languages. Tracts needed by evangelists were being translated into the language of the area and the money raised locally for their publication.

The journal *Les Signes des Temps,* published in the French language, was carrying a knowledge of present truth into nearly every country of Central Europe. It bore a clear, outspoken testimony to the Sabbath, the law of God, the coming of Jesus, immortality only through Christ, gospel temperance, and other important Bible truths. A few tracts had been translated into Arabic. The Danish-Norwegian paper *Advent Tidende,* first issued in 1872, edited by J. G. Matteson and printed at Battle Creek, was being widely circulated. Thousands of copies were sent to relatives and friends in the Old Country by Scandinavian people who had settled in the United States.

During the six months or more that Haskell spent in Europe he visited nearly every country into which the message had found entrance. The various conferences and council sessions held while he was there created a closer unity among the widely scattered missions. His earnest appeals and wise counsel inspired workers and lay members alike with fresh energy and zeal. As he prayed with them his faith in God's leadership, his bright picture of future advance, inspired faith and courage. His practical business ability and his experience in conducting important enterprises with small financial resources and few helpers—all combined to light their way through many perplexing situations and to point them to success.

Haskell's heart was warmed by the courage and loving fellowship of the converts, by their joyful enthusiasm in persuading others to investigate facts of faith which they had found substantial and trustworthy. More than ever impressed with the value of literature evangelism, he strongly advocated local publication of reading matter in the various European tongues. He drew up plans for the establishment of a mission center in London and for the removal of the publishing plant from Grimsby to London. While in Basel he rented a building that contained a good-sized hall suitable for public meetings. Soon after his departure the mission family moved in and Elder Erzberger delivered a course of Bible lectures, which resulted in the addition of new believers to the church.

The two years that followed Haskell's visit witnessed a great forward movement. Periodicals and tracts in the various languages of Europe followed in ever-increasing number. In Basel the Imprimerie Polyglotte ("The Many-Language Printing Office") was established and became the chief publishing center in Europe. The Christiania house also added new books, tracts, and periodicals. As soon as literature was available, tract societies were organized and colporteurs trained. When mission funds were insufficient ministers and members often financed a publication themselves.

When the time came for Elder Haskell to return to the homeland, a letter preceded him expressing the sincere appreciation of the European churches for the willingness of the American brethren to spare one of their leading men to come to their assistance.

On his return to South Lancaster, Haskell's first interest was the school. Then toward the end of the year came the General Conference session, at which he reported on his European journey and the work overseas. The following spring found him in California (for he was also the president of the California Conference as well as the New England Conference). At a camp meeting near Lemoore, California, occurred an incident that proved to be a turning point in the method of evangelism that affected the whole denomination. He had been perplexed regarding certain counsel recently given him by Sister White. As the story is told, he looked up his long-time friend W. C. White and said, "Willie, I want you to come and pray with me. Several times your mother has told me that I should do less preaching and more teaching. I don't understand exactly what that involves." The two went into a nearby grainfield and prayed together, pleading God's promises to give wisdom to all who ask in faith.

Then came a rainy day. During a heavy downpour the drumming of rain on the tent roof drowned out the sound of Elder Haskell's voice. The people crowded into the center of the tent to avoid the spattering rain. Not wishing to lose time, Elder Haskell took his stand by the center pole, and began asking questions and giving out Scripture texts to be read in answer to the questions. The rain continued. Elder Haskell continued also, asking questions and giving out texts. Interest ran high. Scarcely anyone left until the dinner bell rang at one o'clock.

Some of the brethren passed Mrs. White's tent. She called to them and asked what had been going on in the big tent. When they told her she said, "That's what Elder Haskell should do; this is the way the people should be instructed." She later told him that what he had done was in harmony with the light she had received. She related having seen in vision many young people going from house to house with Bibles under their arms, teaching truth in a quiet way.

The 1883 General Conference session recommended this question-and-answer method of teaching and arranged for the publication of the *Bible Reading Gazette* (eventually replaced by a book called *Bible Readings for the Home Circle*, translated into many languages and issued in many editions). The "Bible reading" method was taken up immediately by colporteurs in meeting customers' questions.

The following autumn Haskell was asked to teach this method in a ten-day "Bible reading institute" preceding the General Conference session at Battle Creek. Courses in the method were offered at Healdsburg College and later at South Lancaster Academy. Thus Haskell became an apostle not only of house-to-house distribution of the printed page but also of house-to-house personal evangelism through Bible studies. The "Bible reading" method, though not new, now first became a major development in evangelism, and "Bible reading workers" (now called Bible instructors) were recruited from the lay members.

Beginning also in 1883, a number of "city missions" were opened in New York and other large cities—not, as the term is usually understood, welfare missions for the down-and-out, but forerunners of the modern evangelistic center. Haskell was one of the chief promoters of these, and wrote many articles on the subject in the *Review*. The International Tract and Missionary Society, of which he was the president, sponsored some of these and furnished publications for their use. The mission provided living quarters for the workers and a center for colporteur evangelism, Bible studies, and small public meetings; and it served to train lay workers. Some city missions had reading rooms, others had lecture halls, and in coastal cities ship mission work was included. Wherever a nucleus of converts was gathered, a church was organized.

The typical Seventh-day Adventist city mission of the 1880's conducted a school for the special training of house-to-house Bible instructors. It was launched with the hope that it would cost the conference little or nothing. Every member of the team was expected to earn his share of the living expenses by selling books and periodicals, which would be a means of awakening an interest in the message they had come to bring. By economy and careful planning the cost of running the home must be kept at a minimum. Church members were asked to send contributions of fruits, vegetables, and other foods. However, these missions rarely proved self-supporting.

At the 1889 General Conference session it was recommended that the name "city mission" be dropped, since it was misunderstood by the public, and that such missions become "canvassing stations," with Bible instructors working along with the colporteurs. The training of Bible instructors was to be centered in the Chicago Bible School. During the 1890's many city missions (welfare missions) were operated for the poor. Twenty years after the evangelistic missions had begun in the 1880's, Haskell had the opportunity to conduct such missions, which he called Bible Training Schools, in New York and other cities, and to demonstrate the operation of these on a self-supporting basis (see the chapter "The New York City Mission").

[1] *Review and Herald,* June 27, 1882, p. 409.
[2] *Ibid.,* Aug. 1, 1882, p. 488.

Abram La Rue's headquarters for colporteur work in Honolulu in 1885 (before he began his better-known work in Hong Kong). This building he called the Honolulu branch of the International Tract and Missionary Society. In May of that year Haskell, with several other missionaries en route to Australia, paid La Rue a three-hour visit in the middle of the night while their ship was in port.

Pioneering in Australia

MORE THAN TEN years had passed since Elder Haskell heard Mrs. White relate her vision of the printing presses, in which Australia had been specifically mentioned. He had never relinquished his desire to pioneer the work in that specially designated mission field. A similar desire was cherished by John O. Corliss, who had also heard the vision related. At last their dream came true. On May 10, 1885, a party of missionaries sailed from San Francisco on a seven-thousand-mile voyage across the Pacific, bound for the land down under. Stephen Haskell, director of the enterprise, was accompanied by John O. Corliss, his wife, and two children; also M. C. Israel and family. Two young men, Henry Scott, a printer, and William Arnold, an experienced colporteur, completed the group.

Seven days' voyaging brought them to Honolulu. The steamer, a freighter, arrived a little after midnight and cast anchor, and passengers who so desired were taken ashore. The arrival of the missionaries was entirely unexpected. Because of the threat of war between England and Russia it was supposed that the steamer would not dock. Glancing around in the darkness, and seeing no one at the wharf to greet them, Haskell hired a carriage to take him and his companion ministers to the "International Tract and Missionary Rooms." They found two laymen, Abram La Rue and another colporteur named Scott, who were engaged in missionary operations on the island. By the light of a kerosene lamp they enjoyed a three-hour visit before the ship's siren gave the all-aboard signal.

The visitors were greatly interested to learn of the activities of these two lone workers who distributed literature from door to door, handing it out to any interested persons they met, both on land and on board vessels anchored in the harbor. They had also opened a free reading room to further scatter seeds of truth, and at the same time were supporting themselves by colporteuring. Thirteen persons had embraced present truth. They had also learned of individuals and groups on surrounding islands who were investigating and beginning to practice the truths found in printed messages sent through the mails or dropped ashore by passing ships.

In Samoa the travelers found thriving Christian missions, but no Seventh-day Adventists. The London Bible Society had furnished Bibles to the islanders whether they could read or not, and their teachers had taught them all to carry their Bibles to church with them.

The voyage was restful to the worn and weary workers. Elder Haskell was in special need of relaxation, for his continual travels and incessant toil of the past years, often with poor food and exposure to all kinds of weather, had resulted in physical exhaustion. Only a few weeks before, while he was giving a Sabbath discourse, his strength had failed, and he had been forced to sit down and let another take his place in the pulpit. But after a few days' rest and treatment at the Battle Creek Sanitarium the intrepid warrior was on his feet again and ready to launch out on the Australian mission.

Some time before leaving America he had acquired a typewriter. This he took with him, and from then on it became his constant traveling companion. It served him well and faithfully on this voyage. A few sentences from a typed letter to the *Review* readers will give some idea of his interests during the voyage: "We are privileged to see some things in nature that we have read of, but never expected to see. The 'Southern Cross' . . . is in full view each night. We have the most pleasant evenings ever witnessed. The soft, balmy air and the quiet, gentle breeze felt on the hurricane deck are delightful. The North Star, which has guided so many oppressed fugitives from the land of bondage is not to be seen." [1]

As they were borne forward over the vast ocean, with nothing in sight except blue above and blue beneath, they were led to sense their own littleness and their dependence upon God's care and protection. He was with them on the ship. He would always be with them to guide, instruct, and strengthen as they endeavored to open up a new center of light and blessing in a dark world.

Haskell wrote of soul-inspiring interviews with fellow passengers and of religious services conducted by Elder Corliss in response to requests from the passengers.

When nearing Australia he wrote: "Our last letter was mailed at the Samoan Islands. Since then we have crossed the dayline and had the experience of losing a day in the Pacific Ocean. But it so happened there was no time lost. We reached the 180th Meridian at the close of the Sabbath, May 28. So the proper day to drop from the calendar was Sunday, May 29. Thus, according to the argument made by our opponents against the Sabbath, there is no more Sunday to be kept [Sabbath was May 30; the error may be in his counting back seven days from June 6 across the date line to May 29, then correcting to 28, in the wrong direction, instead of to 30.]. . . .

"We have continued to cast our bread upon the waters by distributing reading matter among the passengers, and preparing Bible readings, which with tracts were placed in empty beer and wine bottles and thrown overboard at points where we had reason to believe they would be washed ashore, or picked up by boatmen."[2]

On Monday, June 1, at 5:00 P.M., the ship anchored at Auckland, New Zealand. The vessel remained at anchor four hours, and the party visited the city and made inquiries about the people and the country.

On the morning of June 6, after a voyage of almost four weeks, the steamer entered the harbor of Sydney, New South Wales, Australia. That evening after the Sabbath, wrote Elder Haskell, they went to a telegraph office and asked when a dispatch would arrive in Massachusetts, U.S.A., and were told, *"To-day,* about this time." The message would have to travel westward, be relayed across Asia, Europe, and the Atlantic cable, and by that time it would be about the same hour in Massachusetts as it had been in Sydney when the message was sent.

Haskell and Israel remained to investigate conditions in Sydney while Corliss and the rest of the party proceeded by coastal steamer south to Victoria to look around in the vicinity of Melbourne. After visiting the free public library Haskell wrote: "We found thirteen of our principal bound books in their catalogue. The library has 60,000 volumes, and during 1884 it had 155,000 readers. In the

Grazing country in Australia, a scene typical of the foothills near the eastern coast; the sort of natural scenery that Haskell described in his reports to the *Review and Herald*.

Sailors' Home we found a small library; but on the table were six of our pamphlets, all much soiled by use. On the front page of each was stamped the following 'From the International Tract and Missionary Society; Free Reading Room, 21 Boylston Place, Boston, Mass. A. T. Robinson, Manager.' 'Sailors' Home' had also been stamped on them. It was like meeting old friends."[3]

After spending a week investigating Sydney and its environs the two men went on to join the others of their company who had preceded them to Victoria. Could we have followed the traveler on those first days while he walked about the wide, stone-paved streets of Melbourne, we doubtless would have noticed a look of satisfaction on his face as he viewed the city's thriving places of business, its comfortable, well-built homes surrounded by exotic shrubs and flowers, and its magnificent government buildings. Perhaps we might even have noticed an amused smile as he recalled a remark made by an American friend to whom he had, before leaving home, expressed pleasure on being included in the pioneer mission group to Australia: The man had asked, "Do you want to go down there and convert those kangaroos?" "We did not know anything about Australia," said Haskell; "we did not think of the English cities there, with nearly a half million English-speaking people in each."[4]

However, four months before the mission party sailed he wrote an article for the *Review* in which he emphasized the fact that its rapidly growing British colonies formed an important center from which the truth might reach millions, and that it could be made an excellent base for missionary work in the South Sea Islands.

Wherever he went he made contact with prominent businessmen as well as industrial, educational, and religious leaders, attempting to learn all he could regarding people and places, thus hoping to find the best possible location in which to begin missionary activities.

In the *Review* he wrote of the large proportion of white people in comparison with the small, rapidly diminishing number of aborigines, who were seen no more frequently than Indians were seen in the United States.

He spoke of the natural beauty and delightful climate of the country, of the variety of brilliantly plumaged birds, and the dense forests. He told of its vast mineral wealth, of its extensive cattle- and sheep-raising industries, which supplied an abundance of raw material for the thriving woolen factories of its cities.

He mentioned especially the orchards of New South Wales. Their fruit was exported to many parts of the world. It had been claimed that Australia produced the largest orange trees in the world. One advertiser maintained that 10,000 oranges had been gathered from one tree within a single year!

He wrote of the many fine buildings in Sydney and of its lighthouse, which stood on a 270-foot cliff, casting a light that could be seen thirty miles out at sea. He mentioned the city's beautiful public parks and botanical gardens.

He noted that the people were eager to keep pace with the rest of the world. "No part of America," he wrote, "unless it be some of the New England States perhaps, has so many libraries in proportion to its inhabitants as Australia and New Zealand."[5] He also found a well-established public school system. In regard to religion he reported the Episcopalians as the most numerous, the Roman Catholics next in number, the Lutherans also quite strong, and nearly all denominations represented.

The colonies and many of the surrounding islands had postal, telegraphic, and shipping communications with one another and with the mainland.

He urged the establishment of the Australian mission and appealed for men and means for that part of the world.

The mission party eventually decided to begin work in the thriving city of Melbourne. Within a month of their arrival they were settled in a large suburb, Richmond, and ready to work. But how should they begin? Rents were exorbitant. To hire a hall would exhaust their limited funds. July winter weather was cold and rainy. Three or four months would elapse before they could hold public tent meetings.

Their only remaining resource was house-to-house evangelism. The three ministers began a home-visitation program, giving Bible readings and holding cottage meetings at every opportunity. The entire missionary company distributed literature from door to door and assisted with cottage meetings. The group organized a Sabbath school and began conducting Sabbath services.

A few weeks after their arrival Elder Haskell wrote: "Sabbath, July 4, was an encouraging day for the Australian Mission. We met as usual at ten A.M. for Sabbath school." Twelve persons were arranged in four classes. As a result of their early evangelism in that area a man came in and announced that he, with his brother and an unmarried cousin, had decided to keep the Sabbath, and that their two wives were considering doing the same. This man had received and read a copy of the *Signs* mailed from San Francisco, had welcomed Elder Israel when he called on him, and had opened his home for Bible studies.

Said Haskell, "We had no fatted calf, but tears of joy were shed as we reaped these first fruits of our Australian Mission."

One of their first concerns was to make friends among the leading business and professional men of Melbourne, and to explain to them their aims in coming to Australia. Many seemed pleased and stated that a new kind of religion might intrigue some who had thus far shown little religious interest. But it was with difficulty that the brethren found access to the common people, especially those who were church members. These Americans with their new doctrines were looked upon with suspicion.

At first the *Signs* and other papers were mostly given away, chiefly because any effort to sell caused the missionaries to be regarded suspiciously as American speculators. The populace looked upon Americans as a people bent upon devising money-making schemes; but by giving away their papers the missionaries allayed suspicion and the people became more friendly.

But difficulty was encountered even in giving papers away. Few places could be found for tract distribution boxes. But the city contained numerous parks, and there, between the tips of ornamental iron fence posts, the workers tucked copies of the *Signs* where men passing to and from work could pick them up. They also left papers in shops and handed them out at railway stations and other public places while continuing to distribute them from house to house.

As soon as a few persons showed an interest in Bible studies the workers began to meet keen opposition. Unfriendly notices appeared in both secular and religious papers; the clergy warned their flocks not to permit these strangers to enter their homes, and a number of them threatened to discipline any who should do so. One preacher who attempted to expose Adventism stated that it arose in the "obscure State of New England," whence everything that was bad had come, and many things that were good; that there was one Miller, in America, who had proved to be a false prophet, and that out of his theory Adventism had developed. In one of the largest papers in the city there were three articles in one issue warning all against Adventists.

Another argument presented by the ministers was that it was dangerous to read the Scriptures without a pastor being present to explain them. This reminded Elder Haskell of the arguments of church leaders in the days of Luther. In a few instances homes were entered and Bible studies interrupted by men determined to break up the meetings. Some of the most influential members of a large Sunday school who took their stand on the Word of God were disfellowshiped without being permitted to say a word in meeting in explanation of their change of views.

During much of this time Elder Haskell was touring the colonies, gathering information that would later be extremely valuable. He carried with him names and addresses of some who had received literature from America; he was made welcome in their homes.

In Tasmania, an island about 200 miles south of Melbourne, he remained ten days visiting, taking subscriptions for the *Signs,* and securing agents for the new paper soon to be published in Melbourne. He was invited to speak to the YMCA and before other gatherings. He left copies of the best Adventist books in the public libraries of Tasmania's two principal cities, Hobart and Launceston.

Henry Scott formed an acquaintance with the overseer of the city library in Richmond, and was soon holding Bible readings in his home. This man was foreman of a large clothing establishment that hired more than a hundred hands. He took a club of fifty *Signs* to distribute among his men, and purchased ten bound books for lending purposes.

Besides holding Bible studies, Scott, being a printer, was investigating the prospects of equipping a printing establishment. When the time approached for opening tent meetings he purchased a small press and some type. Five thousand copies of a *Signs* supplement were printed, with a cover picture of the 40-by-62-foot tent in which the meetings were to be held. These were attached to copies of the regular *Signs* and freely distributed.

In September, the beginning of summer down under, the tent was erected in North Fitzroy, a suburb of Melbourne. Elder Corliss opened a series of Bible lectures. The first night's attendance was two hundred. Some had come from homes where Bible readings were being held. Others were attracted by papers they had taken from shops and parks. Many came from curiosity, to learn what it was that had been so bitterly denounced in the papers.

That summer the tent was pitched in five different places in the vicinity of Melbourne. Every lecture series was well attended; 20,000 copies of the *Signs* were distributed. Quite a number became convinced, followed the light, and began working for relatives and friends, using Bible lessons that the ministers prepared for them to give.

An experience which greatly cheered the workers was that of a Presbyterian deacon who attended a few meetings, purchased some tracts, and embraced the Sabbath. His brother and sister-in-law were displeased that he should accept so unpopular a doctrine. They requested their son, a highly educated man, to visit his uncle and convince him of his error. After an interview lasting nearly all night, the nephew became convinced that his uncle was right and went home a Sabbathkeeper. He began working for his parents, his brothers, sisters, and other relatives; as a result thirteen out of a family of fourteen followed the light of Bible truth.

A well-known, prosperous contractor heard a few discourses and became interested. He and his wife took their stand with others, and began at once to work for their near relatives. Within a few weeks nine of them embraced the Sabbath. The contractor did not stop with this. He notified his workmen that he was not going to have any more Saturday work.

A few were dissatisfied. These were at once paid off and discharged. He told the others that they might put six days' work into five by working overtime. As he was already behind on a government contract, he knew that unless the work was completed on a certain date he would forfeit his pay. The men protested that they would have to work on Saturdays in order to finish at the appointed time. He replied that they could work on Sunday.

Work on Sunday! Who had ever heard of such a thing! The men were indignant.

It looked like trouble for the contractor. He explained the situation to his government employer. His proposition was accepted. They could work on Sunday. But the police were angry and threatened to prosecute; they then went to a reliable lawyer for counsel. He said to them, "The English laws are founded upon the law of God, and if it should turn out that these men are right in their explanation of that law, it might go hard with you." The lawyer advised them to carry the matter no further, and it was dropped.

This affair stirred the community. The people said, "We want to know what has given that contractor the queer idea that he should rest on Saturday and work on Sunday." A time was set for them to meet and talk the matter over. The contractor expected to meet a few individuals, but imagine his surprise when he arrived and found a crowded house! He gave a convincing Bible study on true Sabbath observance. His hearers were deeply interested. Some even asked for further religious instruction.

The Australian mission was prospering; the torch of truth once lighted in the community now shone forth with ever-increasing brilliancy into all parts of the city and surrounding country.

---
[1] *Review and Herald,* June 30, 1885, p. 410.
[2] *Ibid.,* July 28, p. 473.
[3] *Ibid.,* Aug. 4, p. 490.
[4] *General Conference Bulletin,* April 15, 1901, p. 233.
[5] *Review and Herald,* Aug. 4, 1885, p. 490.

In New Zealand

"WHY DON'T YOU publish a paper here in Australia?" This question was often asked by those to whom copies of the *Signs of the Times* were handed, not because they found fault with the *Signs* that came from America, but because of strong sentiment in favor of home production. And there were other reasons why a paper should be printed in Australia. A month was required for the *Signs* to cross the Pacific from America, and forty-two days for *Present Truth* to arrive from England. By that time news was outdated. Then, too, there would be a saving in postage. Local papers mailed from Melbourne to any of the colonies or surrounding islands could be sent for one cent a copy, or packaged for two cents a pound, and from Sydney they could be sent free if mailed within seven days of issue.

But the establishment of a printing plant would require money. The two thousand dollars promised by the General Conference had not yet arrived. In this crisis, as in every other, God had His way prepared to provide the necessary means. William Arnold, the colporteur, on reaching the colonies had at once begun selling books from door to door. At least he tried to sell them. The first six weeks he took not one order for a book. But he refused to be discouraged or to give up. One noon hour he found a retired spot and prayed until he received the assurance of victory. Then he returned to work and "broke all sales records."

Now, when money was needed, he came forward and with his own earnings bought the larger press at a cost of one thousand dollars. Elder Corliss purchased the engine and Elder Haskell the small press to be used for printing supplements and other notices. Friends gave or lent money, and preparations for publishing went forward. Two young converts, W. H. B. Miller and J. H. Woods, sold their printing business and joined heartily in the publishing and evangelistic work.

On his scouting tours in towns surrounding Melbourne Elder Haskell searched for reliable men in the employ of various news agencies who would work for the new journal either by selling single copies or by taking subscriptions. After the tent meetings in Melbourne were well started he decided on a trip to New Zealand. He would look over the territory and size up its advantages or disadvantages for evangelistic efforts. And while there he might be able to secure agents for the forthcoming paper.

So, early in October, 1885, he sailed for Auckland, expecting to be absent only a short time. He carried a letter of introduction from the American consul at Melbourne to the American consul at Auckland. On the ship, while in friendly conversation with the captain, he inquired about a suitable lodging place in the city and was directed to the boarding house of Edward Hare.

He found the place without difficulty and was soon settled in a comfortable upstairs room. With books, typewriter, and clothing neatly arranged, he was ready for work. Now the question was how to begin operations in this strange city. His first concern was to receive working orders from above. When deeply in earnest Stephen Haskell had a habit of praying aloud. At the sound of his voice a boarder in the adjoining room became alarmed. He bolted down the stairs shouting, "Mr. Hare! Mrs. Hare! That new roomer next to me is crazy. He keeps talking to himself. Either get rid of him or I'll leave."

Edward Hare hurried upstairs and listened at the keyhole, and this is what he heard: "Dear Lord, he's such a good man. He already believes in Thy soon coming. Help me to present the Sabbath to him so that he will accept that, too."

Edward found his wife. "Lizzie," he said, "that man isn't crazy! He's praying—praying for me!"

Soon Haskell was conversing with his host on the most friendly terms. He learned that Hare belonged to a family of early settlers who had come to New Zealand from Ireland. The Hares, because of certain peculiar views acquired through independent Bible study, had severed their connection with their former church and had joined a progressive-minded group of Bible believers who designated themselves by the name *Christian*. These people conducted a weekly class in which certain doctrinal points were discussed every Thursday evening. Would Elder Haskell go and present to them those doctrines wherein his church differed from theirs? This was Haskell's opportunity. His first meeting with them ended in free, friendly discussion of the Sabbath question. When another Bible-study class of the same nature was held in a different suburb of the city, he presented the personal, visible appearing of Christ. The Hares were enraptured with the magnificent truths that Elder Haskell brought out so clearly. After those first class meetings they spent every spare moment studying with him at the boarding house. For three weeks they met together at every opportunity, their interest and enthusiasm at fever pitch. At the end of this time Edward and Lizzie Hare were full-fledged Sabbathkeepers.

Said Edward, "I want my father and brothers to hear what you have been telling me." He persuaded his new friend and teacher to go with him on a 160-mile trip to the north of the island and visit his father's large family. There were actually three sets of brothers and sisters. Some years before, after the death of Edward's mother, his father had married a widow with eight children. He already had eleven of his own. Five more were born to this couple, making a grand total of twenty-four sons and daughters! At this time most of them had married and were living near the father's home in a small country town called Kaeo.

Father Joseph Hare had been a schoolteacher in Ireland for twenty years before coming to New Zealand. Both Joseph and his son Robert were Methodist preachers. When Edward introduced Elder Haskell to his father and told what a wonderful Bible teacher he was, Father Hare immediately asked him to occupy his pulpit. Haskell's message that first Sunday was based on Daniel 2. It was well received. But later, when he presented the prophecy of Daniel 7, touched on the change made in the law of God by the Papacy, and stated that the seventh day of the week was the true Sabbath of the Bible, Father Hare thought, This is going too far. He said to Haskell, "You have helped me so much with the studies on prophecy, now I'd like to set you straight on this Jewish Sabbath idea."

Accordingly word was sent out to the five married sons living

The home of Joseph Hare in Kaeo; the childhood home of Edward Hare, of Auckland, who was Haskell's first convert in New Zealand.

nearby, and they all met at their childhood home to hear their father set this American Adventist preacher straight on the Sabbath question. The group sat at the long dining table, Elder Haskell at one end and Father Hare at the other, with the five sons seated along the sides —all with their Bibles.

It is easy to imagine something of how the study progressed. After an opening prayer, Father Hare began by stating that Christ, in honor of His resurrection, changed the Sabbath from Saturday to Sunday. Elder Haskell did not argue the point. When they waited for him to speak he gave out a scripture and asked them to turn and read it; when they had read it, before there was time for argument, he gave out another and asked them to read that. In this manner he proceeded. He spoke few words, but answered every question and met every objection by asking them to find their answers in the Bible. Midnight came, and they were still turning from scripture to scripture. It was becoming evident to them all that neither Jesus nor His disciples changed the Sabbath day, that God had nothing to do with its change, but that a great anti-Christian power—a power which thought itself able to legislate for the Sovereign of the universe—had set up its own institution in place of the one God had commanded.

It was also becoming clear that the law nailed to the cross was not the great moral law of ten commandments, which God Himself pronounced changeless, but the ceremonial law regulating sacrificial offerings, which were a "shadow of things to come." It was this ceremonial law that ceased to be of significance when the true Lamb of God made the sacrifice of His life on Calvary (Col. 2:14-17).

About two o'clock there came a pause in the study. A moment of complete silence settled over the group. Each of those stalwart, earnest, Christian men considered the implications of the truth so recently opened up to him and the solemn duty that it involved.

At last Father Hare stood up and said, "Elder Haskell, by the grace of God, next Saturday I am going to do what I thought I had been doing all my life; I am going to keep the Sabbath of God holy."

Then one by one each of the others said, "I will do the same."

The next day Father Joseph Hare sent out an announcement: "From now on my store will be closed from sundown Friday evening till sundown Saturday evening." Two of the brothers, Metcalf and Robert, arranged to give their ship-building business a twenty-four hour pause; and in the homes of those five brothers preparations were immediately made to keep holy the Sabbath of the fourth commandment.

Robert wrote a letter to his fiancée, giving her what he considered the "good news" regarding the Sabbath of creation, and listing the texts that had led to his conclusion. The following Sunday he made *the true Sabbath* the subject of his discourse at the little church he was pastoring in a nearby village. Imagine his disappointment as, standing at the door to shake hands after the service, he was told by several, "We don't want your Saturday Sabbath." "You need not preach any more for us if you are going to keep that Old Testament rest day."

But the worst came when with eager fingers Robert opened a reply to the letter he had so hopefully written his sweetheart and found her engagement ring within. With aching heart he read the concluding words of her letter: "Robert, you must choose between me and your Jewish Sabbath." He had begun building their home and had purchased some furniture, including a piano, which was already on its way from America. His Emily should have the very best! And now this was the answer.

When Robert told Elder Haskell of his disappointment, the older man said kindly, "Well, it takes some people a little longer than others to see the light—and, of course, some never do." Emily Smith was one of those who never did.

But a happy thought came to the elder, and as a result of that happy thought, Robert, a few weeks later, was on board a steamer headed for California. He would spend a few years at Healdsburg College in preparation for his chosen lifework—spreading the good news of Jesus' coming and sounding the call to obey *all* the commandments of God.

During the three weeks of his stay at Kaeo, Elder Haskell filled Joseph Hare's pulpit each Sunday. The two men visited the townspeople and also held meetings in a hall. Several persons who attended were willing to investigate the "new doctrines," and some took their stand for Bible truth.

Before returning to his publishing interests in Melbourne, Elder Haskell accompanied Edward Hare and his wife to a Maori village where they were holding meetings. The Maoris, the original inhabitants of New Zealand, were an intelligent, superior class of people, whom the Hares had been instructing in Christianity. Joseph Hare served as pastor-evangelist, and Mrs. Hare as physician. On this occasion Elder Haskell preached and Mr. Hare interpreted. After listening to his graphic description of the coming of Jesus, the reunion of loved ones, and the glorious, eternal home of the saved, the listening company expressed unbounded joy at the assurance that Jesus would return and take them to Himself.

A farewell gathering on the evening before the elder's departure from Kaeo, at which time he was presented a generous purse,

The first home of the Bible Echo Publishing House (now the Signs Publishing Company), a rented building in Melbourne, Australia.

evidenced the genuine appreciation of his new converts for the grand truths he had brought them.

En route to Melbourne he stopped at various New Zealand coastal towns to visit families whose names he had brought with him. He reported that in many places there were those who had received our publications from America, and were eager to hear about the Sabbath and the coming of Christ. In this region he found the religious and secular press more friendly than in Australia; the clergy, however, were "as determined to monopolize the ground as they are anywhere else."

January saw him back in Melbourne in time to welcome the first issue of *The Bible Echo and Signs of the Times* as it came from the press. When, a few weeks later, the time came for him to return to the United States, he wrote that at Melbourne there was a church of forty-five members.

On the way home he stopped in New Zealand. As the steamer neared land Elder Haskell's solicitude for his recent converts deepened. Had they remained steadfast? Was their limited knowledge of Bible truth sufficient to enable them to meet the arguments of former church associates? His questions were soon answered. With unbounded joy he wrote: "I found the friends still holding firmly to the truths which they had received at the time of my first visit, and the interest to hear, instead of diminishing, had deepened and extended. At the same time the opposition had grown more fierce from those who had rejected the truth."[1]

Elder Haskell learned that Edward Hare had placed Seventh-day Adventist publications, including bound volumes of the *Signs,* on nearly all the steamers sailing from Auckland. He had given all his time to the selling of our publications and to distributing them on board vessels; and his wife had opened correspondence with persons on the various islands.

From Kaeo, Elder Haskell wrote: "It was on Tuesday at five o'clock P.M. that we met for our last baptism. We then celebrated the ordinances at the house of Father Hare, organized a church as far as we could, arranged for a Sabbath-school, and on Wednesday I left them, and they held their first public Sabbath meeting alone."[2]

It was hard to part with those to whom he had become deeply attached in so short a time. Reluctantly he also left the many speaking invitations he had received and which he would have been glad to fill. But important engagements awaited him in America; his ticket was purchased, and he was obliged to leave on the appointed date.

Of his last days in New Zealand he wrote: "On Monday, while at Auckland, I received the following telegram [from Kaeo]: 'Services and Sabbath-school well attended. Isa. 12:1, 2.'

"We returned the following: 'Telegram received. 1 Cor. 15:57, 58.' Since then we have received encouraging letters from them. They have now organized a course of Bible readings which they hold each night in the week except Sunday. They have also undertaken the task of carrying the truth to every family in that section of the country."[3]

Early on Friday morning on May 7, 1886, Stephen Haskell stepped from a train in the good old South Lancaster station. He stood in the brightening dawn, looking this way and that as if to make sure that he was really home. Then he strode rapidly up the street toward South Hall. Mary had long been awaiting his homecoming. Now, assisted by her attendant, she stepped to the door to greet him. They had been separated thirteen months and seven days. She was sharing a dormitory apartment with a friend and had kept busy during Stephen's long absence writing letters, cheering lonely students, lending them books from her library, and doing whatever she could to encourage her associates.

The two breakfasted together with their friend, enjoyed a brief visit, then hastened to the school chapel, where Elder Haskell related the first of his Australian mission adventures and told stories of the mighty workings of God—stories that were to influence many students to give their lives to the cause he loved so well and had found so rewarding.

---

[1] *Historical Sketches*, p. 105.
[2] *Ibid.*, p. 106.
[3] *Ibid.*

Haskell (rear, fifth from left) at a Nebraska camp meeting, 1880's.

The first Seventh-day Adventist camp meeting in Europe (which Haskell attended), held near Moss, Norway, in the summer of 1887.

Again in Europe

"IT SEEMED a little singular to be where the sun does not set at this time of the year until nearly half-past nine, rising in the morning between two and three, with twilight nearly all night."[1] So wrote Elder Haskell from Moss, Norway, to his friends back home. It was midsummer of the year 1887, and he was attending the very first Seventh-day Adventist camp meeting ever held in Europe. There were only eight family tents pitched in a picturesque grove on an island in the bay, near the border of Norway and Sweden. Many of the campers were obliged to find lodging elsewhere, as the tents ordered from America did not arrive in time for the meeting.

A newspaper, the *Morgenposten,* had this and much more to say about the encampment: " 'The tents are very fine and pleasant, and generally arranged for two families. At first we come into a small every-day room, which stretches across the whole breadth of the tent, and is covered with carpet. The walls are decorated with green leaves and flowers. Altogether we receive the impression that the people occupying these tents must be an economical and well-to-do people. Nothing was seen in the line of taking up collections, for which the Adventists deserve praise.

" 'Besides the one hundred living in the camp, there are about fifty persons taking part in the meetings, who live in different places in the city. There are also in the camp about forty children, belonging to the Sabbath-schools in Christiania [Oslo].' "[2] The article also describes the assembly tent, the "tent for the sale of books," and the "tent where victuals could be obtained." It outlines the daily camp program and states that the campers will stay on the island for a week longer than at first intended, not leaving until June 21.

During this extended week the fifth annual session of the European Council was held. In Basel five years previous, Elder Haskell had assisted in organizing the council. At that time there were only a few isolated believers and groups of Adventists scattered throughout Europe. Now, through God's providence, the last-day message had extended to four countries of Central Europe, the British Isles, Scandinavia, and Southern Russia; the territory had been divided into conferences and mission fields, and a director appointed over each.

Representatives from each area were sent to the council. Stephen Haskell, J. H. Waggoner, D. A. Robinson, and Charles Boyd were some of those from the United States. Ellen G. White and her son William were also there from Switzerland as delegates at large. They had spent two years helping organize and establish the work in Europe.

Cheering reports were brought in from nearly all parts of Europe. Tracts, periodicals, and books in increasing numbers were being published in various European languages. The few ministers spread thinly over Europe traveled from place to place searching for interested persons and groups, holding Bible studies and meetings in private homes, baptizing converts and seeking to establish them in the faith. These workers frequently found people who had read themselves into the message from literature sent them through the various Tract and Missionary Societies.

The reports mentioned a few small but well-established churches in Switzerland, Germany, France, Italy, Norway, Denmark, and Sweden. There was a strong church in Southampton, where Elder Loughborough had conducted evangelistic lectures when he first arrived in England. William Ings had placed tract distribution racks in many public places in Southampton. He had also placed them in more than a hundred London restaurants and in many hotels in Switzerland. He encouraged the Swiss believers to continue this practice, that seeds of the last-day message might be scattered by thousands of homeward-bound vacationers.

It was also reported that at one time R. F. Andrews and S. H. Lane had spent about four weeks in Ireland, searching out interested persons and holding Bible studies with them. They found a few Adventists, including one sister who had been keeping the Sabbath alone for seven years.

Tent meetings were being promoted in Norway and Sweden. There had been some persecution in Denmark, and several colporteurs had been arrested.

A report of experiences in Southern Russia aroused intense interest. As a result of a few evening meetings in private homes, a number had accepted the Sabbath. This set the magistrates in pursuit of the new teachers; but they received warning in time and fled to another city where they continued working quietly until discovered and forced again to flee. Thus they scattered seeds of truth, and a spirit of inquiry was awakened in many places. Even in Siberia, staunch-hearted colporteurs were carrying the message from door to door. L. R. Conradi told the council how almost exactly a year before, he and a German brother in Russia had spent forty days in prison.

At this fifth European Council, conference business and deliberations occupied much time. The publishing work received much attention. Manuscripts must be prepared and translated, then printed. The need for colporteurs' training schools was stressed. The vote was passed to operate a colporteurs' school in each mission for at least three months a year. Two such institutes had been held in Scandinavia during the past year, each extending over a period of three months. Elder Matteson had described one of these training schools: "Instructions in canvassing are given three times a week, and we have recitations in bookkeeping, Swedish grammar, and English twice a week, and in arithmetic, writing, and singing once. At the same time we have lectures on the prophecies and practical religion three times a week, prayer meeting Sabbath-evening, and Sabbath-school Sabbath afternoon. The classes meet every morning at seven o'clock, but the time from nine until three is devoted to canvassing the city."[3]

At the close of the council Elder Haskell, feeling greatly refreshed and spiritually strengthened, took up his new duties in England. Early in July, Ellen G. White and her party, on their way back to America, arrived there. A group of missionaries en route from America to Africa were also in England waiting for their ship to Cape Town. They united in "a praying season," and felt the Spirit of the Lord in their midst as they held the parting meeting.

The next day Mrs. White hired a carriage, and with friends drove to the steamer to visit the group bound for Africa. She wrote: "We could not restrain our tears as we parted with them, not knowing that we should ever meet them again in this life, and not knowing to what they would be subjected in becoming established in their far-off new field of labor." ⁴ A few days later her group sailed for America.

Elder Haskell now entered upon his new assignment in England as editor of the journal *Present Truth*. In anticipation of this he had brought from America numerous cuts with which to illustrate its pages. The printing plant was moved from Grimsby to a suburb of London, thus carrying out a proposal he had made when in England five years earlier. Besides, two rooms were rented in the city in Paternoster Row, then the great book center of the world. One room

Haskell's assistants when he went to England in 1887. Rear: Jennie Owen, W. A. Spicer, Hetty Hurd (who was to become Mrs. Haskell ten years later). Front left, Helen McKinnon. (The picture, made about 1890, also includes Mrs. Spicer.)

would be used as a distributing center for publications—a sort of Book and Bible House—and the other as a place in which to hold Bible studies. His secretary was young William A. Spicer (a future president of the General Conference).

Haskell now focused his attention on establishing a Bible instructors' training school in London. Three young American women—Jennie Owen, Helen McKinnon, and Hetty Hurd—had arrived from America to begin Bible work and to train new converts as house-to-house teachers. After searching several weeks for a favorable location, Elder Haskell rented a large house—The Chaloners—not far from the publishing establishment. The mission family was housed upstairs. On the ground floor a large room was equipped as an assembly hall.

At this time there was only one known Sabbathkeeping Adventist among the millions of London. Elder Haskell visited various places throughout England where efforts were being made to organize companies and churches. The work was progressing steadily, but not as rapidly as in his homeland. Yet he wrote in his usual cheerful vein:

"God selected this nation to be the guardian of the Bible. It is here that the first Bible society was organized, which has sent out over 112,000,000 volumes of the word of God. The Bible has been sent by this people to all the nations of the earth. God will not pass by a nation that has done so great and noble a work, without giving them the light of the closing work of the gospel."[5] He joined Elders Loughborough, Durland, John, Lane, and others who were conducting evangelistic campaigns in halls and tents; and he himself conducted Bible lectures for several weeks in Southampton.

The paper *Present Truth* was prospering. Its circulation had reached five thousand. From London it was sent to the far corners of the earth. One thousand copies went to South Africa and six hundred to Nova Scotia, filling subscription lists that had been worked up largely by the New England tract societies.

As always when new centers of light and truth were opened, there was bitter opposition. Elder Haskell later wrote: "It would seem that Satan had laid every plan to prevent the establishment of the work in this country. But God is greater than the power of the enemy; and with the united prayers of nearly a thousand Sabbath-schools and 25,000 individuals (including children), for God to open the way here in London, we shall expect that something will be accomplished."[6]

That winter Elder Durland conducted a training school for colporteurs; in the spring William Arnold arrived from Australia and began selling books and giving new colporteurs a practical field training in salesmanship.

D. A. Robinson and his wife came from Africa and joined the Bible instructors' training school. About a month after their arrival the first baptism took place. Working quietly and praying constantly, the mission family was beginning to makes its impression.

Elder Haskell wrote: "Individuals come nearly half a mile to the training school to attend a class in history connected with prophecy, which is held at six o'clock, A.M. They return to their homes for breakfast, and come again at half-past nine for another exercise in Bible reading. It is more difficult to gain access to houses here than in America; but when once this is effected, the people are found to have a regard for the Bible that is not found there."[7] Before the end of that year, 1888, a church had been organized in the great city of London.

Elder Haskell's report from the European field when, early in September, he made a surprise appearance at the Maine camp meeting, was one of steady progress. A few weeks later, October 17, he was appointed temporary chairman of the twenty-seventh session of the General Conference in Minneapolis, Minnesota. G. I. Butler, who had served for eight years as General Conference president, was ill and unable to attend.

It had been about eighteen years since Stephen Haskell attended his first General Conference. Then there had been 22 delegates; now there were 91. The last gathering message was extending to all nations of earth, and its light was penetrating earth's spiritual darkness.

---

[1] Haskell, in *Review and Herald*, July 19, 1887, p. 457.
[2] Quoted in *Review and Herald*, Aug. 2, 1887, p. 492.
[3] *Review and Herald*, Feb. 22, 1887, p. 124.
[4] Manuscript 36, 1887, p. 5.
[5] *Review and Herald*, Sept. 20, 1887, p. 601.
[6] *Ibid.*, April 10, 1888, p. 233.
[7] *Ibid.*, May 8, 1888, p. 298.

Scouting for Missions

THE COMMISSION to carry the three angels' messages "to every nation, and kindred, and tongue, and people" had met with the response of faith by Seventh-day Adventists; a beginning had been made here and there. But now numerous appeals coming from all parts of the world indicated that it was time for a great forward movement. The immensity of the task was completely out of proportion to the material resources of those responding to the call. Therefore there must be not only undaunted faith but also wise and economical planning in organizing and carrying out the most fruitful methods of labor.

The General Conference now planned to send Stephen Haskell abroad to inspect the world field and bring back information for guidance in their immediate missionary movements. He accepted the appointment with the understanding that he would have the company of a younger man to act as his secretary and traveling agent. A brilliant Battle Creek student, Percy T. Magan, was chosen for this; and it was arranged that he should join the elder at the close of the spring term of school. Accordingly Elder Haskell, on February 15, 1889, took passage from New York. He would spend some time holding evangelistic meetings in England and attending councils and conferences in the Scandinavian countries, in company with the newly elected General Conference president, O. A. Olsen, who had not yet taken up his duties in America. Then, with L. Johnson, Elder Haskell visited Nordland, Norway, a picturesque country described as "an alpine region by the sea." They found the land occupied by a sturdy people, the greater portion of whom live along the coast on coastal islands and who make fishing their chief industry. The principal exports of the country are codfish and cod-liver oil; the world is their market. The two ministers traveled mostly by water. Their steamer, plying between the islands, made twenty-seven stops on the trip.

Usually it anchored some distance from land and little rowboats would paddle out with a cargo of fish and other island products and return with passengers and freight.

Here the traveling brethren again witnessed the midnight sun. Elder Johnson wrote: "We found no difficulty in keeping the Sabbath there, the position of the sun showing very plainly when it was night."[1] The travelers saw huge glaciers, and were almost constantly within sight of a hundred-mile range of snow-capped mountains, presenting a panorama of sparkling glory by day and of fairyland enchantment at night. At Bodo, a bustling shipping port within the Arctic Circle, Elder Johnson disembarked to hold meetings with a company of Adventists. Haskell sailed to Tromso, two hundred miles north.

In Tromso, on Sunday morning, he left his hotel room looking for someone who could speak English. He found a man who said he could "talk a leetle," and it was a very little. He came across another who could talk a little more, and this man went in search of another who, they said, had spent eight years in America. While passing down the street, Elder Haskell was recognized by a colporteur from the school in Christiania. He came to the hotel, bringing two other colporteurs with him. The elder had learned a few words of Norwegian and the young men knew a few words of English. But their combined linguistic ability did not furnish them the vocabulary necessary to facilitate conversation. Finally the man who had gone in search of the man who had lived in America found him and brought him to the hotel and they had an excellent visit.

Early in August the older missionary was joined by his young companion, Magan, who had started late and had stopped on the way to visit his childhood home in Dublin. With more than ordinary pleasure Percy anticipated the three weeks' voyage to Cape Town in company with Elder Haskell and Mr. and Mrs. A. Druillard, who were scheduled to reinforce the pioneer group there. Mrs. Druillard had been "Aunt Nell" to the young man ever since she had found him, a lonely, almost penniless immigrant lad working for a farmer, and had directed him toward Battle Creek College.

Percy's duties were numerous; they included securing reservations, arranging transportation of baggage, exchanging coinage, watching to see that none of the seven pieces of hand luggage were lost, stolen, or left behind while being transported from hotel to carriage, to train, to tramcar, bus, or whatever vehicle was to take them to the steamer. All this he dispatched with alacrity, not relaxing his vigilance until the numerous parcels were tucked away under cabin bunks and the overflow stored in the ship's hold.

Then began the real work of the secretary—taking dictation and typing letters and articles. This task occupied many hours of each day and sometimes of the night, especially when urgent matters required immediate transcription in order to catch homebound steamers passing them on the high seas. One of Magan's tasks was to obtain information with which to amplify the Haskell articles. This necessitated the spending of much stopover time at ports searching for books and statistical records in shops and travel agencies.

Percy contributed a series of forty-nine articles to the *Youth's Instructor* in which he described their travel experiences and the places they visited. Well does the author remember how, as a child, she eagerly implored any adult who seemed to be enjoying a little unnecessary leisure, to read aloud those Round the World stories signed P. T. M. On Sabbath, as soon as the table was cleared and the dishes stacked, she would bring out the *Instructor* and, in imagination, tour the world, while her five-year-old sister colored pictures. When, a year later, Percy himself returned from his world-circling tour, he often visited the two little orphans, whose mother was dead and whose father was in faraway Australia. Percy would take Mabel on his knee, and Ella would sit close by listening to fascinating tales of what he had seen on that memorable journey he had made with Elder Haskell.

When, en route to Africa, their steamer docked at Lisbon to take on coal, the passengers were permitted to go ashore. The travelers saw buildings that had been demolished by the great earthquake of 1755 and left in their ruined condition for nearly one hundred and fifty years—a fulfillment of Bible prophecy which foretold devastating earthquakes as a sign of the near approach of Christ's coming.

The water carriers in Lisbon (called *Gallegos,* from Galicia, in Spain) numbered three thousand among the city's population of 400,000. Said Haskell: "It is surprising to see what heavy weights they carry suspended by a rope from a strong, wooden barrel resting on a horse-shoe-shaped collar, placed on their shoulders, as they trudge along in pairs, always out of step to neutralize the oscillation of their bodies. Two men are said thus to carry half a ton. The Portuguese . . . have a saying: 'God made first the Portuguese, then the *Gallego* to wait on him.' "

They saw many primitive ox wagons with solid wooden wheels, also many modern conveyances drawn by horses and mules. Of the pedestrians he wrote: "The fish-women are the most picturesque, having a broad-brimmed, felt hat, indigo blue, closely pleated, short, woolen skirt, a loose jacket, and bare legs. Many of them are adorned with a profusion of gold ornaments. In this lies their wealth, which they ever carry with them. . . .

"The city is scrupulously clean, and there are Protestant places of worship, with the 200 public houses for that purpose. The Portuguese are noted for their politeness. The greatest liberty is granted to all, from all parts, to express their sentiments in the papers and by public speech, both in political matters and on the subject of religion." [2]

The next stop for the travelers was the island of Madeira. "Here, as in other places, there is quite a proportion of English people, many having been recommended by physicians to come for their health." As soon as the anchor is cast, swimmers surround the boat "like so many sea birds, waiting for the passengers to throw over any coin from a half penny upward, when from one to half a dozen will dive for it, and the most expert will bring it up. They will also dive from the boat over the upper deck, a distance, we should judge, of not less than fifty feet." [3]

August 9, 1889, was a happy day. As the *Warwick Castle* steamed into Cape Town Harbor they recognized among the crowds thronging the wharf a number of friends whom they had recently seen in England and America.

The very next day after their arrival, Haskell, assisted by his secretary, launched into the task of gathering facts and general information that would serve as a guide to the General Conference in shaping foreign-mission policies. In such a survey he sought first to become acquainted with the country, taking particular note of features contributing favorably or otherwise to Adventist missionary enterprise. Haskell, a keen observer and a tireless gatherer of facts, whose conclusions were generally sound and practical, now considered what opportunities Africa might offer for literature evangelism. In this case, his conclusions were not encouraging.

The English-speaking inhabitants were few as compared with multitudes of Africans, most of whom were illiterate. A large proportion of the white settlers were Dutch, a very religious but conservative people, who spoke Afrikaans. At first our colporteurs had worked successfully among them; but their predikants, or ministers, alarmed lest they lose members, warned their congregations against the Adventist salesmen—many even named the colporteur and the title of the book he was selling. Most of the European towns were small and even in them the Coloured and African population predominated. Food prices were high, traveling and living expenses exorbitant. The farmers lived on large tracts of land, their homes being on the average ten miles apart. About one tenth of the Cape population were literate Moslems whose religion forbade the reading of Christian books.

There was no way of making even an approximate count of the African population of the continent; some estimated it to be 200 million and others twice that number. This multitude was divided into numberless tribes, each with its own language or dialect; they were scattered the length and breadth of the continent.

It was obvious to Elder Haskell that self-supporting colporteur evangelism would not be the answer among the African tribal people. But there must be an answer. What was it?

The two men focused their attention on the educational systems of South Africa. They learned that the government maintained a high standard, using a system of grants and aids by which mission schools were encouraged and assisted, but not supported, by the government. Education among all classes was promoted, with liberty to operate each school in any particular denominational pattern.

It was reported that there were seven hundred mission schools in South Africa, all prospering, besides fifty-four special training schools for mission workers. Haskell and Magan decided to visit as many of these schools as their time would permit.

One of the nearest was the Huguenot Seminary, about forty miles from Cape Town. It was patterned after Mount Holyoke Seminary, an American college, and prepared young women for mission careers as well as more general aspects of Christian service.

The two visitors found a beautifully landscaped campus in the midst of rugged mountains. They were warmly welcomed by the principal, Miss Furgeson, who devoted several hours to her guests. She told them that the school had first opened in 1874, with forty students. An early rule was that each girl should be alone for half an hour every morning and evening. The first hour each day was given to religious instruction and discussion. Every evening a fifteen-minute prayer meeting was held. At the beginning of that first year, only one third of the forty students were Christians. By the close of the first year every girl was rejoicing in the Saviour's love.

"At present," said Miss Furgeson, "we have two-hundred-fifty girls in attendance." As she toured the institution with the visitors, she noticed that Elder Haskell was especially interested in the classes where, under supervision, students were gaining teaching experience. They were also studying methods of conducting mission schools and of training African workers to do the same.

When she discussed the school's high literary standards, the men were interested. But when she showed them students actually baking bread, washing dishes, setting tables, laundering, and cleaning, she noticed that they were greatly impressed.

The grand purpose of the school was preparation for mission service. Their missionary society was supporting two European workers and corresponding with missions in various parts of Africa. Each Monday morning replies were read before the entire school. The students also conducted branch Sunday schools in the vicinity for both white and Coloured children.

Religious prejudice had no place there. One teacher observed the seventh-day Sabbath, and was enabled to do so without embarrassment or criticism.

Elder Haskell wrote: "Our interest in the school work has been greatly revived since we have visited some of the schools in South Africa, and learned of their history and practical workings. The noble men and women who are engaged in this work will reap a harvest of souls for the garner of the Lord."[4]

"If all of our schools under the control of religious teachers kept before their pupils some such missionary work, they would accomplish ten times as much for humanity as many now do. It is sowing for eternity, planting seeds that will blossom in the earth made new. We are in the world for the benefit of humanity, and it would be bigotry in the extreme to suppose that all good methods of instruction, in this enlightened age of the nineteenth century, are confined to any one denomination or class, or even to people whom God has called to a special work."[5]

After an intensive study of South Africa and its problems, both Haskell and Magan were firmly convinced that the imperative, immediate need of that land was Christian education, including practical training in farming, mechanics, industries, and trades. Large undeveloped tribal areas desperately needed instruction in sanitation, healthful living, and the care of the sick.

Doors to medical missionary work were open on every side; but where were the self-sacrificing workers equipped with knowledge and a great love of humanity, enabling them to minister to soul and body? Many times Percy asked himself this question. It eventually led him to devote the latter half of his career to the building up of the College of Medical Evangelists (now the Loma Linda University School of Medicine) and to endeavor to plant in the hearts of its students a love for and commitment to mission service.

What Elder Haskell had learned of the work accomplished by various Christian denominations greatly rejoiced his heart. It had also increased his interest in the enterprise of training Adventist youth to fulfill the divine commission given the remnant church—that of proclaiming the *special message* due the world in this last hour.

---

[1] *Review and Herald*, Sept. 3, 1889, p. 554.
[2] *Ibid.*, Sept. 24, 1889, p. 602.
[3] *Ibid.*
[4] *Ibid.*, Dec. 3, 1889, p. 761.
[5] *Ibid.*

Zulus of South Africa, a people described admiringly by Percy Magan.

An Adventurous Journey

DURING AN extensive trip up the eastern coast of South Africa, the two world travelers visited Lovedale, the largest mission station in the area. As Elder Haskell has failed to leave any detailed account of their journeyings at this time—probably because of being fully occupied in fulfilling the purpose of his "mission-scouting trip"—it will be given here in Magan's graphic language.

"At 6:00 A.M. the coach was advertised to start from the depot with passengers and mails, but it was more than an hour after that time when it put in an appearance, and all *voyageurs* were requested to 'hurry up and take seats.' We did hurry up, but to take seats was altogether another matter. The coach, or rather cart, . . . was a two-wheeled concern, with sitting space for six, arranged three abreast, on two seats, one behind the other. But these were hardly visible for the multitude of mail sacks that covered everything. They were piled on before and behind, under the seats, and over them, and out onto the pole in front of the dashboard. One of the party [apparently Elder Haskell] crawled in behind, and after making his legs perform a sort of corkscrew movement, managed to seat himself; the writer found a corner at his side, a young colonist perched himself beside the jarvy (driver), and a gold-digger took up his position on a heap of stable cargo in front. This completed the list.

"With the usual amount of shouting and yelling from the postboys and grooms, the start was effected, and soon the vehicle was under way, and whirling down the main street of the sleeping city. Six Cape horses pulled us merrily along, the whole team being so poor that they scarcely made one good shadow. Our driver was . . . [an African], and armed with the typical bugle and two whips, he performed his duty with great adroitness. One of these scourges, for they are little less, consisted of a light bamboo pole, about twenty feet in length, and with a rawhide lash some ten feet long. This was applied to the leaders and mid-team; the other was hardly quarter the length, with a short, thick thong, for the benefit of the wheel horses.

"The night had been rainy, and we soon became painfully aware of the fact; for the road was a case of alternate truck-holes and camel's humps, over which the chariot bumped in a merciless manner. The kneading and percussing and vibration received was sufficient to digest the heaviest dinner that mortal ever ate, but was to hygienists something totally unnecessary.

"With brakes set, at full speed the descent is made down one hill, across the railroad track, and then in a gallop the steeds make straight up another. The cart reels and sways, and tips heavily backward, and the Jehu with a most complacent smile informs the passengers that 'another one of them, sir, and she'll tip over; so if you value your lives, sit forward.' But we can't; for there's no room for our feet, and our knees are curled up in close proximity to our noses, so the risk must be run, and all relapse into silence, and devote all their energies to holding on.

"A mountain range now appears in the offing, with a deep can[y]on running through it. Into this we enter, the road winding along on the side of the precipice. The scene is one of wild and almost gigantic grandeur,—above, on one side, tower rocks and crags for many hundred feet, some of them looking as if a touch would send them crashing down onto the road, from thence to be precipitated into the gorge beneath. This is filled with a jungle of euphorbias and cactuses, and many tropical trees, covered with beautiful jasmine and a creeper known as monkey rope. The speed is breakneck, and when the bottom of Pluto's Vale is reached, all breath[e] more freely.

"At Fish River a halt is made for a change of horses, as these which have pulled thus far have commenced to show signs of weariness. ... Many ostriches are feeding by the way-side, but in appearance they are far different from the pictures in the old school readers. White feathers are much more profuse in the portrait than on the bird itself, and the ostrich that ran away from the hunter, and buried its head in the sand, thinking that, because not seeing, it could not be seen, never breathed on the plains of South Africa, its native home. ... One blow of their foot is sufficient to break the back of a horse.

"The road now lay over a rough bush country, peopled for the most part by natives, their little round huts looking like bee-hives dotted all over it.... All the afternoon we journeyed, and at set of sun, on reaching the top of a small hill, beheld the village of Alice lying beneath, and just beyond the Chumie River stood the massive gray stone buildings of the Lovedale Mission station. We were soon comfortably ensconced within its walls."[1]

"Lovedale is more of an educational institution than a mission station proper. All classes of the African race are here, and representatives from almost if not every tribe. The Bible is made the main object of study, and a good common school education is imparted....

"There are at present some four hundred students; the majority of these are native boys, with a comparatively small percentage of girls, and a few English. In age they vary from six or seven to twenty-seven or thirty. English and Kaffir are the languages mainly used. The latter is a very soft and musical tongue, and it is touching to hear them at their missionary meetings....

"It is wonderful and praiseworthy the eagerness which some of them manifest to acquire an education. Grown men, who have spent all their early days in the heathen kraal and at hard work in the diamond mines or at the gold reefs, will take their little earnings, and deposit it at a mission station or school, and beg to be taken in and taught. They care not for the ridicule of those of their race more fortunate than themselves, and will cheerfully enter classes with little children of from seven to eight years, and commence to learn the alphabet. ...

"[The man] lives in his kraal, surrounded by his family, smokes his pipe, ... while his wives, with pick and hoe, cultivate the ground for his sustenance. His food is corn and milk and Kaffir beer. He acquires his cattle by the dowry he receives from the suitors of his daughters. ... [A] girl is worth six or eight cows, and one of attractive qualities sometimes doubles that amount.

"[These people have] no knowledge of the true God, and, in

fact, the missionaries found it necessary in order to introduce the gospel, to create a word in the Kaffir language to signify God."[2]

"Stage traveling in fair weather is something by no means enviable, but when it is wet, in South Africa at least, it is not only unpleasant but positively dangerous. Bridges are scarce, and almost all the rivers have to be forded. These are short, and the altitude of their source considerable, so that in dry seasons there is hardly any water flowing, and in rainy weather there is a flood.

"It had been raining for a few days previous to our leaving Lovedale, and on the morning when we expected to start, the clouds looked very dubious, and we were informed that it would be hardly safe to go.... But start we must, or we were liable to miss the steamer at East London, the southeastern port, which we could not afford to do, as time, when one is traveling, slips rapidly away. So despite the unpleasantness of 'trekking,' as the Dutch style it, in a drizzling rain, we determined to start. The Chumie [River] was crossed, the water reaching to the steps of the carriage, the force being so great that for a while the conveyance was carried by the current, but to no great extent. The horses, realizing the danger, pulled with a will, and soon reached the opposite bank in safety. The Keiskamma was also forded, and only just in time; for all the next night it rained torrents, and it was three days before the crossing could be made again.

"A few miles from King William's Town, the road winds along near the base of the Pere range.... At evening the Buffalo River was crossed on a fine iron bridge, and King William's Town entered. Our stay there was short.... A short trip by rail brings the traveler to East London, where the steamers call for passengers for Durban, Natal, the seaport town of the growing little colony on the eastern coast.

"On December 23, the good ship *German* arrived, and cast anchor outside the bar of Buffalo River, as there was not enough water for her to cross. The tug went off [to the ship] to take in her passengers and the mails, but leaving those who wished to embark for a second trip. The sea was running very high, and it was with considerable difficulty that the little *Midge* crossed the breakers, and gained the vessel's side. But to come in again was another thing, as the waves were increasing in size every moment; and even had her commander wished to enter, he was prohibited from doing so at sight of the black ball on the yardarm of the harbor flagstaff, which signifies that the port-captain forbids any ship to leave or enter. For several hours she tossed to and fro outside, looking like some pilgrim seeking admittance to a city of refuge, and denied it.

"Toward noon the storm abated somewhat, and the passage was safely made; then came the turn of those wishing to embark. We steamed down the river, which was as calm as a sheet of glass; the sky was clear and blue above, but ahead was the ominous bar. The huge green waves were leaping over the breakwater, seemingly threatening at every moment to wash it away. The captain said it was the worst sea they had had since '74. All the passengers were ordered below, and the hatches battened down overhead. This is an unpleasant sensation at any time, but especially so when, added to the stuffiness of a launch cabin, there is a vague feeling that 'she may go down.'

"It was easy to tell when the first sea struck her; with a bang it came over the decks, washing them fore and aft, at the same moment lifting her high on its crest, and then with a whirl she went down into the trough on the leeward side. Sea after sea came over the deck, and it seemed sometimes as if nothing could save her from being washed up against the breakwater. In cases of this kind, the helmsman never tries to steer his course, but devotes all his energies to running away from the waves, and dodging in and out between the swells, so as to avoid being capsized. Once across [the bar], the motion was not so rapid, and the hatchways were opened, and passengers permitted on deck again.

"The next thing was to get on board the *German,* and the way she was rolling made it no easy matter. It took a long time to get the tug made fast to her side, and then a basket was lowered over the side by means of a derrick from the mast. Into this, two at a time, we were placed, and then hoisted up and let down with a bump on the deck.

"At set of sun the good ship was under way, and running close to the coast, with her bows toward the east, under full steam, she sped along. At break of day we were off the borders of Pondoland. There was but little to be seen on the shore that was of interest. Hardly a house, or sign of life of any kind, although the hills looked green, as if there was good pasturage for cattle. By the middle of the afternoon, the Durban bluff was in sight, with the white light-house on its summit, and after rounding it, anchor was dropped in the bay." ³

It was Christmas Eve in Durban; the thermometer registered nearly 100 degrees in the shade. The weary travelers were exhausted by heat and high humidity. After a short stay in the city they began making excursions into bordering territories.

Percy wrote: "The Zulus are by far the finest race of all the South African tribes. In physique they are much in advance of the average American or European, and their strength is something marvelous. They will take a box weighing nearly two hundred pounds, place it on their heads, and trot off with it as if the weight were nothing, and they will carry this for a mile or more without stopping to rest....

"A Zulu in full dress wears a 'moucher,' or loin cloth, which is generally made of skins, the ankles and arms covered with bangles, and the neck profusely decorated with beads. The hair is twisted into small pig-tails, which are often threaded over with beads, or little pieces of quill, giving a remarkable appearance to the wearer. A hole is punched in the lobe of one ear, and in this is stuffed a snuff-box about as thick as a man's index finger, and three inches in length." ⁴

As the men traveled along in a slow-moving ox wagon, with their African guide and driver, they passed numerous banana, sugar cane, and tea plantations, owned by settlers of various nationalities. The green grass, the luxurious, brilliantly colored wildflowers, and the thriving eucalyptus, cypress, and acacia groves proved that this was a well-watered country. However, sharp, strong thorns covered the underbrush and many shrubs. One close contact with the *wag-'n-bietjie* ("wait-a-bit") bush led Elder Haskell to remark that all Africa seemed to be on the defensive.

While Haskell and Magan were exploring South Africa, gathering ideas for successful methods of gospel labor among the heathen, the *Review and Herald* and *Youth's Instructor* readers were following them in their wanderings. Many hearts were throbbing in response to their numerous appeals for volunteers for mission service. Here is one typical heart-stirring appeal from Haskell which reached Seventh-day Adventists before the days of mission budgets:

"God has offered no grander opportunity to those who would be His servants, and labor in His vineyard, than to go into a foreign country, there to educate the young, and instill into their minds pure and sound principles, which will fit them, not only for the practical duties of after life, but for a place of radiant brightness in the kingdom of God. . . .

"The glorious truths of the gospel are to be presented before kings, and nations, and tongues, and peoples. God will adopt His own methods, He will select His own servants, He will use His own agents to accomplish His own work. He is not limited for means to carry it forward, but His providence is over all, and the message will be carried to the lengths, and breadths of the earth. He is using men and women in various situations and stations in life to accomplish His purposes, and these bear the stamp of the divine."[5]

---
[1] *The Youth's Instructor*, May 14, 1890, p. 78.
[2] *Ibid.*, May 21, pp. 81, 82.
[3] *Ibid.*, May 28, p. 86.
[4] *Ibid.*, June 4, p. 90.
[5] *Review and Herald*, Dec. 3, 1889, pp. 761-763.

Calcutta and Beyond

THE TWO TRAVELERS sailed from South Africa for India on the cargo ship *Umtata*. They now wrote from Calcutta, capital of India, the city said to have been named for the hideous, four-armed goddess, Kali, and at that time residence of the "great man," the viceroy. Riding through the narrow streets in the humbler section of the city, they held their breath as they observed the careful maneuvering of their driver in passing other vehicles in space no wider than the gharry in which they rode. The streets were lined with crude mud-and-thatch shops with open fronts, exhibiting their wares to passers-by, and so close that the men could almost reach out and touch the merchandise.

Magan later wrote, describing the manner in which the Hindu merchant often conducted a very profitable business: "His store is also bamboo, matting, and mud, and at first sight one would hardly think it capable of containing stock to more than the amount of a few hundred dollars. But once inside, it is found to be a perfect labyrinth of shelves, pigeon holes, and other nooks and corners, which are filled with the most costly merchandise, every space being utilized, from floor to ceiling. In the middle of the room, sitting on the floor, and almost entirely destitute of clothes, is the proprietor. . . . If the truth were only known, he has gold enough hidden away to build him a palace, and clothe him like a king, should he desire it." [1]

At the first halt of the gharry, a street hawker spotted the two Americans and accosted them with the offer of a pair of handsome peacock-feather fire screens; "Three rupees, master, three rupees."

"Give you half a rupee."

"All right, me sell them to Sahib for half rupee!" Evidently the seller did not expect so large an offer at the first bid.

"Backsheesh! Backsheesh!" they heard, and saw a fakir, dirty,

A bathing ghat at Calcutta, the first city Haskell visited in India.

unkempt, scantily clad, his body daubed with mud, extending his skinny hand for a coin. On every side people could be seen perhaps sitting with extended arms hour after hour in the burning sun, or lying on beds of spikes, or torturing themselves in some other hideous manner. Many bathed in the murky river, hoping to wash away their sins and gain an entrance to Paradise.

The visitors found the foreign quarter less than a tenth of the city, but much pleasanter, with wide streets and attractive homes, most of them having spacious verandas. Their guide informed them that only twenty-five miles away were dense jungles where tigers and other wild animals roamed at will. These fierce beasts caused hundreds of deaths annually.

As in Africa, the men visited Christian missions and conversed with missionaries who had devoted their lives to the task of carrying the gospel to the people. After a few weeks in Calcutta they boarded a British mail train en route to Benares, India's most sacred city. How long? Oh, how long must India await the good news? was the thought that traveled with them.

Elder Haskell's mind was fully occupied with the one great question, What can be done by Seventh-day Adventists to hasten the proclamation of the gospel in this land?

Percy Magan, assigned to describe their travel experiences, wrote:

"Coronetted palms, toddy-trees, and wide-spreading banyans were dotted here and there. . . . We passed through some fairly large cities. . . . At a place with a name that sounded something like Moghal Serai, we changed trains. . . . At one town we were entertained by a snake charmer, who fondled the . . . serpents as a mother would her infant. He wound them around his neck, played with them and after the performance was over, informed us that he had broken all their teeth. . . . Their teeth are broken by enticing them into a sack, and then they will try to bite their way out again. But here lies the trap; their fangs are caught in the strands of the material and easily broken." [2]

At Benares, they were told, more than half a million idols were worshiped, and there were a thousand temples. The idols were "a heterogeneous mass representing everything in nature and out of it, from a jellyfish to a gorilla," some with "noses like an elephant's trunk" and faces a "combination of man and monkey." They visited the Monkey Temple, where thousands of monkeys venerated as gods enjoyed luxurious living, and a temple where many of the sacred cows were kept, pampered and petted.

From Benares the men traveled on to Lucknow and Cawnpore, where during the Sepore Mutiny many Christians became martyrs. At Lucknow they saw evidences of the long and painful siege, which had occurred less than forty years before.

"In many places," wrote Magan, "there is hardly a square inch not dotted over with the marks of the bullets from the murderous rifles, and huge gaps still remain where cannon balls tore away the masonry, causing pain and death to those within. We walked in the dungeons where women and children were placed for safety and where they remained through all the siege, without a change of clothes and with scant provisions. We could but think of the early Christians in the catacombs, and we wondered how many fervent prayers had ascended to our Father's throne during that fearful time." [3]

"At Agra the scene changed, and the brightest pictures ever seen in the most vivid day-dreams of an imaginative and beauty-loving mind were more than realized."

The city was built by Akbar, a famous Moslem conqueror. Space will not permit full reproduction here of Magan's graphic description of its wonders.

At Agra they saw "the pavilion overhanging the river," where rest the "precious caskets of marble, glittering all over with . . . precious stones." The Shish Mahal, or palace of glass, was an oriental bath. "Its chambers and passages are adorned with thousands of small mirrors, disposed in the most intricate designs. The water fell over brilliant lamps in a broad sheet into a marble pool, and the fountains are so constructed as to be lighted from within."[4]

At Agra they also saw the famed Taj Mahal, the white marble tomb built in the seventeenth century by one of the rulers of India to honor the memory of his favorite wife.

The Taj Mahal, one of the most beautiful buildings in the world, visited by Haskell and his secretary, Percy Magan.

Magan described the graceful structure: a central-domed building on a raised platform with a tall minaret at each corner—all of pure white marble; decorated with lacy carving and inlaid with colored marble and other stones, and inscriptions from the Koran. He called it "a masterpiece of architecture, equaled by no other building on earth."[5]

But since the aim of our world travelers was "scouting for missions" rather than portraying material grandeur amassed by ruthless conquerors, they hastened on to Delhi. There Magan described the famous Peacock Throne, so called because its back was formed by jeweled representations of peacocks' tails.

"The throne," he wrote, "was six feet long and four feet broad, composed of solid gold inlaid with precious gems. It was surmounted by a gold canopy, supported on twelve pillars of the same material. Around the canopy hung a fringe of pearls, and on each side of the throne stood two chattahs, or umbrellas, the symbol of royalty; they were made of crimson velvet, richly embroidered with gold thread and pearls, and had handles eight feet long of solid gold studded with diamonds."

From the palace the two men drove to the Jami' Masjid, "one of the largest and most beautiful mosques in the East." "The interior of the mosque proper is paved with slabs of white marble, three feet long by one and one-half broad, each decorated with a black border, which gives it an extremely beautiful appearance. . . . In the northwest angle is a little chamber partitioned off by a beautiful white marble screen, in which are deposited some spurious relics of the prophet Mahomet. . . . The relics consisted of some hair that was said to be from Mahomet's beard. . . . Then there were the crumbled remains of his shoes, . . . part of the Koran, hand traced, said to be the work of Mahomet's grandson, . . . [and] a footmark in solid stone, . . . supposed to have been made because Mahomet stood there to pray so often."[6]

"After a two days' rest at Delhi," Magan continued, "we once more boarded the train, and started on our journey southward. . . . In the morning arrived at Jeypore. . . . In the afternoon we drove to Amber, or Old Jeypore, four miles from the present city. Arriving at the confines of the place, we were met by an elephant sent out by the Maharaja to take us up the mountain. This is customary, and a courtesy shown to all visitors desiring to view the halls of his ancestors.

"We had often heard about riding on elephants, and had seen pictures of the performance, but this was our first attempt. The driver sat behind the animal's ear, which was almost large enough to cover him, and certainly to form a good sunshade, could it only be brought into the right position. At a word from the driver and a prod from a grappling-iron by means of which he steered the beast, the giant knelt down. Then a seven-foot step-ladder was unslung from his side, and placed on end, and up we clambered. It was now Jumbo's turn to arise. . . . The effort seemed greater than that of a ship crossing the breakers of a billowy bar. With another prod, and some inexpressible lingo from the jarvy, our steed commenced to waddle. I shall never forget the sensation; the motion is indescribable. He seemed to plow along worse than a brig in a gale of wind. . . . It nearly made me seasick, and every little while he would sneeze, or something of the kind, wetting his deck-like back fore and aft, and completely submerging us. But to his praise be it said, he did steer well, and would tack his huge, clumsy feet round the sharpest corners among the rocks, as we ascended the mountain-side, without once grazing our toes. . . .

"After surveying the ruins, we once more mounted and started down grade, and the motion was, if anything, worse than when ascending. If you want any bones dislocated and set again, try a ride on an elephant; or if you wish your teeth loosened prior to visiting a dentist, take a jog on Jumbo down a can[y]on, and it will insure 'painless dentistry.' Safely landed once more at the foot of the gulch, we vowed we would never go elephant riding again.

"We slept again that night on wheels, the iron horse whirling us down to India's great seaport. A reverend gentleman disturbed our peaceful slumbers during the night with a 'Hurry up and get out, I want that carriage for my daughter.' But we had been elephant riding and were weary, and didn't propose to get up, dress, and shift about thirteen pieces of baggage, so we bade him depart to find a resting-place for his daughter elsewhere. . . .

"We sincerely hope that the night which followed will be our last on an Indian railroad in the hot season. The heat was something fearful. H[askell] took the upper berth, and tried to sleep, but how well he succeeded he alone can tell. A British army officer and myself disrobed, and sat in our sleeping suits gasping for air. . . . At last the brakes grated on the rails in the Bombay depot. We hurried to the post-office to see if there was not feed for folk who have undergone letter-starvation for nearly three months. Nor were we disappointed. We were glad we had a carriage, for we could not have carried it all home in our arms."[7]

In Bombay a fair was in progress. The entire city was illuminated in honor of Prince Albert of England, grandson of Queen Victoria, whose visit was expected soon.

Magan wrote: "All public buildings, monuments, and stores were ablaze with lights of many colors. . . . Everywhere they glistened, those near the ground casting a soft light across streets and squares, while those on the cornices and h[e]ights of the towers had, as they flickered in the wind, more the appearance of twinkling stars. In the harbor I suppose there were as many as a thousand ships, and from the masts and rigging of nearly all of them gleamed these fairy scintillations, the light streaming over the water, and producing a resplendent effect.

"We thought of the honors that men bestow on their fellow-beings, and remembered what a cold reception was accorded to the world's Redeemer when He came to earth to die for humanity. But so it has been ever, and will ever be, until He shall come whose right it is to reign, and shall claim His own. And then celestial rays, far brighter than anything ever conceived in the mind of man, will flood the heavens and bathe the earth in glory."[8]

In Bombay, the Parsees attracted the travelers' attention. Outsiders were prohibited from entering their temples, where sacred fire burned perpetually on their altars. Anyone could watch them perform their devotions as they came down to the seashore to pray.

"They come, men and women," wrote Magan, "and stand facing the mighty ocean, with their eyes upturned to the sky, praying frequently for half an hour at a time. But before commencing their adorations and supplications, a very curious ceremony is performed. Around the waist every Parsee has a cord, called the 'kusti.' This is made of pure white lamb's wool, and is composed of seventy-two distinct strands, denoting seventy-two doctrines of religion, while the material and color signify the character of the people professing such a religion.

"Their morality and uprightness in deal exceed that of the English-speaking races. Nearly all of them are wealthy. The national love existing between them is very strong, and they never allow one of their own name to come to want. They support a large number of hospitals, homes for the friendless, and other kindred institutions. As a rule, they are well educated, not only speaking their own language, but also English and Hindoo...

"The gospel of Christ has made little headway among the Parsees, who now number about 100,000 in India. They say that they do not see that the lives of those professing Christianity are as moral or as upright as those of their own people, and therefore they see no need of forsaking the doctrines of Zoroaster and accepting those of the Christian's Bible." The young missionary must have sighed regretfully as he typed these words, "The basis of their reasoning is only too true."[9]

Too soon it was time to leave India; from there the travelers sailed for the Far East. Tropical nights on shipboard were beautiful. Passengers forsook their staterooms; mattresses and blankets were spread on the hurricane deck. "What a treat this is!" they exclaimed. "After city hotels and stuffy indoor rooms, to be sleeping under the star-lit canopy of heaven!" At Hong Kong all passengers were glad to see land, for the last day of the voyage had been a stormy one.

After a short stay in the city Haskell and Magan sailed for the "Kingdom of the Rising Sun." Percy devoted seven articles to Japan and its people. He seemed entranced with its beauties, which he declared no other country could rival.

He wrote: "Chains of mountains rise majestically all over the landscape, and they are clothed with an almost eternal verdure.... Lower down their slopes waves the golden grain on terraced ground, such as we believed could only exist in a fairy-tale. The little bam-

A tile-roofed village among scenic mountains in Japan.

boo houses, with their pretty thatched roofs, nestle cosily in the ravines, and are only exceeded in uniqueness by their inmates.

"The climate is delightful and bracing, and the winter months are just cold enough to impart that vigor to the human frame which seems to be essential in order to make a nation enterprising and successful. It is in this country of majestic splendor that the Japanese have lived for centuries upon centuries." [10]

He described the people, the houses, the streets; their own visit to an exhibition, their rides on streetcars and in jinrikishas, their attempts to eat with chopsticks.

From Japan, Haskell and Magan sailed for China in June, 1890.

In China, as in India and Japan, the two travelers encountered highly educated people. Haskell made the following remark on their superior intelligence: "Imagine a child at the age of twelve, mastering

5,000 characters, one after another! And this is necessary before the Bible can be read understandingly in Chinese."[11]

He found many missionaries struggling with seemingly insurmountable obstacles to the reception of Christianity, the greatest being ancestor worship. He wrote: "Imagine a nation that for centuries has had its shrine in every house of the rich and poor, high and low, and whose every member from babyhood, both by example and theory, has been taught to bow before it, offer incense, and do sacrifice."[12]

When told that it was considered a great sin to refuse to burn incense and paper money before the little images adorning the home, he realized the vast courage required of a lone Oriental Christian.

Haskell and Magan spent two weeks in the cosmopolitan city of Shanghai. There the British, French, and American settlements each had its own municipal government and laws. Business houses, even post offices, were operated separately. The men found the missions in which they were interested mostly in the Chinese part of the walled city. In China a door seemed to be wide open for literature evangelism, for many men and some of the women could read.

Because of a talk he had with a man who for eleven years had been a colporteur in and about Shanghai, the Father of the Tract and Missionary Societies was greatly encouraged regarding this phase of denominational endeavor. This man had met with good success as he traveled among the villages selling Christian tracts and leaflets.

Haskell stressed the importance of mission schools. "To have a school of some kind," he writes, "and a place to gather the people seems to be a necessity for successful work. . . . Some boarding schools take children, but it is with the understanding that they are not to be taken from them till they are twenty years of age, neither are they to be betrothed to any one without the missionary's consent. Day schools are more numerous than boarding schools. Training schools for teachers and missionaries are also established."[13]

Ever an admirer of the British and American Bible Societies, he was glad to learn that during the past year (1889) more than 66 million Bible portions had been distributed in China.

At Hong Kong he again met Abram La Rue, the former seaman

who had been engaged in ship mission work in Honolulu, where, on his way to Australia, Haskell had met him for the first time. Now La Rue had come to Hong Kong, and though his years were telling upon his strength, he was still supporting himself selling books to English-speaking people on the island. He spent much time distributing literature among sailors on board vessels anchored in the harbor. Longing to spread the gospel among the Chinese people, La Rue engaged a Chinese scholar to translate a tract by Ellen G. White telling of the love of God (a chapter from her book *Steps to Christ*). He then had it printed and distributed it widely. This was one of the first pieces of Seventh-day Adventist literature to be circulated in Chinese and by La Rue. As that country's first Adventist missionary, he had already visited mainland China in 1889 with books in English.

The trip from Hong Kong to Sydney was made in a small cargo ship, laden with tea for Australia. Tea was piled in every vacant cabin and in every other available space. There were only five passengers —Haskell and Magan, the "tea man," and two women tourists who had been visiting Japan.

Five years had passed since Haskell had first visited Australia and New Zealand, and had begun his pioneer labors there. What joy was his, on returning, to meet many former associates and to witness the blessing of God upon their early seed sowing. Churches and companies of believers had multiplied.

In Australia the two world travelers parted. Magan returned to America, where, later, he would become a strong promoter of industrial and medical education. Elder Haskell remained in Australia and New Zealand to help for a time in holding institutes and conferences.

---

[1] *Youth's Instructor*, July 16, 1890, p. 114.
[2] *Ibid.*, Aug. 27, p. 138.
[3] *Ibid.*, Sept. 17, p. 149.
[4] *Ibid.*, Sept. 24, p. 153.
[5] *Ibid.*, Oct. 1, p. 157.
[6] *Ibid.*, Oct. 8, p. 162.
[7] *Ibid.*, Oct. 15, pp. 165, 166.
[8] *Ibid.*, Oct. 22, pp. 170, 171.
[9] *Ibid.*, Oct. 29, pp. 173, 174.
[10] *Ibid.*, Nov. 19, p. 186.
[11] *Review and Herald*, Oct. 28, 1890, p. 665.
[12] *Ibid.*, Oct. 7, p. 617.
[13] *Ibid.*

Alone, Yet Not Alone

THE SABBATH of February 28, 1891, was a memorable day in Battle Creek. The Dime Tabernacle, capacity of nearly four thousand, was rapidly filling. The north, south, and east vestries, which had been vacated after Sabbath school, were fully occupied again.

"It looks as if all the Adventists in town have turned out," the ushers said to one another as they hurried about, trying to find seats for latecomers. In addition to the usual attendance from the city, the college, the sanitarium, and the Review office, there were present on this occasion delegates from distant parts of the world to attend the twenty-ninth session of the General Conference, which would open March 5. All were eager to hear Elder Haskell, the veteran missionary, and to welcome him home after his two-year world-encircling tour.

A stillness fell over the great congregation. Stephen Haskell rose in his usual dignified manner and began to speak in low, measured, impressive tones. The theme of his discourse was, "The abundant grace given by the Father to Jesus Christ, and through Him to the world." "This supply of grace," he said, "is sufficient to meet every emergency and thwart every attempt of the enemy to embarrass or overthrow the work of God. Every difficulty only opens the door for another installment of the infinite grace of Christ prepared to meet it." He dwelt on the history of the apostolic church and the mighty work that the early Christians accomplished in an incredibly short time when they linked themselves to the great promises of God.

In the afternoon he spoke again to a crowded church, telling about his visits to distant lands and relating incidents that he saw as showing that the Lord had gone before His people, "to prepare the way for His gospel in its last special phase of the third angel's message."

No less inspiring was his sermon the following Sabbath, also in the Tabernacle. He told of islands in the Pacific, apparently ready for the light of God's Word, where no missionary had yet visited.

The General Conference session continued from March 5 till March 25. Reports of progress were brought from nearly all the States, and from six overseas fields—Central Europe, Denmark, Sweden, Norway, South Africa, Britain—and from the new missions, including the Polynesian Mission, which had been organized during the year. The ship *Pitcairn* had been built, equipped, manned, and started on her mission to the Pacific Islands.

A brief review of the world field was given by the General Conference president, O. A. Olsen.

During this General Conference there were meetings of various associations directing the activities of the denomination—Publishing, Sabbath School, Health and Temperance, Tract and Missionary, and Religious Liberty—at which comprehensive reports were rendered either by the chairman or by the secretary.

One of the earliest reports to be rendered at that time and one that thrilled the heart of the Father of the Tract and Missionary Societies was brought in by Mrs. S. L. Strong, general correspondence secretary for the International Tract and Missionary Society. One item in her report revealed the secret of rapid advance of the Adventist message in the West Indies. In 1889 the Tract and Missionary Society had received from William Arnold, who had been selling Adventist literature in the Lesser Antilles, 1,100 addresses of persons to whom he had sold Uriah Smith's *Thoughts on Daniel and the Revelation.* Letters had been written to these people. Responses began to come in, sometimes as many as twenty-five letters in one mail, expressing gratitude for what they had received. Most of the writers were requesting more literature, not only for themselves, but also for friends whose addresses they were enclosing. Soon an additional five hundred names brought the list to a total of sixteen hundred correspondents in the West Indies alone! Brother Arnold told of one man on the island of Antigua who, on receiving his book, was so thrilled with the message it contained that he engaged nineteen persons to distribute literature in thirteen villages.

As might be expected, Elder Haskell made numerous and valuable contributions during the conference. At an early session he spoke on the subject, "The Education of Missionaries," dwelling especially on the importance of their being adaptable. Part of his address is given here: "In such fields as India, China, et cetera, we find customs which to us appear as nonsense, but not so to the . . . [local inhabitants]. And when they see in the foreigner a disposition to conform as far as possible to their ways, it disarms prejudice, and awakens a feeling of friendliness in their hearts. Many of the disasters which came upon the first efforts of the missionaries were due to the failure to appreciate this principle."[1]

In India, Elder Haskell had once intimated to an experienced missionary that his church was interested in the education of missionaries, and that perhaps some of those trained for foreign service would go to India; and he inquired as to the most essential ingredient in their preparation. This is the answer he received: "First, adaptation; second, adaptation; third, adaptation; and fourth, adaptation. When they get that learned, let them come here, and I will find them work."

Elder Haskell commented further that those who conduct mission schools find that the only successful plan is to educate nationals in their homeland, as teachers, "instead of sending them to England or America to put on the ways of foreigners, and to lose touch with the customs and feelings of their brethren. . . . We should have our schools right where we want our workers, and every missionary should be an educator."[2]

At this same General Conference session Elder Haskell appealed earnestly for workers to be sent to distant lands that he had recently visited. He pleaded that teachers be chosen to open a school in Australasia; and also that Ellen G. White and her son W. C. White spend some time in that field. The Mission Board, immediately after the conference, invited them to go in the autumn. Thus one of the most far-reaching results of Elder Haskell's visit to Australia was the work and widespread influence of Mrs. White and her helpers, who responded to the invitation of the General Conference to work there.

That summer Elder Haskell visited churches and camp meetings, preaching faith and courage and seeking to arouse interest in foreign missions. In September he was again elected president of the California Conference. Near the end of that year he sent a progress report to the Seventh-day Adventist Publishing Association (later renamed the Review and Herald Publishing Association) regarding the California Conference, which in 1891 included California, Nevada, Utah, and Arizona, and had eighty workers. The conference tract society was prospering, with a capital of six thousand dollars, and was sending literature far afield.

Healdsburg College was overflowing with students. Several young men from overseas had graduated and returned as workers to Australia, New Zealand, and England.

A rapid increase in patronage at the St. Helena Sanitarium had required an addition to its facilities.

The Pacific Press was employing about 175 hands and had nineteen power presses. An average of one carload of paper, costing $1,500, was required weekly. Two branch offices had been established —one in New York City, the other in London. Both were thriving. The Pacific Press had, with the blessing of God, been able to make donations to home and foreign missions amounting to $35,000—more than its original capital stock. These donations were in the form of their own publications. Pacific Press had also begun to publish the *American Sentinel, Our Little Friend,* and the *Sabbath School Worker.*

Elder Haskell found it restful to be free from the distressing sights and sounds of paganism. He was thankful that he was no longer required to make frequent long trips away from home. Because of Mary's physical needs he had rented a cottage on the grounds of the St. Helena Sanitarium. In a letter to Mrs. White he wrote, "We are living in the St. Johns' cottage. . . . Wife takes treatment each day. . . . I think that it is my duty to spend more time with her than in the past although she never says a word against my going away, only she clings to me as never before. . . . I owe her a debt of gratitude and have a duty to her. . . . I have concluded it is not duty for me to leave her when she is sick." [3]

We read from another letter: "She wanted to come with me to California as never before, more to be with me or where I could come to see her once in awhile. The only reason I did not take her was our failure to provide a woman that we could rely upon to take care of her while here." ⁴

A helper was found, Anna Rasmussen. At St. Helena Mary's health improved. Her husband traveled to San Francisco and bought a carriage for her use. For a few months she and Anna rode out every day. "That is her life," wrote Haskell. "But she has to be helped up and down stairs and also into the carriage. She has a horse that is perfectly safe and is in no sense a lazy one but is full of life, but afraid of nothing and would not run away if left entirely alone. And it seems the angels watch over it and her. I believe the Lord does have a special care for her." ⁵

With Mary feeling better and happily situated, Elder Haskell could travel again. He was called to assist with camp meetings in the Upper Columbia and North Pacific conferences, and reported from there that the foundation had been laid for a college at Walla Walla. Then he was home again, attending a health convention especially for ministers and workers, at a camp on the sanitarium hillside.

"The tents are not pitched in any regular order, as the stones and trees prevent it," he wrote, but they looked as if they had "come down in a hailstorm." The assembly tent measured only 27 by 30 feet, making it necessary to place seats outside the tent to accommodate the overflow. He further records that the sanitarium had bought twenty acres of hill land, and was grubbing out the trees. A landscape gardener was employed to improve the place, although the work moved slowly, "like pulling a cat by the tail over a carpet, if you know how that is." ⁶

In their Bible class the subject of the week was the Holy Spirit. So intense was the interest in these devotional meetings that some days they ran from six-thirty in the morning until one o'clock, eliminating the regular morning service! At this time a six-month nurse's training course was organized. Even though it was distinctly stated that only those who had consecrated themselves to the work of God were invited to attend, the enrollment reached forty.

Early in the spring of 1893 Haskell was called to assist with European camp meetings. Mary was again weak and nearly helpless. Their months together at St. Helena had been enjoyable. Haskell de-

Above: St. Helena Sanitarium, showing the original building (with additions) at left. Below: View from the sanitarium roof overlooking the Pratt Valley, which leads into the Napa Valley beyond the small hills in the middle distance.

scribed how she had enjoyed being there so much, going out in the morning on the porch of the St. Johns' cottage, looking down upon the Pratt Valley, and singing. But her husband was wrestling with problems that must be solved before he could go; he was still paying rent on their home in New England, at South Lancaster, and also paying rent in California. "I had so long lived in New England and kept such a large and open house for our brethren, that it becomes very difficult for me to adjust myself to the renting of two or three rooms or rather, a small house of a few rooms, scantily furnished, and having my library scattered all over the country."[7]

Next he faced his problem at St. Helena. He described it to Mrs. White: "It has been suggested that I go to Europe. . . . Should I go I would not feel free to leave Sister Anna Rasmussen with my wife and a team to drive around on these hills. So I felt that it would be best if it could be brought about to move from here to a place where the roads are more level. . . . Napa was on my mind."[8] He traveled to that valley town. In a providential manner he found a furnished house, with even a cow in the barn and hens in their enclosure. Best of all, the rent was the same as he had been paying at St. Helena. But Anna loved the hilly country around the sanitarium. Haskell invited her to inspect the property he had found. When she saw it, she was so carried away with it that she wanted to move immediately.

On May 19 he wrote that they had moved from St. Helena to Napa. His personal affairs now in order, he prepared for the European trip. How could he leave Mary? Would he see her again? Courageously, holding back her tears, she bade him, "Go, do God's work, and may He reward you with many souls. We will have a long eternity together." And so, following his life practice of placing the work of God first, he left California on May 25.

At the camp meeting at Moss, Norway, he became very ill. "Sometimes it seemed I could not walk to the house after I got through speaking," he wrote. "But before the meeting was over, I was better. I simply lie in His hands. If I go whether I feel well or not, . . . while speaking I am strengthened. God truly helps me."[9]

From there he visited camp meetings in other parts of Scandinavia and in Central Europe, then returned to England, planning to embark for America. All the time he was thinking of Mary. Reports from home were not reassuring, and one day he received a telegram requesting his immediate return. Without further delay, he was on his way. His arrival revived Mary's failing energies; husband and wife enjoyed a few days together between frequent absences made necessary by his administrative duties.

Finally, on January 29, 1894, at the age of 81, Mary passed peacefully to her rest, leaving a record of long years of cheerfulness and fortitude, frequently under intense suffering. She was buried not far from her last home, in the cemetery at Napa, California.

At first Stephen was relieved, knowing that Mary could never again experience pain. But immediately this feeling was followed by a sense of unutterable loneliness. For more than forty years they had loved each other. Even when separated by his travels, he had known that she was thinking of him and praying for him. Now he felt that he was alone in the world, for he had no children.

Then, one night soon after Mary's death, he had a strange and distressing experience. He told it a few months afterward to the A. T. Robinson family, while visiting them in Cape Town, South Africa:

"One night soon after my wife's death, I fell asleep repeating the promises of God, for I felt very lonely. I had not been asleep long when I was awakened by a light in the room. Opening my eyes I saw, standing beside my bed, a bright, shadowy form. I heard a voice speak: 'Stephen, I have come to bring you comfort. I shall ever watch over you to comfort you, for I am nearer to you now than when I lived on earth.' It was Mary's voice, so natural, so sweet.

"My first impulse was to reach out my arms to her. But at that moment there sounded clearly in my consciousness, though no audible words were heard, *'The dead know not any thing.'* I drew back in fear.

"'O Stephen, don't you know me?' Love, longing, and pathos were in the voice.

"I gathered all my strength, and answered boldly, 'No! I never knew you! You are not my Mary. You are an evil spirit sent by Satan to deceive me; and, in the name of the Lord Jesus Christ, I command you to depart, and to trouble me no more.'

"The spirit vanished. But in the going, for one brief instant, the gentle expression on that face turned to one of baffled rage, the most malignant that I ever saw on the face of any man, or in the pictured likeness of any evil demon. It left me all of a tremble and in deep distress of mind. Why had such an experience come to me? Had I failed somewhere and shown some weakness, that the devil dared to approach me in this manner?

"I prayed and asked God to reveal to me any unknown sin. But instead of the conviction of some unrepented wrong there came into my mind clearly and emphatically, words that I had read many times in the book *Early Writings:* 'I saw that the saints must have a thorough understanding of present truth, which they will be obliged to maintain from the Scriptures. They must understand the state of the dead; for the spirits of devils will yet appear to them, professing to be beloved relatives or friends, who will declare to them unscriptural doctrines.... The people of God must be prepared to withstand these spirits with the Bible truth that the dead know not anything' (page 262).

"So with the knowledge that these evil spirits will appear even to the saints, we need have no fear that such experiences indicate God's displeasure, but that they are permitted as a test of our faith in the revealed instructions from heaven.

"I thanked and praised God that He had warned us against our subtle enemy, who is seeking our destruction. 'For the living to the dead?' Never! What light can come from that source? Bright, shining messengers, direct from the throne of God bring us light, comfort and joy, even in the time of our greatest sorrow."

---

[1] *General Conference Bulletin,* 1891, p. 45.
[2] *Ibid.*
[3] Letter to Ellen G. White, Aug. 10, 1892.
[4] Letter to Ellen G. White, April 28, 1892.
[5] *Ibid.*
[6] Letter to Ellen G. White, Oct. 5, 1892.
[7] Letter to Ellen G. White, Jan. 27, 1893.
[8] Undated letter to Ellen G. White, 1893.
[9] Letter to Ellen G. White, June 30, 1893.

With the Pioneers in Africa

SHORTLY AFTER Mary's death Stephen was requested by the General Conference to spend the spring and summer of 1894 attending camp meetings in Europe. Then he journeyed on to South Africa, landing in Cape Town August 29. He was welcomed by his old friend, Asa Robinson, president of the South African Conference.

Almost immediately Haskell inquired as to the progress of the work in South Africa during the five years since his first visit in 1889. Robinson replied, "Haven't you heard? We are no longer a mission field. We are now an independent, organized conference." Then for two hours Haskell listened to a thrilling account of progress. A company had been organized in Cape Town and a church building erected, the first Seventh-day Adventist church in that city. It was only a few doors from his home on Roeland Street. Treatment rooms had been opened and the construction of a sanitarium in the nearby suburb of Claremont was under consideration. A college had been opened at Claremont, and a church school started in connection with the college. A home for orphans had also been opened. Colporteurs and evangelists were busy in many South African towns, and they had succeeded in establishing several companies of converts.

But Elder Haskell was most interested in Robinson's account of the securing of land for the establishing of a mission for African tribal people—the station that proved to be the first permanent Seventh-day Adventist mission to the pagans. A 12,000-acre tract of land had been secured from the British South Africa Company, which was now apportioning land in Matabeleland and Mashonaland to settlers. Robinson recounted the circumstances connected with the securing of a site for this mission (later known as Solusi Mission).

"The General Conference Foreign Mission Board . . . voted to make an effort to secure a portion of this land. . . . As I was in Cape

Town at that time, the Mission Board asked me to . . . see Mr. [Cecil] Rhodes. Mr. Rhodes, . . . one of the greatest of English statesmen, was somewhat abrupt in his manner. . . . He replied, 'Very well, then, come next week, Wednesday, at ten-thirty.' . . . I prepared a very carefully worded memorandum. . . . [I stated] that we were Seventh-day Adventists. I told him our object would be to establish schools, teach the natives habits of civilization, take into the country American farm machinery, teach them how to cultivate the soil, clothe themselves, and build houses.

"While I was reading this memorial to Mr. Rhodes, he sat at his desk very busily writing. Fearing that he was paying no attention to what I was reading, I paused for a second or two. He looked up and said, 'and.' I then went on reading, and he kept on writing, until I paused the second time. He again looked up and said, 'and.' I then proceeded until the third time. I was so dead sure that he could not be listening to me, while writing just as fast as he could make his pen go, that I again stopped to get his attention. He looked up, and with a bland smile on his face, said, 'and.'

"I then went on to the end of my chapter and sat down. . . . I sat very much embarrassed for what seemed to me about five minutes, . . . while Mr. Rhodes kept on with his writing. He then hastily folded together several sheets, placed them in a large envelope, sealed it, wrote the address on the envelope, and handed it to me, saying, 'Hand this to Doctor Jamieson when you get to Bulawayo.' After a little conversation regarding the new country he politely bowed me out of his office.

"We outfitted a party, composed of Brother Druillard, formerly of Nebraska, and Peter Wessels, of Cape Town, with several helpers, sixteen mules, a large covered wagon, an abundant supply of foods, and started them off. They were six weeks on the way. They carried Mr. Rhodes' letter, but were ignorant of its contents. When they arrived in Bulawayo they handed this letter of introduction to Doctor Jamieson. He read it and said, 'Gentlemen, how much land do you people want?' . . . Brother Wessels said, 'Well, doctor, the facts are we ought to have around ten or twelve thousand acres, but it will depend on the terms, whether or not we can handle that much.'

Above: An early picture of the Solusi Mission site. Below: A celebration at Solusi College in the 1960's with faculty and students lined up before the church building.

" '*Terms!*' The doctor replied, 'Rhodes commands me to give you all the land you can make use of. Do you want better terms than that? I will give you a guide, and you may go east, west, north, or south, and wherever you find such a tract of land not already taken, it will be yours.' " [1]

Members of the scouting party had not yet returned to the Cape, but Elder Robinson had letters from them, and a telegram sent over the new telegraph line that had been completed as far as Bulawayo while they were searching for a site. They wired the news that land had been secured in Matabeleland for a mission (later named the Solusi Mission). In a later report Haskell wrote about the friendliness with which the party had been received by the local tribesmen. When told about the God who had sent them, the Africans asked, "Where does He live? Is He young or old? Have you seen Him?" After talking awhile through our interpreter they went away, and returned leading a fine, large goat as a present, saying, "If this great Boss who has sent you here will be good to us, take care of us, and protect us against the English, we will be glad to have you come and live among us." [2]

Robinson regarded it as providential that even worldly statesmen were helping make it possible to bring the gospel to the Africans. It was soon after the General Conference took definite action to open a mission in Central Africa that the British conquered the fierce Matabeles, who were a terror to all the surrounding tribes. "With God's message in our hands," he said, "and the divine commission to carry that message to 'every nation, and kindred, and tongue, and people,' it seems evident that whatever motives may have prompted the opening of this country to civilization and the gospel, God's providence overrules it all." [3]

Haskell wrote that Bulawayo was suddenly experiencing a tremendous boom, due to a report of gold diggings in that part of the country. A rumor was afloat that this was the land of Ophir, where King Solomon's gold came from. The railroad was now within a few hundred miles of Bulawayo; telegraphic communications were now complete. And so, as the brethren were saying, "the lightnings of God have come down to hasten the proclamation of His last message to the world"; and He had opened the way to establish a mission station among a people who had not even a vague conception of God.

On October 15, an early spring day in South Africa, Elder Haskell started out with the Robinsons on a visiting tour among the South African believers. After a train ride of thirty-six hours, they reached Beaconsfield, where was one of the first Seventh-day Adventist churches in South Africa. Here Elder Haskell again met Sister Hetty Hurd. Several years before, she had assisted him in establishing the Bible Teachers' Training School in London. Two other women were now associated with her in literature evangelism and house-to-house Bible instruction. Many books had been sold in this area and a mission church school was being conducted by Sarah Peck, with an attendance of over fifty children, more than half from non-Adventist homes.

The brethren remained two weeks at Beaconsfield and held twenty-four meetings, which Elder Haskell states were attended by the people of the community and by every member of the thriving little church. This seemed extraordinary to him, considering that some meetings were held at five-thirty in the morning to allow the busy members a full day for work, and that most members had to walk from one to two and a half miles to attend.

A revival followed these meetings at Beaconsfield. Many were convinced of the truths presented. Arrangements were made for them to receive special Bible studies with Sister Hurd. With his usual hopeful, forward look Elder Haskell wrote: "I can see how it was when Christ was on earth, and *how it will be in the end* when we, as ministers and people, are in the place where the Lord can speak through us and glorify His name without the instrument taking any of the glory; then will people be stirred to listen and take their stand for God and heaven."

One Sabbath service an educated African was walking past the Beaconsfield place of worship. Desiring to see a Seventh-day Adventist service, he stepped inside. He listened to the sermon, which convinced him that here was a Christian church built on the foundation of God's Word. He went home with one of the brethren who spoke a language that he could understand. They prayed and talked together. In a later meeting he bore his testimony, which had to be translated. He said that he had thought himself pretty good because he did not smoke or drink, and had no bad habits; but he found it was all self-righteousness. He said that now he felt like a bird let out of a cage. He fully embraced the Sabbath that very day although he had never heard a word on that subject before.

In an address given at the 1901 General Conference session, Elder Haskell told more about this African man, Richard Moko. He was an interpreter and understood several languages. After uniting with the Adventists he received large salary offers from other missions with the stipulation that he give up the Sabbath and preach their doctrines. He suffered persecution. His own wife turned against him, and every influence was brought to bear to turn him from the truth. But he remained faithful and his wife was converted.

The party from Cape Town next visited Cathcart, the nearest railroad station to James Tarr's four-thousand-acre farm. Though they arrived at midnight, they were welcomed by Brother Tarr. With the help of his drivers and one or two lanterns they were loaded, bag and baggage, into a farm wagon drawn by eight bullocks, and started on the fourteen-mile trek to "Tarsus," the farm. In one of his newsy letters Haskell describes this midnight ride: "Over the hind axle . . . by actual measurement there was a width of two feet and ten inches for us to get into. Each one except the [Robinsons'] baby went down narrow-side first, Brother Robinson in the middle and the baby on top. It was very rough and there [were] no springs, and we were over the hind axle. So as we had wedged in as tight as it was possible, there was no danger of our rolling round. We had the satisfaction of knowing that three sides of us were warm all the rest of the night. But in the morning about six we felt as though a breakfast would do us good. And a warm bath might take out some of the soreness."[4]

He then tells about James Tarr's family: Tarr was fifty-four years old, and had sixteen children, besides seven others orphaned by the death of his brother. All were Christians; two were in America attending college, and four in Claremont—all preparing to take a part in the Lord's work. They conducted a regular day school and Sabbath services in their house. It was really a church in the home, gathering morning and evening for Bible study around a long table. The father and some of the sons canvassed much of the time. He had many African helpers, whom he treated with the greatest kindness.

His flock of sheep numbered five hundred, and he had one hundred and eighty head of cattle. They fed on the rolling prairies, and at night were shut into kraals, with walls topped with thornbush to discourage a colony of lions that had their den in a ledge of rocks not far from the house.

After this the group traveled on to the seaport town of East London and from there to King William's Town, where Fletcher Tarr had gathered a group of sixteen converts. He had secured an appointment for Elder Haskell to deliver a lecture at the regular meeting of the Good Templars, a temperance society, and the elder gladly complied.

Much of the traveling in the eastern provinces was by ox wagon or two-wheeled postcart. This afforded the travelers a good opportunity to view the country. Elder Haskell described the land, owned in large tracts, where many thousands of sheep and cattle were seen grazing on the hillsides in every direction. When there was plenty of rain there was plenty of feed and everything was in a prosperous condition; but in case of drought, which was common, there was a scarcity.

The Robinson-Haskell party reached home Friday morning, November 23, after an absence of five weeks. Soon they were engaged in preparations for a Bible institute, scheduled to begin November 30. The institute was held at Claremont Union College, with one hundred present. Since it was vacation time at the school, workers and members attending from elsewhere were comfortably housed in the dormitories. This was the largest gathering of Seventh-day Adventists ever held in Africa up to that time.

Early the following year Elder Haskell, with several other brethren, had the privilege of interviewing Khama, king of the Bechuanas. This people, a peaceable tribe numbering about sixty thousand, were protected by the British Government. French missionaries had established several Christian missions among them.

In Khama's country the rains had failed and crops were poor. To prevent famine among his people, the king had forbidden them to sell to any other tribe garden or farm produce they might raise. Some of his subjects protested this law. Khama, knowing that the British Government always upheld the chiefs if their demands were reasonable, had come for the first time to the Cape, to solicit aid in upholding his authority. He was accompanied by his interpreter and the British Commissioner, the Reverend Mr. Moffat.

Of this Christian chieftain Haskell wrote: "Chief Khama evidently is a man of about sixty-five years of age, . . . about five feet ten inches in height, slim, but well built and of more than ordinary appearance. His step is light and quick. . . . He neither snuffs nor smokes, although many of his people do. . . . We learned from him that nearly all of his people are educated to read and write in their language, and now they are making an effort to learn the English language. He also was much interested in the suggestion of our plan of Christianizing the Matabeles. . . .

"[The Bechuanas] are strictly temperate; no liquor is sold in the country, nor is the making of Kaffir beer allowed. The penalty of banishment is rigidly enforced upon all, both white and black, who violate this just law. They are loyal to the king and to the principles he inculcates among them."[5]

Mrs. Druillard (Mother D to nearly everyone who knew her) now mothered this African chief, who in his endeavor to uplift his tribe had made strict laws against intemperance and was endeavoring to keep drunkenness, debauchery, and the sale of intoxicants out of his country. She even wrote to Queen Victoria, as secretary of the WCTU in South Africa, presenting the temperance principles of Khama and requesting that she instruct her representatives in Africa to uphold him in his efforts to prevent liquor dealers from debauching his people.

One of Haskell's most exciting experiences was his trip into Basutoland in a two-wheeled postcart drawn by four horses. "Language cannot describe the roads," he wrote, "the hills we went over, the gorges we went through, the steeps we climbed, the ditches we went into in crossing streams. . . .

"Imagine our feelings when we learned that the driver had not been over the road for four years—and such a road! There were no guideposts to go by—nothing but one's sight and the instinct of the horses. . . . In vain was the candle-lantern lighted and hung in the center under the cart; for the jolting of the cart, first to one side and then to the other as it struck some boulder, would put it out. A number of times the horses stopped, and although spirited, refused to move . . . until the driver got out and found the path and directed them to the right way. Then, without any urging, they would make haste to get in the right path, evincing a knowledge of the situation. . . .

"Sometimes, contrary to the reining of the driver, the leaders would spring more than the distance of the width of the cart, and lead the wheelhorses by the right road down into a gully; when, had they gone directly forward, we would have plunged over an embankment." [6]

After seventeen hours of continuous travel, stopping only to exchange horses, the postcart drew up at the home of a resident missionary, a member of the Paris Evangelical Missionary Society. A warm welcome, a satisfying meal, and a sound sleep put the exploring traveler in condition for a tour of investigation the following morning. He was shown through chapel and classrooms, through printing and book-binding departments, where religious books and textbooks were printed for the mission; then he was conducted through numerous other buildings where students were trained in such industries as blacksmithing, gardening, stonemasonry, and carpentry.

He was told that there were seventeen mission stations in that part of the country, all conducted by white farmers, besides one hundred and forty-one outstations or Christian schools conducted by trained African evangelists. Results of such practical education were evidenced by the many brick or stone houses instead of the usual pole-and-mud thatched huts.

In a letter to Ellen G. White, Elder Haskell related an amusing experience that concluded the Basutoland excursion. He had decided to visit Lady Grey, a quiet little town of four or five hundred homes, completely surrounded by rugged mountains, its only access being by a wagon road. Nearly every family in town had subscribed to our new African journal the *Wachtor* ("Watchman"), and Elder Haskell thought that an opening might be found there for meetings. Accordingly he hired a horse, intending to make the thirty-five-mile trip to the town by horseback.

But the old horse proved to be "notoriously lazy," as the story goes. "I used up all the switches I could get, and ruined my cane I had carried for years, lost my eye glasses in his jolting, as well as had my pockets emptied of letters, which I dismounted to get, and also passed through five gates, . . . and after a nine hours' ride I reached Lady Grey. I had engaged the horse for a number of days, but the next morning I sent him back. . . .

"On Friday Bro. and Sister Rogers came on their bicycles. We spent Sabbath on the mountains, among the rocks, reading the Bible and letters or copies which you sent me in the last mail."[7] He had hired an easier-riding horse, a "gentle" creature, and had turned him into the yard to graze during the night, intending to start back with the Rogerses at one o'clock in the morning, there being a full moon. But when the time came to start, the horse was gone. The garden gate had been left open.

In the morning the horse was found; but when Haskell attempted to mount, the "gentle" creature—wise as well as gentle—looked appraisingly at the ponderous proportions of his would-be rider, pulled back, then doubled up his knees and rolled over on the ground, breaking the bridle and girth. This is the last record that can be found of Stephen Haskell's attempting to ride horseback. He wrote that he was remaining with the family where he was lodging and would trust Providence to get him back to Cape Town and his typewriter.

Finally the postcart came by, enabling him to make connections with the train, which after two days and nights of travel landed him where he wanted to be.

In South Africa Elder Haskell traveled extensively, sometimes alone but oftener with an African teacher or translator who acted as guide and interpreter when he visited with the tribesmen in the villages. Richard Moko, who was with him for a time, introduced Haskell to a fellow Christian, David Kalaka. Kalaka was an intelligent Basuto who had been educated by the French missionaries and then employed as their translator.

Two mountain scenes in Basuto-land, a region in which Haskell traveled while scouting for missions.

Haskell engaged Kalaka to conduct him through Basutoland. Together they visited the paramount chief. They sat outside his royal hut and talked. The chief poured out a long story of grievances. His counselors, the underchiefs, did not agree with him; and in their council meetings they could not agree among themselves. The chief said, "I see how things ought to be done, but my counselors do not agree with me."

Haskell pointed to a tree and asked, "Do you see that tree? There are no two limbs just alike." The chief could not see any two that were exact duplicates. "Then can you expect that men will be alike in their opinions?"

The idea was new to the chief and struck him favorably. "Yes, I understand," he said; and before the visitors left he said, "I wish you could come here, and start a mission in our country."

At one mission station Kalaka introduced Haskell as an Adventist missionary. Said the director, "I know about your people. One of your papers was sent to me for some time. You make a great deal of the books of Daniel and Revelation. Students are asking me to explain these books, but I know nothing about them. I wish you could stay here long enough to teach my theological class and make a special study of Daniel and Revelation." Telling the story years afterward, Elder Haskell said, "I thought I could not stop very well then; but I could [have] if I had had half faith enough." He always regretted his failure to recognize this as an overruling providence of God, and that he had not stopped right then and taught those two books to the inquiring students.

During his associations with Kalaka, Haskell "was careful not to say the word 'Sabbath' to him, and not to say anything to him to try to proselyte him over to our faith. But," he wrote, "we read the Bible together every day; and as I selected some portions where the truth stood out prominently, I simply emphasized the words we read.

"For instance, we took the subject of baptism at one time, reading from that chapter in Acts about Phillip's baptizing the eunuch. I wondered how he felt about it. . . . We came to a stream of water, and Brother Kalaka wanted to be baptized; but there was not water enough in the stream. We made arrangements for him to translate

141

Steps to Christ [into Sesuto], and to come over to Cape Colony to be with our brethren."⁸ He decided to keep the Sabbath, and accepted all our faith. During a general meeting at Kimberley he was baptized by O. A. Olsen.

Several years afterward J. M. Freeman was sent to work in Africa. When he came to Basutoland he went to the chiefs to ask for land on which to build a mission. These men, who had the right to say who could work in their country and who could not, had been instructed to refuse land to the Seventh-day Adventists. This they did. But the paramount chief asked some questions and soon discovered that Missionary Freeman believed and taught the same religion as Elder Haskell. To make sure, he asked, "Are you of the same beliefs as the old missionary that came here some years ago and talked with me about the trees?"

"Yes, I am," answered Freeman.

"Then you can have any piece of land in my country," he declared. Thus he reversed the decision of his underchiefs. So the Basuto Mission was established.

David Kalaka joined Missionary Freeman and assisted as a teacher at the mission. He also sold hundreds of copies of *Steps to Christ* all through Basutoland. By horse and cart he would visit from fifteen to twenty villages each trip. He died about the age of sixty, leaving a son who also became a Seventh-day Adventist teacher and minister.

---

[1] As Robinson recounted it fifty years later in *Review and Herald*, July 20, 1944, p. 19.
[2] *Ibid.*, Oct. 23, 1894, p. 666.
[3] *Ibid.*, Sept. 18, 1894, p. 598.
[4] Letter to Ellen G. White, Nov. 8, 1894.
[5] *Review and Herald*, March 5, 1895, p. 153.
[6] *Ibid.*, Jan. 21, 1896, pp. 39, 40.
[7] Letter to Ellen G. White, Dec. 3, 1895.
[8] *General Conference Bulletin*, April 15, 1901, p. 233.

Teaching at Avondale

IT IS EARLY Monday morning, April 5, 1897. We are on the Avondale school estate in the heart of the eucalyptus forest that borders the small town of Cooranbong, New South Wales, Australia. The site of the new Australasian training school (now Avondale College) is a scene of unusual activity. Carpenters are siding up an unfinished building; men are hauling and shoveling sand and mixing concrete; bricklayers are working in an underground cellar; and—what is this?—a girl handing them the bricks, and another girl passing bricks to the first young woman! At a short distance from this building we see still another girl sliding bricks down a wide plank into a deep hole in the ground. The hole is in the process of becoming a cistern. Two men are down there building a double brick wall that is to be cemented and made waterproof, ready to receive refreshing showers and to store them for future use.

And here is another girl busily unloading bricks from a cart and piling them on the ground within easy reach of the one who is sliding them down the plank. The driver of the cart is Milton, son of Metcalf Hare and grandson of Joseph Hare, the old patriarch. Metcalf has been appointed business manager of Avondale and has brought his wife and two boys, Milton and Robert, to live in a small cottage he has built near the school.

We notice nearby another building that seems to have been completed. Attracted by the laughter and chatter, and the rattle of buckets and pans, dustpans and brooms, we enter the building and find that the joyful noise is coming from boys and girls who are busily scraping and scouring plaster from floors and paint from windows,[1] using nearly any kind of tool they can get, from putty knives to sixpenny coins.

We decide to satisfy our curiosity by going back and looking

Haskell and his second wife, Hetty.

around in the unfinished building. A FRESH PAINT sign warns us, and we enter cautiously. An elderly gentleman is applying paint to a front window sash. He lays down his brush and pauses for a word of greeting. His name? Joseph Tucker, a painter by trade. His age? Eighty-two. An employee? "No, just one of the volunteers! We're helping to get the building ready so school can begin on time," he says.

Stepping farther inside, we come across two middle-aged women down on their knees, both of them vigorously swinging hammers. A man is forcing floorboards into position with a floor jack while the women fasten them securely with nails. We ask a boy hurrying past carrying floorboards who these two lady carpenters may be. He informs us that one of them is Sara McEnterfer, Mrs. White's secretary and traveling companion; the other one is Hetty Hurd Haskell, a bride of two months. The man handling the jack is Iram James, Mrs. White's helper on her farm. He is an honored consultant of the families who are moving into the neighborhood and beginning to transform a portion of the fifteen-hundred-acre forest into a community of thriving homesteads.

We learn that all this is in response to an appeal from Mrs. White for help in finishing the building and readying it for the opening of school. A six-o'clock meeting of the church had been called for Sunday morning, the day before, to consider what could be done to hasten building operations so that the school could be opened on the day announced. Everyone connected with the enterprise had abandoned hope that it could possibly begin on the day set for its opening —everyone except Mrs. White. She knew that the building funds were exhausted; but the people had waited long for the school, and there ought not to be another postponement. In response to her appeal for help thirty eager volunteers went to work with a will.

But why was money so scarce at this time? A severe and widespread drought following a prolonged financial depression had brought on hard times. Cattle and sheep died by the thousands; crops were poor; work hard to obtain; banks closed; business firms failed. There was poverty and suffering. Mrs. White wrote in her diary of constant appeals from families who "had not money to buy bread." It grieved her that she could help them but little. Her own office staff had been put to the inconvenience of waiting months for their wages. It was at such a time—a time to test the faith and endurance of everyone, especially the new Australian believers—that the school project was launched.

But what about the bride carpenter and the groom who were temporarily occupying a tent near Sunnyside, Mrs. White's home? In response to an appeal from Mrs. White, Stephen Haskell had joined the pioneer workers in Australia. She had also invited Hetty Hurd to become a worker at Avondale. But it seems that a special request from Stephen in the form of a proposal of marriage was required to bring her there from Africa.

When the ship bringing Hetty finally arrived in Sydney, Stephen Haskell was at the docks, waiting to greet his bride-to-be. He was informed that the Sydney passengers were all in quarantine because of a smallpox scare on board. He requested the privilege of calling on his intended wife and was readily given permission, but told that if he did so he himself would be quarantined! The wedding had to be postponed while the lady languished in quarantine and the groom filled appointments in connection with an evangelistic series in which he was engaged.

Mrs. White rejoiced to see the two united in marriage and working where they were most needed, ready to help in starting the new school.

At the age of sixty-three, and after nearly three years of loneliness, the veteran missionary had found a second companion, on February 24, 1897. Hetty was destined to stand by his side and render valuable assistance for twenty-two years.

Stephen Haskell's second wife was a California girl. She had been converted early in life but had lost interest in religion. In 1884 a brother-in-law persuaded her, much against her own inclination, to accompany her sister's family to a camp meeting in Oakland. She consented to go, but declared that she would not attend the meetings. One day while resting in her tent on the campground she was attracted by singing coming from the pavilion close by. She approached, and stood outside listening; then she slipped inside and took a seat at the edge of the tent. The talk on Bible prophecy that followed the singing interested her. Never had she heard anything like it before. After that first meeting, Hetty was a regular attendant at the tent.

One day while listening to a sermon by Elder Loughborough on the subject of the saints' inheritance and the New Jerusalem, she said to herself, "I'll be there!" She had just concluded a term of teaching in a large district school near her sister's home, and was engaged to teach the following year at a handsome salary. She had also been solicited to sign a life contract with the school. But now, inspired with a great longing to carry to others the good news that had brought unspeakable joy to her own heart, Hetty resigned from teaching and joined a group of young women who were learning how to give Bible studies.

She put heart and soul into the work and soon became so proficient that she began helping others to acquire the art. A few years later, with two other young women, she was sent by the General Conference to assist in opening the training school for Bible instructors in London. There as we have seen, she first met Elder Haskell. Her work in England was successful. When a consecrated teacher was needed to train Bible instructors in Africa, Hetty Hurd was chosen for that post. There Haskell renewed his acquaintance with his old friend. He said of her work in Cape Town:

"Sister Hurd runs what she has on her hands with a stiff team. . . . She is competent in her work, and she goes ahead and drives her own horses when she can find a field to work in and can have a number of workers with her." [2]

On the day announced—April 28, 1897—the Avondale School for Christian Workers opened its doors. The buildings were ready, but where were the students? Only ten presented themselves on that opening morning, with four teachers. Elder Haskell wrote: "During the first few days there were only two students in the home, and it did not look very encouraging; but our faith took hold of the Lord, and many earnest prayers ascended to God to send us students." [3] During the first four weeks, while awaiting the arrival from America of Prof. C. B. Hughes, who was to take the principalship of the school, classes were conducted more as a Bible institute than a regular school. Haskell taught Bible, and his wife was matron and assistant in Bible.

In the meantime ministers and workers throughout the entire Australasian Union Conference were struggling with the problem of filling the school with young people to be trained as workers for Australia, New Zealand, and the great Pacific Islands field. Many young people were eager to receive a Christian education that they might be qualified to give the gospel message. During the years, when the need for consecrated workers had been presented from the pulpit, young men in the audience would often be seen weeping because they could not afford to cross the ocean and attend an Adventist college at Battle Creek or Healdsburg. Now there was a school in their own land, but few had the means to attend it; and the church had no money to assist them.

"For a time the prospects looked very dark," wrote A. G. Daniells, president of the Australasian Union Conference. "We could not learn of one person in New South Wales who was planning to go as a boarding-student. We heard of but one in New Zealand, and we knew of only three or four in this conference [Victoria]. In our perplexity we prayed over the matter. In our councils various suggestions were made from time to time, and finally light came in, and we began to work with all our might. A suggestion was made that we ask our brethren in all our churches to each pledge six pence a week for twenty weeks towards the students' aid fund. . . . The amount thus raised would pay for the tuition of one student for the present term of twenty-two weeks. We proposed that what was contributed should always belong to the fund. . . . This was to be loaned to the students with the understanding that they would return it when it became possible to do so. Then it would be loaned to other students selected by the committee.

"This plan greatly pleased our brethren, and they have responded very cheerfully. Not only this, but it has seemed to bring new life into our midst. We first presented the plan to the North Fitzroy church. We asked the church to raise enough to send one student, with the result that they raised enough to send two. These have been selected, and are on their way to school today. Other churches have taken hold in like manner, and there is a real stir in the camp. One week ago tonight we sent six young men and women off by Cook's excursion. This morning at six o'clock we sent six more. One went alone in the middle of the week. This makes thirteen that we have sent from this conference, and we are expecting to send four more." [4]

And so, because individual church members took hold to help, it began to appear that "that school, way out there in the wilderness," was going to be a success after all. God blessed the many small gifts of money and labor, accompanied by prayer and an ever-increasing faith in the sure promises found in His Word.

Sister White described how another problem was solved: "For some time the country had been suffering from a drouth, but our cistern was only finished a few days when we had blessed showers from heaven which filled the tanks, and half filled the large cistern. . . . After a few weeks another downpour of rain came, which filled the cistern to overflowing. If there is no more rain during this term, the school has enough for all its needs. Thus the Lord has favored us." [5]

As soon as accommodation was available, Elder and Mrs. Haskell joined the school family on the campus. About two months after the opening he wrote: "The blessing of God has rested on the school from the first; everything connected with it is calculated to bring peace and harmony. There are about forty students in the home; this makes a nice little family. Professor Hughes is the principal, and teaches history from 'Empires of the Bible.' Sister Hughes teaches grammar, elocution, reading, rhetoric, and one Bible class. Brother Lacey teaches arithmetic, geography, physiology, and music; while Sister Lacey has the primary department. Sister Haskell is matron, and has one Bible class, a verse-by-verse study on the book of Revelation; and the writer has lessons on the book of Daniel daily, besides a general study at the opening of the school [each day]. Besides these, there is a practical cooking-class which meets once a week." [6]

The daily program was strenuous: "Rising bell is at 5:45 A.M.; prayers, 6:15; breakfast at 7:00; school opens at 8:45; regular class-work begins at 9:15, continuing until 1:15 P.M., and dinner is at 1:30. Then come three hours of labor. The work of the boys has been the clearing of the land and the building of the roads; and as the season of planting vegetables comes on, they will be engaged in cultivating the soil. On each Sunday afternoon, boys, girls, and teachers engage in preparing the front yard for flowers of every description that will grow in this climate, and all seem happy in this work." [7]

"The school buildings are about one mile from the public road, and over two miles from the nearest post-office. Cooranbong, our post-office, is a small country village consisting of one store and a very few houses.... There is a space of about sixty feet cleared around the buildings, and the rest of the yard is covered with trees. It is a common sight to see a kangaroo go leaping across the space laid out as our future lawn." [8]

"The location of the school could not be more desirable; it is in the woods, where the heart can listen to the voice of God in nature." Haskell then described the birds, flying foxes, opossums, little koala bears, iguanas, and wallabies—diminutive members of the kangaroo family. He mentioned the large eucalyptus trees, whose timber is so hard that holes have to be bored in which to drive the nails, and which, in dry weather, will "sometimes strike fire under the planer." [9]

He was charmed with the Avondale River (Dora Creek) as it wound its way through semitropical foliage, past Dora Creek Station, to the Pacific, its calm surface reflecting the trees on the banks and the small houses and orange groves.

In his Bible classes Elder Haskell took the book of Daniel verse by verse and dug into it with the purpose of getting all the meat there was in any particular scripture, using other portions of the Bible to help interpret difficult passages.

One day when he stated in class his belief that every portion of Scripture contained some valuable spiritual lesson, a student raised his hand. "I can't agree with that statement," he said; "I am sure that some portions of the Bible have a purely material significance."

"Will you give us an example?" asked the teacher. The young man stood up and read Paul's words to Timothy: " 'The cloak that I left at Troas with Carpus, when thou comest, bring with thee, and the books, but especially the parchments.' Now what spiritual lessons are we supposed to get out of that?"

Without hesitation Elder Haskell replied, "One of deep significance, especially for self-supporting workers in God's cause. The apostle Paul had brought the imperishable riches of heaven to thousands of souls; yet he was so poor in this world's goods that he preferred to wait an indefinite length of time while Timothy made the uncertain journey from Troas to Rome rather than to have money expended in purchasing a new coat and writing materials." He could say with a depth of experience known to but few, "as poor, yet making many rich; as having nothing, and yet possessing all things" (2 Cor. 6:10).

In the realm of personal sacrifice Haskell could speak from experience. Economical almost to a fault, he and Hetty were ever more careful of the Lord's money than of their own. It was not unusual for them to share their wages with others who were eager to do service for God, supporting them from their own meager allowance until the efforts of these new workers proved fruitful and their names were placed on the conference payroll.

Nor did the Haskells ever knowingly lose an opportunity to help a person in need. During their first year at Avondale, they had made room in their own home for a wayward child who had been expelled from school.

Elder Haskell remembered how he and his first wife, Mary, had worked for twenty years to own a home of their own. Just after securing a clear title to a house in South Lancaster, while still rejoicing that the mortgage was no more, they received word of a financial crisis in Battle Creek. Three thousand dollars was needed immediately. Uncomplainingly they remortgaged their property and sent the money to headquarters. Elder Haskell said afterward that although at the time it was a great trial to him, God had rewarded him ten times over in every sense of the word.

The prosperity of Avondale was never measured in dollars and cents. Mrs. White wrote: "There are many things in this world that cast bright lights into our life experience. We have the evidence day by day that the Lord is working through the ministration of His angels in our school in Cooranbong. In His Word the Lord is giving the most precious, noble thoughts to our students. . . . All have every advantage in the school to have their minds carried upward to a higher level, and to a purer, clearer atmosphere, where the Lord can communicate with them individually." [10]

Elder Haskell also wrote that all the teachers and students appreciated the light given through the gift of prophecy respecting our schools, and that they were anxious in every particular to make an application of the same. One of the students was from Raratonga, where she had held the position of government translator for some time. But she had come to gain a better knowledge of the Bible and of our work in order to go forward in translating the truth into the Raratongan language.

"In Brother and Sister Haskell," affirmed Sister White, "the Lord has sent us the right kind of help. . . . He presents truth in a clear, simple, earnest manner that carries its own evidence with it to the hearts of those that hear it. As matron and teacher, S[iste]r Haskell could not be excelled. She is firm as a rock to principle, and she has no special favorites. She loves all, and helps all." [11] "She takes hold most earnestly, not afraid to put her hand to any work. She does not say, 'Go,' but she says, 'Come, and we will do this or that'; and they cheerfully do as she instructs them. We have had most precious instruction from the word from both Bro. and Sr. Haskell." [12]

Everyone looked forward with pleasure to Mrs. White's frequent chapel talks. She spoke appreciatively of both staff and student body, who, she said, were working in cooperation with one another, under the instruction of heavenly angels.

The first room utilized by the Avondale community for Sabbath services was a rough loft built over the sawmill and approached by a narrow, steep, outside stairway. In winter, cold winds entered through cracks in the floor and walls, and in summer the heat under the tin roof was almost unbearable. When a new dormitory was finished, its dining room became a place of worship, and later the assembly room served the same purpose. Mrs. White often presented the need for a suitable place of worship, and one reason she gave was that in their present location the crowded arrangement of seats and school desks interfered with kneeling in prayer. This need was sometimes discussed by the school faculty and the church board; but each discussion usually ended with the question, Where is the money with which to build?

One Monday morning in her chapel talk Mrs. White surprised everyone. The preceding evening she had favored not hastening the building of the church. But she now stated that during the night she had been instructed that the time had come to "arise and build." On Friday a council was held, and although only one hundred pounds ($500) was available, it was decided to walk out by faith and make a beginning. That very night in the mail a draft for two hundred pounds arrived from their friends in South Africa.

The next Thursday Elder Haskell and others conferred on the size and style of the prospective church building, and the kind of materials to be used in its construction were decided upon. The location was selected near the main road, about fifteen minutes' walk from the school. Miss McEnterfer took Mrs. White and Elder Haskell in the carriage to mark out the exact location. They chose, as Mrs. White wrote in her diary, "the most beautiful spot upon the whole grounds. We cannot see where there can be a spot that will have greater advantages, and as all our advancement and favors come from God, we will present to Him the very best offering we have, and say, 'Of Thine own we freely give Thee.' " [13]

The next day, Sabbath, Mrs. White addressed the united college and community groups from the words of Haggai the prophet, and the response of the people who "came and did the work in the house of the Lord of hosts." Elder Haskell also spoke.

On Sunday morning he walked over to Sunnyside in the rain and breakfasted with the White family. The horses were again harnessed to the phaeton and the three—Elder Haskell, Mrs. White, and Miss McEnterfer—started out in the downpour to find Brethren Hardy and Lamplough, two experienced carpenters who could oversee building operations. Estimates were made and a list of necessary materials was drawn up. Within a day or two Haskell and Lamplough were on their way to order timber and other building supplies.

Meanwhile, Mrs. White and Miss McEnterfer called on members of the community and secured promises of assistance with the labor. Two carpenters each volunteered to give two weeks' free time, others

Above: The original girls' dormitory (right) at Avondale. Parallel to it, but almost hidden by it, is the dining hall, built at the same time and several years later joined across the front by the building at the left. Below: The Avondale campus in the early 1960's. Visible at the extreme left are the buildings shown in the above picture, but seen from the opposite direction.

to give their unemployed days, and some with families to support, unable to donate labor, offered to work for half wages.

Preparations progressed rapidly. The ground was cleared and leveled. One day when Mrs. White and Miss McEnterfer went again to the chosen spot they found nearly the entire student body at work. In response to their own request, the school had been closed for a day that all might have part in erecting a temple to the glory of God. Men were struggling with the roots of immense trees; some were sawing their trunks in sections for removal; others were clearing away the undergrowth; still others were digging foundation holes. "All seemed to work cheerfully and with great pleasure," wrote Ellen White in her diary account of August 30. She lent a carpenter's bench, which was loaded onto a cart and taken to the grounds where the chapel was to be built. There were no idle hands at the school.

Building materials were slow in arriving. Yet in spite of a ten days' delay, hope was entertained that the church might be finished within seven weeks. School would close then and visitors arriving from Melbourne and New Zealand to attend the Sydney camp meeting would want to inspect the school.

When difficulties arose in the building process, as they sometimes did, Elder Haskell called the workmen together for earnest prayer that God's special blessing might rest upon them and upon the building. Many testified that they had never seen work progress more rapidly than it did on that church which was being built so largely by volunteer labor. Often the sentiment was expressed that "angels of God were beside the workmen" and that "the Holy Spirit was helping them." There was thanksgiving and rejoicing when, within the time limit, the building was completed and dedicated without debt.

The church was built of wood. The main auditorium seated three hundred, but the total capacity of the church was over four hundred, for two large wings were connected with the auditorium by double doors, so arranged that when they were thrown open on special occasions those seated in the wings could see the speaker.

The dedicatory service was held October 17, four days before the opening of camp meeting. Elder Haskell gave the discourse and Mrs. White offered the dedicatory prayer. Herbert Lacey conducted the singing. It was a solemn and joyful occasion. Referring to it Mrs. White said, "We felt indeed that the Lord Jesus was in our midst as we presented our chapel to God and supplicated that His blessing should constantly rest upon it."[14]

The Avondale School for Christian Workers belonged to the entire Australasian Union Conference. It was the product of prayer, faith, labor, and sacrificial giving of the entire membership throughout the conference. God had showered rich blessings upon the school and all connected with it. He had also provided for all their material needs. Even the shortage of money was a means of blessing, serving to develop in the prospective workers those most essential and indispensable qualities of economy, industry, and patient endurance of privations and hardships.

The young men had worked diligently. They had cleared land with mattock and ax. They had drained swamp areas, leveled ground, built fences, made roads, plowed, planted, set out a large orchard, cared for livestock, and performed many other duties comprising the life of the settler and farmer. The girls had done cooking, laundering, general housework, mending and sewing, and had often engaged in gardening. In his report of the school's activities Professor Hughes commented that it was cheering to hear them singing about their work.

As soon as school closed for the summer Elder and Mrs. Haskell were out again, assisting in evangelistic meetings, organizing companies, and building churches. Then when the second term opened they were back in the classroom ready for another year's teaching.

During vacation a boys' dormitory was built, accommodating fifty students and two teachers and providing one classroom, an office, and a large assembly room. The orchard was beginning to produce; and the garden, unaffected by the drought, was yielding vegetables, melons, and berries, all of a superior quality. A generous supply of honey from their own rapidly multiplying hives was stored for the coming year.

By the next year the enrollment had climbed to 117, including day students and the primary department. There were fifty boarders, as compared with two when school opened the year before. The faculty was increased by one member. Sarah Peck had arrived from South Africa to organize a teacher-training department. A class was also begun in home nursing.

Before the close of the first term (1897) Elder Haskell reported that all except two boarding students had made their decision to follow the Saviour. Among them was a young Tahitian prince who during the year had been traveling abroad and was led to visit the school. Desiring to perfect his knowledge of English, he remained to study Bible and language. Soon he stopped smoking, gave himself to God, and was baptized. Haskell informed the readers of the *Review* that he felt God had had a part in selecting the students who came to the school. The baptismal font was a quiet, clear pool in nearby Dora Creek. At the close of the second year thirty-two, mostly students, were baptized.

The next year, reporting again concerning the school, Haskell told of a Japanese who came for the purpose of studying English and was asked about God. Pointing to himself, he said, "Me God." In teaching him to read, Mrs. Hughes began with the New Testament. He became so interested that he declared he would never give up reading that Book. One day in conversation with her he said, "Man made a book, and it said, 'Man evolved; world long, long time being created.['] God made a book and he said, *he* made the world *in six days,* and *he* made *man.* Me believe God."[15] He was baptized. When school closed he joined a tent company with the purpose of gaining an experience that would enable him to carry the gospel to his own countrymen.

Elder Haskell wrote more about the curriculum: "The Bible has had the foremost place in the school. It has been the foundation of all study. Textbooks have been used for terms and descriptions, but the Bible for authority. . . . Nature study was also made prominent. Science and revelation were shown to be in harmony." "In some respects this school is different from any other of our schools, or from any other school I ever visited. Missionary work is a prominent feature. Two societies have been organized, one for the young women, and the other for the young men. Nearly every student has taken some part in practical missionary work. Meetings have been held in

Sunnyside, Ellen G. White's home at the Avondale school, as it looked in 1967, after restoration.

all the surrounding country. Temperance meetings have been conducted where the prejudice was strong, Bible readings have been held, and the Christian Help work has been taken hold of with a zeal not always seen. This, in part at least, may account for the desire of so many of the older students to enter the work. . . .

"The character of the prophets' school has been studied; and with the counsel of Sister White, the blessing of the Lord has rested on our efforts. Whatever success has been attained is attributed to the endeavor to follow the light that God has given respecting this school." [16]

The teachers, however, were human and equally subject to faults and imperfections of character as any of God's struggling children. At one time the Haskells received a message of reproof from Sister White for manifesting a harsh, critical spirit toward certain other members of the faculty.

The reproof was accepted in a spirit of humility. That it accomplished its purpose is not to be doubted. It did not lessen in the least the deep and tender Christian fellowship ever maintained between Ellen White and Hetty Haskell, the one more severely reproved.

At about this same time another teacher one afternoon walked out alone into the woods surrounding the school buildings, searching for a secluded spot where he could pray. He heard voices, and in a clearing he saw a small group of teachers on their knees. He joined them in prayer and in making confession to one another. Some had harbored the same spirit toward one another for which the Haskells had been reproved. As the group prayed together, a wave of spiritual blessing came upon them. On the campus it resulted in a rapid increase of student conversions.

The Haskells spent more than two years in Australia, and returned to the United States in the summer of 1899.

---

[1] The author of this book was one of them.
[2] Letter to Ellen G. White, July 26, 1895.
[3] *Review and Herald*, Oct. 26, 1897, p. 679. W. C. White reported forty students, eleven boarding in the home, on the opening day (*ibid.*, June 22, p. 396).
[4] *Ibid.*, June 22, p. 396.
[5] Letter to Mrs. Wessels, June 24, 1897.
[6] *Review and Herald*, Aug. 17, 1897, p. 521.
[7] *Ibid.*
[8] *Ibid.*, Oct. 26, p. 679.
[9] *Ibid.*, Aug. 17, p. 521.
[10] MS 175, 1897, pp. 3, 4.
[11] Letter 99, 1897.
[12] Letter 33, 1897.
[13] MS 175, 1897, p. 15.
[14] Letter to J. E. and Emma White, Oct. 18, 1897 (Letter 178).
[15] Haskell, in *Review and Herald*, Nov. 29, 1898, p. 768.
[16] *Ibid.*, pp. 768, 769.

The Sure Foundation

HETTY HASKELL stood at her tent door. She had gone out on the campground searching for her husband, had found him, brought him back to their tent, and insisted that he take a rest. Now she stood guard, making sure that no one would awaken him by knocking on the tent post. She explained, "I think my most important duty just now is to see that my husband gets a little rest. His old friends are so glad to see him that they would keep him talking all the time if he would do it." This guard duty was her self-appointed task as the Haskells, back in America, traveled to various late summer and fall camp meetings of 1899.

After spending a few days at the Kansas campground, at Wichita, they found G. A. Irwin, General Conference president, burdened over the spiritual declension and lack of practical godliness among the churches. He felt that earnest effort must be put forth to present before the people their need of careful, prayerful study of the Bible and the *Testimonies to the Church,* and of a more conscientious application of their principles to daily Christian living. He invited Elder Haskell to join him in this endeavor, and they traveled together in the latter part of 1899 and early 1900 holding special meetings in various places.

The Kansas camp meeting program opened at five-thirty in the morning with Bible study, followed after breakfast by group prayer meetings in family tents. During the day there were conference sessions in the assembly tent, with testimony meetings, Bible studies, and preaching. In the evening and on Sunday the meetings were of a character to interest the general public.

Elder Haskell presented daily Bible studies on the great fundamental doctrines, the "pillars of the church." Elder Irwin devoted an hour every day except Sabbath and Sunday to the conveying of important instruction and presenting urgent appeals from Sister White in Australia.

From the Kansas camp meeting the Haskells journeyed on with Elder Irwin, visiting Union College and attending the Nebraska camp meeting. They spent a few days in Chicago to visit the Life Boat Mission, the Working Men's Home, and the Rescue Home for Women, established by Dr. John Harvey Kellogg. Here Elder Haskell spoke to about sixty young men and women, mostly students in the American Medical Missionary College or the nurse's training school at Battle Creek, who, as a part of their training, were working in Chicago. They attended an evening service conducted especially for the city's "down and outers"; after which a street meeting was held, continuing till past midnight.

In Battle Creek Elder Haskell met with the employees of the Review and Herald and the sanitarium. He attended committee meetings and spoke every night in the Tabernacle "to more Sabbathkeepers than there are in all Australia." His wife conducted classes for Bible instructors.

One day they dined with Dr. Kellogg and his wife in their pleasant home, situated in a grove on the outskirts of the town, near the Seventh-day Adventist orphanage. The kindhearted doctor had taken about twenty orphans into his own family. Thirteen were seated at the table on that occasion. In ages they ranged from a two-year-old to young men and women.

Elder Haskell loved to tell of his Australian experiences. At that particular time he was appealing for funds to be applied toward the erection of a sanitarium building near Sydney. He had thus far secured one thousand dollars and was sending it on with the promise of more when pledges were paid.

Some were able to give hundreds of dollars, but many gifts compared in loving sacrifice with the widow's two mites. Elder Haskell was deeply moved when old people at the James White Memorial Home for the Aged came with twenty-five-cent pieces, all they had to give. One little girl gave her last ten-cent piece. When her father rewarded her liberally with a dollar bill, she exclaimed happily, "I'll give the dollar, too!"

People brought gifts of money, requesting that the elder send them to Sister White. He accepted their offerings, assuring them that such money would never be retained for her personal use. Every penny was invested in the cause. When asked whether Mrs. White intended to return to America, he usually replied, "The best way for you to get her to return will be to send her enough money to accomplish the work the Lord has shown her must be done there; then I think she would be willing to return."

Haskell's first year after returning to America was filled with difficulty. One cause of great anxiety to the General Conference leaders was the eagerness among a few younger ministers to invent and teach new and startling doctrines, intended to create a sensation but actually diverting minds from the important, testing truths of the Word. Strangest of all was the idea that those who were to receive the seal of God must experience complete physical "restoration" before the seal would be placed upon them.

It was affirmed by certain ones that if the children of Israel had lived right in every respect, the promises God made to them would have been fulfilled by their entering the land of Canaan and never dying, being made immortal in this present world. It was suggested that the same promises are for God's people today—that those who experience this physical restoration will receive the seal of God and will not die but will be made immortal in this present life. It was even believed and taught by some of the younger men that the seal of God would never be placed on any diseased, crippled, or deformed person, or even upon one who had gray hair; for in the closing work, God's people would reach a state of perfection, both physically and spiritually, where they would be healed from all deformity, and then could not die.

One conclusion of this restoration doctrine was that God would restore the land when, under the cultivation of men who have this faith, there would be no insect pests in the wheat, and nothing to hurt or destroy in all the farms thus cultivated. Connected with this idea was the theory that it would be wrong to kill anything that has life.

As Elder Haskell witnessed "the whole brood of errors" being taught, some of them even from the pulpit, he declared that he would give the third angel's message straight on the old lines, drawing from it principles that would dig out the roots of all such errors. He stated that the cause and foundation of such fanatical positions were the superficial study of the Bible. His own thorough knowledge of the Bible enabled him to counteract these false interpretations and to make sound applications of the divine principles of Scripture.

He proved that the theory that it is wrong to take life in any form whatever savored strongly of pantheism, that heathen philosophy which identifies God with His material creation. In reality it does away with that God whom Christ revealed to His followers as a loving heavenly Father.

When Elder Haskell was asked, "Is it not the life of God that is in all His creatures?" he answered, "Yes, that is true; and so is the life of Satan God's life." But, he contended, when a created being gives himself over to sin, his life becomes a curse, and is forfeited, and God proposes to take it back. Then when we remove the things that are only a curse, whether they be poisonous plants or hurtful insects or beasts that live only to destroy, we are cooperating with God in ridding the earth of that which is evil. However, Elder Haskell always made it clear that human life should be taken only at God's express command, for God is the only one who can read hearts and discern motives.

At times there was manifested a strong desire for supernatural demonstrations in the healing of the sick. At one camp meeting all the feeble and sick and infirm were brought to one tent, and for some length of time fervent prayers were offered for a special manifestation of the Holy Spirit in their restoration to health. Expectations of immediate healing were expressed by many, but their hopes were not realized.

The effect of this experience was depressing. It led Elder Haskell, who had little sympathy with such movements, to ask the question: What should be the underlying motive in praying for a manifestation of the Holy Spirit? Should it be a desire for supernatural manifestations? Or should it be, rather, that hearts might be cleansed of sin and given clear understanding of the Word of God? When we get hold of the Word of God and see its importance, then there is a power that does heal the sick.

The question was often asked, Why does God not grant the remnant church a fuller manifestation of the gift of healing? The following statement from a testimony concerning the school where he was on the faculty answered this question: "At times, restoration would not be best, either for the friends or for the church, but would result in wild enthusiasm and fanaticism, leading some to the conclusion that impulse is the ground of our faith. The only safe course is to follow the written Word."[1]

At this time Irwin, Haskell, and other leading ministers who were struggling against these fanaticisms were receiving letters from Mrs. White in Australia. One message brought Haskell extra encouragement. She had written: "I am glad you are where you are. Do not become discouraged. Meet the people with a courageous front. Keep the eye steadfastly fixed on your Leader. Dark and cloudy faces will confront you, but the bright beams of the Sun of Righteousness will melt away this feature, and you will have the victory in God. . . . Expect everything possible that God can give. Do not talk doubts; do not ponder doubts. God has a people true as steel to principle, but they are confused. They are walking like blind men. Help them, for Christ's sake, help them."[2]

A few weeks later Haskell and Irwin received another lengthy letter from the same source which contained much ammunition to use in his war against fanaticism. Sister White said: "The things of which you write are simply foolish imaginings. . . . The teachers who cherish them need to learn anew the principles of our faith. . . . To make the statements they make, and hold the notions they hold, is like descending from the highest elevation to which the truth of the Word takes men to the lowest level. God is not working with such men. Having lost the grand truths of the word of God, which center in the third angel's message, they have supplied their place with fables."

There were a few ill-balanced minds, she said, that were ready to catch at anything of a sensational character, but many who are as true as steel to principle would be helped and blessed. The great principles of the third angel's message must stand out, and the great pillars of our faith would hold all the weight that could be placed upon them.

She continued: "The Lord has afflicted ones, dearly beloved in his sight, who bear the suffering of bodily infirmities. To them special care and grace is promised. Their trials will not be greater than they can endure.

"Paul had a bodily affliction; his eyesight was bad. He thought that by earnest prayer the difficulty might be removed. But the Lord had his own purpose, and he said to Paul, 'Speak to me no more of this matter. My grace is sufficient. I will enable you to bear the infirmity.' "[3]

There were many believers, she said, who showed the natural results of old age, but God loves them; He honors their gray hairs because they have fought a good fight and kept the faith.

"Young men must be educated to keep within the bounds of, 'It is written.' ... No one is to put truth to the torture by cheap imaginings, by putting a forced, mystical construction upon the word. ... I have words to speak to the young men who have been teaching the truth: *Preach the word.* ...

"Let those who are tempted to indulge in fanciful, imaginary doctrines sink the shaft deep into the quarries of heavenly truth, and secure the treasure which means life eternal to the receiver. In the word there are the most precious ideas. These will be secured by those who study with earnestness; for heavenly angels will direct the search: but the angels never lead the mind to dwell upon cheap nonsense, as though it were the word of God. ... He desires us to seek for a pure, clean soul, a soul washed and made white in the blood of the Lamb. It is the white robe of Christ's righteousness that gives the sinner admittance into the presence of the heavenly angels. Not the color of his hair, but his perfect obedience to all God's commandments, opens to him the gates of the holy city. ... In the great day of God all who are faithful and true will receive the healing touch of the divine Restorer. The Life-giver will remove every deformity, and will give them eternal life."[4]

During the greater part of a year (1899-1900) Elder Irwin and the Haskells visited among the churches, schools, and district sessions, where they were the principal speakers. The Spirit of the Lord attended the meetings and great blessings were received by those who attended.

In January, 1900, at the close of a meeting in Graysville, Tennessee, Haskell had an attack of influenza, the effects of which persisted. He took a rest by visiting the Oakwood school at Huntsville, Alabama, and spending a week on J. E. White's Mississippi River mission boat *Morning Star,* but further preaching in Texas, Arkansas, and Kansas drained his strength. At Lincoln, Nebraska, Elder Haskell was laid low with weakness and fever and with a vicious carbuncle in the groin that made walking excruciatingly painful. For five days his condition deteriorated until serious doubts were expressed as to his recovery. One day the doctor said, as he came from the sickroom, "It will be over in a day or two, unless the Lord heals; blood poisoning has already set in." When the patient requested special prayer, Elders Irwin, Olsen, Johnson, and others met at his bedside and anointed him with oil, at the same time directing their petitions to the Great Healer. The course of the disease was stayed. He was carried to a meeting in a chair and was able to speak for about twenty-five minutes. The following day, Sabbath, he was able to speak for nearly an hour! Then on Sunday the abscess came to a head. When Dr. Kellogg, of Battle Creek, who had just arrived, was called in, he opened it at once. The operation brought immediate relief, followed by sleep, and there was definite improvement in the patient's condition.

A month later Elder and Mrs. Haskell were at Boulder with their old friends, the Druillards. Mrs. Haskell was following doctor's orders, and the hydrotherapy treatments she was administering were hastening his recovery. But one part of the prescription she could not follow because of the patient's lack of cooperation. The orders were *complete rest,* but he was trying to salvage his convalescent days by writing and preaching.

By midsummer the campaign was inaugurated to sell Mrs. White's new book *Christ's Object Lessons* to raise funds for schools. Elder Haskell received a personal letter from Mrs. White telling of her gift of the book, and of her hope that profits from its sale might benefit the schools.

Mrs. White gave her writing of the book; the publishing houses gave the printing; our brethren contributed money for illustrations, book plates, and material; the tract societies (Book and Bible Houses) handled the business without profit; church members were either to give or to sell the books to friends and neighbors, returning the full retail price to the educational fund. Every individual in the church would be called upon to help with some part of the project.

The great missionary leader saw much more in this enterprise than a means of decreasing the indebtedness threatening to crush our educational institutions. What an opportunity this was for all, even those who had become apathetic and indifferent, to renew their loyalty and devotion to the cause of truth! Had the day come for a revival of the old-time missionary spirit among our people? He and Hetty entered heartily into the plan to promote widely the sale of the book.

By the late summer of 1900 they were again in Battle Creek, busy as ever. But Haskell, not feeling well, had placed himself under Dr. Kellogg's care. The doctor took a personal interest in his old friend, attended him in his weakness, provided him with medications, health foods, grape juice, and whatever else his condition required. The heart of the old missionary was deeply disturbed as he saw the doctor drifting from the foundation truths of the message and questioning some of the personal testimonies sent him by Mrs. White. They had earnest prayer together, sometimes extending late into the night.

---

[1] Ellen G. White, MS 67, 1899; printed in *Selected Messages*, book 2, p. 348.
[2] ———, Letter 218, 1899, to S. N. Haskell, Nov. 29, 1899.
[3] ———, Letter 207, 1899, to S. N. Haskell and G. A. Irwin, Dec. 15, 1899.
[4] *Ibid.*

Meeting the Holy Flesh Fanaticism

AFTER THE brief period of recuperation in Battle Creek, Elder and Mrs. Haskell, at the invitation of the General Conference, went to Muncie, Indiana, to assist at the camp meeting to be held there September 13 to 23, 1900. A. J. Breed, the superintendent of District Number Three, comprising five States, of which Indiana was one, and member of the General Conference Committee, also attended this meeting. What the Haskells had found in the way of fanatical teachings during the preceding months as they visited churches and attended camp meetings was now eclipsed by what they found in Indiana. They could sense something peculiar as they came onto the campground at the opening of the meeting, as Mrs. Haskell reported to Mrs. White. Elder Haskell said he knew that spirit well, though he had not seen it for twenty years, and that it was very hard to deal with. A few days later Mrs. Haskell wrote to Sara McEnterfer, describing what was happening in the meetings:

"We have a big drum, two tambourines, a big bass fiddle, two small fiddles, a flute and two cornets, and an organ and a *few* voices. They have *Garden of Spices* as the songbook and play dance tunes to sacred words. They never use our own hymnbooks except when Elders Breed or Haskell speak, then they open and close with a hymn from our book but all the other songs are from the other book. They shout 'Amen' and 'Praise the Lord,' 'Glory to God.' . . . It is distressing to one's soul. The doctrines preached correspond to the rest. The poor sheep are truly confused."[1]

What the Haskells did not know was that a full eight months before, while Mrs. White was in Australia, this very situation had been opened to her in vision. While this camp meeting was being held, Mrs. White was on shipboard, returning to the United States. On reading the letters from the Haskells soon after her arrival in California she wrote on October 10:

"Last January the Lord showed me that erroneous theories and methods would be brought into our camp-meetings." "The things you have described as taking place in Indiana, the Lord has shown me would take place. . . . There will be shouting, with drums, music and dancing." [2]

But what was back of this strange experience? How could such things take place on a Seventh-day Adventist campground, and what would the outcome be? From several eyewitness accounts the story can be reconstructed.

The conference evangelist, S. S. Davis, developed and promulgated the teachings that led to these strange happenings. In time he was joined by R. S. Donnell, president of the Indiana Conference. Nearly all the conference workers followed. The basic features of this strange doctrine, which was called the "cleansing message," were that when Jesus passed through the Garden of Gethsemane He had an experience which all who follow Him must have. It was taught that Jesus had holy flesh, and that those who followed Him through this Garden experience would likewise have holy flesh. They were then "born" sons of God and they had "translation faith." Having holy flesh like Christ, they could not see corruption any more than He did; thus they would live to see Him come. Those who did not have this experience were "adopted" sons. They did not have translation faith. They must pass through the grave, and thus go to heaven by "the underground railway."

Attempting to gain this Garden experience by which holy flesh could be obtained, the people gathered in meetings in which there were long prayers, strange, loud instrumental music, and excited, extended, hysterical preaching. They were led to seek an experience of physical demonstration. The bass drum and the tambourines aided in this. It was expected that one, possibly more, of their number would fall prostrate to the floor. He would then be carried to the platform, where a dozen or more people would gather around and shout "Glory to God" while others prayed or sang. When this person regained consciousness it was declared that he had passed through the Garden experience—he had holy flesh, he had translation faith!

The conference president, who was responsible for planning the camp meeting program, was deeply involved in this doctrine, and was unwilling that the two visiting brethren, Elders Haskell and Breed, be given much opportunity to reach the people. He warned his workers that these men did not have "this experience," and the ministers should not allow themselves to be influenced by them. As the president stood one evening speaking, he held his arms outstretched toward the congregation, and later reported that he had felt great power coursing down his arms and passing through his fingers, out to the people. Elder Haskell reported that there was indeed a power, a strange power, in this new message. The people were bewildered. None wished to miss the experience of the outpouring of the Spirit of God. Translation faith seemed desirable. The teaching was a mixture of truth, error, excitement, and noise.

Between meetings many of the campers would gather around the tents where the two visiting brethren were staying. These people were frightened. They plied the brethren with questions, and in turn received instruction and warnings. Haskell and Breed declared the experience to be fanaticism, a repetition of what had been met among certain extreme fragments of the Millerite movement in 1845, against which the Seventh-day Adventist founders had contended.

It was especially unfortunate that these strange teachings were presented during the evening meetings when non-Adventists from the city were present. To many this was their first contact with Seventh-day Adventists. The two men were heartened, however, to see that some of the people discerned the true spirit of what was going on. "One new sister," reported Mrs. Haskell, "who had come from the Quaker church eighteen months ago came around the other day and said, 'You can tell by the sound whether a bell is cracked or not. Much of the preaching sounds cracked; but when you General Conference workers speak it sounds firm.' "[3]

It seemed to Elder Breed and the Haskells that there was little they could do to help the bewildered people. They wished that Mrs. White could be present to reprove error and help the members through this distressing experience. In agony of heart they left the campground on the closing day of the meeting, feeling that they had accomplished little.

Then on October 10, Mrs. White, from her newly acquired home, Elmshaven, in northern California, wrote quite fully of what had been revealed to her while still in Australia early in the year.

"The Holy Spirit never reveals itself in such methods, in such a bedlam of noise," she wrote. "This is an invention of Satan to cover up his ingenious methods for making of none effect the pure, sincere, elevating, ennobling, sanctifying truth for this time. . . . No encouragement should be given to this kind of worship." [4]

Through the remaining months of 1900 and the early part of 1901 the "holy flesh" teaching spread through the Indiana Conference. Churches were divided and adjoining conferences were threatened. It was asserted that this was the cleansing message, the beginning of the outpouring of the latter rain. One conference minister lost his credentials because he refused to go along with the teaching. To be out of harmony with this new movement, which was defended as hastening the day of Christ's coming, was to be in a very unpopular position with the Indiana Conference leaders. Thus it was until April, 1901, when the General Conference session was held in Battle Creek.

For nine years Ellen G. White had been in Australia. Now, invited to attend this session of the General Conference and motivated by instruction given her more than a year before, she crossed the continent and was ready to take her place at the meeting. The conference began on Tuesday morning, April 2, with Mrs. White as the speaker. She also met various appointments throughout the conference; then on Wednesday morning, April 17, she met with the ministers to read a testimony she had written entitled "Regarding the Late Movement in Indiana."

Elders Donnell and Davis were both present. Others from Indiana were delegates. Many ministers from the Indiana Conference were in attendance also. Mrs. White read:

"Instruction has been given me in regard to the late experience of brethren in Indiana, and the teaching they have given to the churches. Through this experience and teaching the enemy has been working to lead souls astray.

Ellen G. White speaking at the 1901 General Conference at Battle Creek (Haskell seated on platform at rear, to the right of vacant armchair).

"The teaching given in regard to what is termed 'holy flesh' is an error. All may now obtain holy hearts, but it is not correct to claim in this life to have holy flesh. The apostle Paul declares, 'I know that in me (that is, in my flesh,) dwelleth no good thing' (Rom. 7:18). To those who have tried so hard to obtain by faith so-called holy flesh, I would say, You cannot obtain it. Not a soul of you has holy flesh now. No human being on the earth has holy flesh. It is an impossibility. If those who speak so freely of perfection in the flesh, could see things in the true light, they would recoil with horror from their presumptuous ideas. . . .

"Let this phase of doctrine be carried a little further, and it will lead to the claim that its advocates cannot sin; that since they have holy flesh, their actions are all holy. What a door of temptation would thus be opened! . . .

"I have been instructed to say to those in Indiana who are advocating strange doctrines, You are giving a wrong mold to the precious and important work of God. Keep within the bounds of the Bible. Take Christ's lessons, and repeat them over and over again. . . .

"Those who meet Christ in peace at His coming must in this life walk before him in humility, meekness, and lowliness of mind. It becomes every human being to walk modestly and circumspectly before God, in harmony with the great testing truths He has given to the world. But the late experience of brethren in Indiana has not been in accordance with the Lord's instruction. I have not during this conference held conversation with any one in regard to this matter, but the Lord has given me a definite testimony that a strange work is being done in Indiana, the results of which are not after His order. This phase of religious enthusiasm is a dangerous delusion. The sentiments and exercises are not prompted by the Holy Spirit. They have led to very sad results.

"Again and again in the progress of our work, fanatical movements have arisen, and when the matter was presented before me, I have had to bear a message similar to the message I am bearing to my brethren from Indiana. I have been instructed by the Lord that this movement in Indiana is of the same character as have been the movements in years past. . . .

"The manner in which the meetings in Indiana have been carried on, with noise and confusion, does not commend them to thoughtful, intelligent minds. There is nothing in these demonstrations which will convince the world that we have the truth. Mere noise and shouting are no evidence of sanctification, or of the descent of the Holy Spirit. Your wild demonstrations create only disgust in the minds of unbelievers. The fewer of such demonstrations there are, the better it will be for the actors and for the people in general.

"Fanaticism, once started and left unchecked, is as hard to quench as a fire which has obtained hold of a building. Those who have entered into and sustained this fanaticism, might far better be engaged in secular labor; for by their inconsistent course of action they are dishonoring the Lord and imperiling His people. Many such movements will arise at this time, when the Lord's work should stand elevated, pure, unadulterated with superstition and fables. We need to be on our guard, to maintain a close connection with Christ, that we be not deceived by Satan's devices.

"The Lord desires to have in His service order and discipline, not excitement and confusion."[5]

Mrs. White stood before the congregation for an hour, first reading from the manuscript she had prepared for the occasion, then bearing impromptu testimony, which was also reported in the *Bulletin* and published in the *Review and Herald*. She spoke of how we still had in our midst "a few of the old pioneers who know something of the fanaticism which existed in the early days of this message. Here is Brother [J. L.] Prescott; he knows something about it. He is acquainted with phase after phase of the fanaticism which has taken place. Here is Brother Haskell. He knows something about it, and there are various ones of our older brethren who have passed over the ground, and they understand something of what we have had to meet and contend with. Then there is Brother Corliss; I speak of him because he knows something about fanaticism, not only in the early days, but in our later experience. . . .

"At great expense to myself, in sickness and feebleness, I have come a long way to bear this testimony before the congregation which was presented to me before I left Cooranbong [Australia]. If this had not been presented to me, I should not have been here today. But I am here, in obedience to the word of the Lord."[6]

The group sat in silence, pondering God's providences. Elder Haskell said in his heart, "Surely the Lord has spoken to us this day."

The next morning at the workers' meeting, Elder Donnell rose and asked if he might make a statement. It appears in the *General Conference Bulletin* under the title, "Confession of Elder R. S. Donnell." He spoke in measured words:

"I feel unworthy to stand before this large assembly of my brethren this morning. Very early in life I was taught to reverence and to love the Word of God; and when reading in it how God used to talk to His people, correcting their wrongs, and guiding them in all their ways, when a mere boy I used to say: 'Why don't we have a prophet? Why doesn't God talk to us now as He used to do?'

"When I found this people, I was more than glad to know that there was a prophet among them, and from the first I have been a firm believer in, and a warm advocate of, the Testimonies and the Spirit of prophecy. It has been suggested to me at times in the past, that the test on this point of faith comes when the Testimony comes directly to us.

"As nearly all of you know, in the Testimony of yesterday morning, the test came to me. But, brethren, I can thank God this morning that my faith in the Spirit of prophecy remains unshaken. God has spoken. He says I was wrong, and I answer, God is right, and I am wrong. . . .

"I am very, very sorry that I have done that which would mar the cause of God, and lead any one in the wrong way. I have asked God to forgive me, and I know that He has done it. As delegates and representatives of the cause of God in the earth, I now ask you to forgive me my sins, and I ask your prayers for strength and wisdom to walk aright in the future. It is my determination by the help of God, to join glad hands with you in the kingdom of God." [7]

With this confession the holy flesh fanaticism was broken. All the workers involved, except S. S. Davis, who had introduced the teaching, gave it up. Immediately after the General Conference session leading workers went to Indianapolis, the headquarters of the Indiana Conference, for meetings with the conference constituency. Mrs. White was asked to accompany them, which she did. The conference committee resigned and was replaced by men who had not been weakened by the teachings of holy flesh. The cause of God had been saved. God by His hand had guarded His church. But it was a bitter lesson.

This experience shows the length to which the great adversary will go in his attempts to thwart the work of God. The instruction given in connection with this has proved helpful in succeeding years, and as found in *Selected Messages,* book 2, will continue to guard the church.

During the crisis at the Muncie camp meeting, Elder and Mrs. Haskell had again and again expressed the wish that Mrs. White might have been there, confident that her testimony would have gone far to straighten things out. They knew not that God had opened up the whole situation to her months in advance. They rejoiced that her testimony given personally at the General Conference session, then at Indianapolis, showed up the specious error, specified what was truth, and preserved unity in the church.

---

[1] Mrs. Haskell, letter to Sara McEnterfer, Sept. 17, 1900.
[2] Ellen G. White letter 132, 1900, to the Haskells, Oct. 10, published in *Selected Messages*, book 2, pp. 37, 36.
[3] Mrs. Haskell to Ellen G. White, Sept. 22, 1900.
[4] Ellen G. White letter 132, 1900, in *Selected Messages*, book 2, pp. 35, 36.
[5] *General Conference Bulletin*, April 23, 1901, pp. 419-421 (reprinted in part in *Selected Messages*, book 2, pp. 31-35).
[6] *Ibid.*, April 23, 1901, p. 426.
[7] *Ibid.*, p. 422.

The New York City Mission

SINCE THEIR return from Australia in mid-1899 the Haskells had traveled extensively in the homeland. In addition to attending camp meetings, Elder Haskell and G. A. Irwin, the General Conference president, for more than a year held Bible institutes in each of the six General Conference districts in America. Elder Haskell was exhausted and for a time had been seriously ill. Physicians warned him that if he desired to continue a life of usefulness he must have rest. The Haskells planned to accept an invitation from an old-time friend living in nearby Massachusetts, Mrs. Melvin Bradford, for them to spend a few weeks at the Bradford country home near Acushnet.

In this retreat, far from the stir and bustle of the great city and from even more wearying committee sessions and continuous interviewings at Battle Creek, the two could rest, free from the pressures of work; they could sit by the window and look out over the snow-covered landscape while enjoying the comfort of a wood-burning heater, and Haskell could give undivided attention to writing. But a call to fill an emergency vacancy in New York City delayed them. Then after the new year began, they went to their Massachusetts haven.

Almost as soon as they arrived he was threatened with pneumonia. Hetty put her patient to bed and tried to keep him there under all the treatments prescribed earlier by Dr. Kellogg. She applied fomentations to his chest and charcoal poultices to his legs, massaged his aching back and limbs, and kept him inhaling medicated vapors and sipping the fruit juices that their attentive hostess brought to the room. But resting was the most arduous task Stephen Haskell ever had to perform. Though for a few days Hetty managed to keep him in a prone position, she could not slow down the operations of his restless mind. He was eager to get to work on his writing—to finish an assignment that had been given him while teaching Bible at Avondale.

During a conference session at Avondale, Mrs. White had remarked to Elder Irwin that two books were especially needed by the denomination—one on Daniel and one on the Revelation. They should be simpler and briefer than Uriah Smith's *Thoughts on Daniel and the Revelation* and adapted to busy people engaged in the everyday occupations. She had named Stephen Haskell as the one who should do the writing. He had written several drafts in the previous two years, but could never devote sufficient time to the work to finish it.

"Now's my chance, Hetty! Now's my chance to write those books," he declared. In spite of her protest, he was up and at work; she was meekly bringing writing materials and arranging them with his Bible on the table before him. He had the editorial help of Bessie De Graw. On January 31, 1901, the manuscript for the first chapter on the book of Daniel was in the mail on its way to Elmshaven, with the request that Mrs. White read it critically and offer suggestions. Before the end of February he had completed the manuscript for the book on Daniel. It was written in story form, with the proposed title *Story of Daniel the Prophet*. Working from his earlier drafts, he had completed the task in about four weeks. (The book on Revelation was finished later.)

During his first weeks there, when he was sick, he was heard to say, "If I can only live to finish this work, I will be content." As he completed the last chapter his wife said that the effect was as good as a medicine, and he felt that he had a new lease on life. The Haskells were now ready for their next assignment—New York.

After attending the General Conference session in April they spent some time in South Lancaster repairing their house, readying it for renting, and fitting up rooms in the attic for their own use. Then about July 1 they returned to New York City. After four days of house hunting they found an apartment for their mission. We can picture them looking with satisfaction around their unfurnished rooms and out of the sixth-floor window on the traffic below—sidewalks thronged with pedestrians and streets crowded with horse-drawn vehicles, bicycles, and streetcars.

"Well, Hetty, I think we have found the right place for the mission at last. How good God has been to reserve this retreat right here in one of the best residential sections and six stories above the noise, dust, and confusion."

"Yes, this is ample reward after four days of house hunting. But if we succeed in securing the number of helpers we need we shall require even more space than we have here."

Elder Haskell sent the following report to the *Review:* "This is Tuesday morning, and two workers are already on hand. As yet we have not even a bed or a chair; but we expect before the week closes to have our mission family together, and the house in running order. Our rent is required in advance, and many things must be bought to begin keeping house. If any of our brethren have a stray dollar which they wish to give to home mission work, it will be duly credited and a receipt returned, should they send it directly to us or to any of the secretaries of the tract societies." The report closed with a reminder: "Do not let our brethren forget to pray for us. Do not forget the address. It is 400 West 57th Street, New York City." [1]

What was the emergency that had brought the Haskells to New York? Soon after they closed their work with Elder Irwin, Elder Haskell had been called to go there late in 1900 in place of A. G. Daniells, who had been sent to California instead. Then the next April, in the General Conference session of 1901, Daniells was elected General Conference president. So the Haskells had been invited to make New York and vicinity their future field of work. There were already two churches in Manhattan and four in Brooklyn (one Scandinavian, two English, and one German). But they were to conduct a training center in evangelism and personal work among some of the millions in the city yet untouched by the churches. As Mrs. Haskell wrote, there lived within an hour-and-a-half ride of their new home two or three times the number of people as in the entire State of California.

Elder Haskell was conducting an evangelistic "city mission" in New York. It was a combination of an evangelistic mission such as had been promoted in the 1880's, and a mission among the poor, such as had flourished in the 1890's. He was well acquainted with the established methods of administering these missions. He was also regretfully aware that their maintenance was so expensive that some of the conferences in which they had operated were brought close to bankruptcy. But he was sure that he could succeed in carrying out the original plan of making the city mission self-supporting, or largely so. He would make it an experimental station for devising methods by which this could still be done. His energetic wife entered into this endeavor enthusiastically.

Elder Haskell appropriated a large part of his salary as a conference worker; gifts and favors came from businessmen and other citizens to whom Haskell explained the purpose of their work. They were there, he told the men, to assist them in their efforts to reach all classes and to raise Christian standards by setting forth pure religion and the importance of obedience to the commandments of God.

No time was lost in beginning operations. Inexperienced newcomers were given a few brief instructions in the art of selling books and periodicals. Then after earnest prayer, they started out in trembling faith to ring doorbells. They found this experience much less frightening than some had anticipated. One young girl who had never sold a thing in her life returned one evening and exuberantly announced that she had sold nine books.

The Bible Training School was operated on a regular routine. Forenoons were given to study. The elder held an early morning Bible study from six-thirty to seven-thirty, followed after breakfast by Mrs. Haskell's Bible instructors' classes, one at nine o'clock for experienced workers and one at ten for beginners. The afternoons were spent in visiting the people. The classes were open to any church members desiring to receive instruction in literature evangelism.

The young women in the mission family took turns preparing the meals and doing the housework. Sabbath school was conducted in the parlor. In warm weather classes were sometimes conducted on the roof, away from street noises; occasionally the group enjoyed a day's outing in the country for rest and relaxation.

After their initial efforts, the workers were much encouraged. They were thankful that they did not have to walk far in the hot sun or climb long flights of stairs to reach their neighbors, for they began in their own apartment house and those nearby. A touch on an elevator button lifted them to within a few steps of any particular family they wished to visit. The building in which the mission home was situated contained fifty-five other apartments. Most of the adjacent buildings housed from five to twenty-five families each, making it easy for the workers to hold two or more Bible studies in one afternoon.

Yet in spite of these favorable conditions there were many experiences during those first weeks that required a stiff battle against discouragement. Funds were scarce, almost nonexistent. In July the most severe heat wave in years struck the city. Newspapers reported numerous deaths from heat exhaustion, and it was not unusual for the workers to see dead or dying horses lying along the streets. Then, most distressing of all, several of the workers became seriously ill, but prayer and careful nursing brought healing and new courage.

Elder Haskell did not diminish his labors even during the period of intensely hot weather, but he did not go out often in the heat of the day, and he did not need to walk, since he could take a streetcar at the door to any part of the city.

That month, so unfavorably begun, brought three new openings for mission advance. A wealthy owner of a funeral home became so interested in the Bible after a conversation with the elder that he offered the free use of his chapel for Wednesday night Bible studies. The room seated about one hundred persons. As there were no visible evidences of its being a funeral chapel, Elder Haskell gladly accepted the offer, and Wednesday evening classes were arranged. At the conclusion of that first interview the elder sold the man several books, that he might continue studying the subjects they had been discussing.

Some local church members desired to receive instruction in methods of house-to-house evangelism, but for various reasons they could not attend classes at the mission. One of these lay members offered the use of a room connected with his shop where such instruction could be given.

A member whose husband owned a large apartment building persuaded him to provide as many spare rooms as might be needed to equip a mission for the colored people of the city. Mrs. Haskell and one of the city mission girls went to look over the place. They visited the occupants of the building and suggested opening meetings the following week, but were told that there was no reason why they should wait. A room could be prepared and seated, and they could begin at once. So it was planned to hold Sabbath school the next Sabbath; and that same day several copies of J. E. White's *Gospel Primer* were sold, from which the children could study their lesson. This school later grew into a branch of the central establishment, and came to be known as the 62nd Street Mission.

Thus within a few weeks of the opening of the New York mission three other centers of endeavor were operating. The aim of their founders was to develop many of these branch missions, and to place them under the management of consecrated laymen who would, with the assistance of workers from the central mission, be gaining an experience in leadership.

The new workers, launching out in faith, were thrilled and inspired by some of the experiences they met. When one woman stated in a positive manner to the young man who called at her door, "I am a Christian already; I don't need your literature," he asked, "How about your husband?" She answered, "Oh, he is an avowed infidel. I don't want you to meet him, for he abuses every professed Christian he meets." The young man asked, "Have you ceased praying for him?" "No," said the woman, "I pray for him every day."

"Then how do you know but that the Lord is answering your prayers in sending me to you?" Finally the woman reluctantly named a time when the worker might call and find her husband at home. This he did, and their interview resulted in an appointment for Bible study. The topic, "The Glorious Coming of Christ," was presented by a young woman who in turn was receiving her first lessons at the mission. This was the first Bible study she had ever prepared. Both the infidel and his Christian wife sat spellbound throughout the study. When asked at its close if they would like to have the worker come again the man replied, "Yes, this is the most intelligent and reasonable view of the Scriptures I have ever heard." Regular studies followed, and before their conclusion the one-time infidel was rejoicing in the message of salvation.

The mission chief was ever on the lookout for idlers in the

church. To these he would extend the invitation, "Come, work in the Lord's vineyard." Whenever he heard of a promising member not definitely connected with any soul-saving enterprise, he would visit or write, inviting that person to join the Bible Training School. Many responded, and the mission family rapidly increased in number.

There were times when funds were scarce, with no cash on hand to meet current bills. In such crises the situation was laid before the group for discussion. The workers usually solved the problem by resolving to devote more time to selling books and periodicals; in this way all would help to make up the deficit. Often, too, Elder Haskell would run across a well-to-do friend of the mission whom he would persuade to extend assistance in the form of welcome cash.

In a personal letter he relates a conversation with such a person during one of these crises: "I told him that we are trying to enlarge our work and that this would require funds, that we are trying to obtain a thousand dollars from ten hundred-dollar men; this thousand dollars is to aid us when we fail in donations from other quarters. He says that is a good financial scheme.

"I told him that I have a friend on 87th Street W.; . . . told him that I thought of calling to see him one of these days to have him help us out; he said, 'Call over; your work shall not stop for want of means.' "[2]

There were two scriptures which the elder knew how to use convincingly—one, "The silver is mine, and the gold is mine, saith the Lord of hosts" (Haggai 2:8); and the other, "The liberal soul shall be made fat" (Prov. 11:25).

In October the mission was able to secure the use of the centrally located hall called the Metropolitan Lyceum, on 59th Street, in which to conduct a series of Bible lectures. The hall had rented for five hundred dollars a month, but in the providence of God, Elder Haskell secured it for one tenth that amount simply by meeting the monthly payments on a mortgage.

Other favors were readily obtained from friendly businessmen. These included lumber required for building the platform, the printing of announcements, and the loan of a good organ and five hundred chairs for use in the auditorium. Sunday evening Bible lectures were given by two young ministers, J. A. Brunson and Luther Warren. There were several rooms in the building suitable for weekday classes, Sabbath school, and other special meetings and gatherings.

The first baptism was held in a beautiful spot on the East River. A church was organized, with Haskell as elder, known as Church Number Three. It was a lively, wide-awake group of people active in soul winning even before baptism.

A widowed Adventist sister drove the Haskells to her home in the country, near the East River, a mile and a half beyond the electric railway terminal, where, surrounded by the beauties of nature, she was conducting a private boarding school. During their visit Mrs. Haskell remarked, "You must charge high tuition to be able to maintain such an elegant home and so fine a pair of horses!"

The sister replied, "No, we charge only twenty dollars a month for board, tuition, and the care of clothing, and only half that amount for some children who come from poor families. But we do plan carefully." She let the Haskells in on some financial secrets which, she had discovered, worked well in New York.

She offered them the loan of a small hand printing press. This was thankfully accepted, and was set up in a room at the mission. With the saving in printing expense the workers were able to enlarge their announcements to include the sermon outlines, with the usual notice of time and place. Thus the eighteen thousand handbills distributed over the city that week carried the outline for the coming Sunday evening discourse, "What is true Sabbathkeeping?" with the texts; and therefore everyone who was handed a notice received a brief Sabbath tract.

Before starting out to distribute announcements, it was the workers' practice to spread them out before the Lord to ask Him to send angels to watch over them and bring them into the possession of truth-seeking people. The workers had many evidences that these prayers were answered.

Officials of the elevated railroads permitted them to distribute handbills freely, either in the cars or at the stations. By this means thousands of notices flowed in all directions throughout New York City.

In 1902 health-education classes were conducted for the public. Many intelligent, progressive people attended and showed their appreciation in the form of voluntary contributions. Many of these people deplored the practice of drug dosing, so common among physicians at that time. They appreciated the demonstrations of simple home treatments, given by capable nurses in these health classes.

At times in the evening classes instruction was given on the selection and preparation of plain, wholesome, nutritious, yet appetizing foods. The advantages of a meatless diet were presented. Both men and women were encouraged to attend; it was important that all should understand the principles of healthful living.

A six weeks' school of health was held, the leading feature of which was a series of twelve lectures by Dr. Geisel, of the Battle Creek Sanitarium.

A class was also taught in designing and constructing healthful clothes for women. Mrs. Luther Warren, whose husband was engaged in public evangelism in Brooklyn, conducted this class, assisted by lay members of the church. The woman's world was at that time emerging from the deadly tight-lacing epoch. Hoops and bustles were relics of the past; however, corsets and other constricting garments were still worn. Numerous skirts, suspended from the waist, dragged heavily upon the internal organs; and the free use of the limbs was impeded by the long dresses. Efforts to design a dress convenient and healthful and at the same time graceful and beautiful were receiving favorable notice from many fashion-weary women. Mrs. Warren's dressmaking classes were well attended.

As an outgrowth of friendships which Elder Haskell made with New York newspapermen, the mission received favorable mention in some of the leading papers. Occasionally a reporter would be sent to gather firsthand information by actually attending classes.

Calls began coming to the mission for efficient, trained workers to fill important posts in other cities. It was not easy for the Haskells to release workers upon whom they had bestowed much time and labor and whom they could ill spare. But they willingly gave up some of their most capable helpers, happy in the thought that they were thus helping to build up God's work in many places. Then they would search out new recruits and begin again the joyous but arduous task of training beginners in their Bible Training School.

It was during the summer of 1902 that a new periodical was born. Mrs. Haskell had received several requests for written outlines of the lessons she was teaching. The thought came to her, Why not print these lessons, send them out through the mail, and thus extend the influence of our Bible Training School here in New York City? It was natural that the paper should be called the *Bible Training School,* launched in June, 1902.

A special issue of Haskells' journal, *Bible Training School.*

Because there was no time for such occupations during the day, Elder and Mrs. Haskell sat up nights preparing copy. At first it was printed in New York, but later sent to South Lancaster, Massachusetts, to be printed by the academy press. Each issue contained several prepared Bible lessons to aid lay members who wished to give studies in private homes. Besides using the topical Bible lessons, readers could learn how to construct and give their own Bible studies. The paper also contained brief, crisp articles on important phases of Bible truth, instruction on healthful living and home nursing, Bible quizzes, and other items intended to stimulate interest in Bible study. The journal filled a real need in our ranks. Thus was begun a publishing enterprise that was to grow and become an integral part of the Haskell missionary program. It paralleled their labors to the close of their active ministry.

The subscription list grew steadily. Tract societies used clubs in their missionary efforts both in the homeland and abroad. Letters of appreciation arrived from church members who were using the Bible-study outlines. Some letters came from individuals in other churches who were using the lessons as guides in Bible-study groups.

Longing to see the Bible truths in the little paper made available to a larger number of people, the Haskells prayed for men and women whom they might train as salesmen to sell it on city streets and in business offices. For a year they continued praying. They were determined not to divert any regular colporteurs who were selling truth-filled books for the denominational publishing houses, but to find men and women in secular employment whom they could initiate in gospel service.

In time their faith was more than rewarded. Among those volunteering to sell the *Bible Training School* were men, women, and children. Some worked full time, others only occasionally. There were also the halt, the lame, and the blind. Mrs. Haskell later wrote about two girls who spent their summers together selling the papers from city to city. She wrote of a crippled lad who signed himself "Wandering Willie." This boy had taken ten thousand journals and was beginning to sell with the objective of founding a home for cripples. She also told of a "blind Brother Bahler" who, with his wife and small son, was supporting a seven-member orphan's home from the profits, besides buying a gospel tent and assisting in other missionary endeavors.

Selling *Bible Training School* was to become a favorite method of raising money for the starting of home and foreign missionary enterprises and of maintaining them during lean years. In lots of ten thousand, salesmen bought the special issues for three cents a copy and sold them for ten. Regular copies were a bargain at five cents apiece. If he was endeavoring to aid some special missionary project, the worker would give a part or all of his commission to the object of his endeavors.

Much of the responsibility of assembling material for this paper was carried by Mrs. Haskell. The opening article in practically every number was from the pen of Ellen G. White. Elder Haskell was a frequent contributor. Haskell's own articles and outlines were interspersed among contributions by such writers as J. N. Loughborough, H. W. Cottrell and his wife, W. A. Spicer, and others. Illustrations and poetry were not lacking. One poem, representative of the aim of the whole endeavor, is found in *Bible Training School* for May, 1906:

MY DAILY PRAYER

"May every soul that touches mine—
Be it the slightest contact—get therefrom some good,
Some little grace, one kindly thought,
One aspiration yet unfelt, one bit of courage
For the darkening sky: one gleam of faith
To brave the thickening ills of life;
One glimpse of brighter skies beyond the gathering mists,
To make this life worth while,
And heaven a surer heritage."

—*Selected*

---

[1] *Review and Herald,* July 9, 1901, p. 448.
[2] Letter to W. C. White, Sept. 23, 1901.

The Crisis in New York

IN JANUARY, 1902, about six months after the Haskells had established their mission headquarters on West 57th Street, another evangelist in the city, E. E. Franke, began meetings in Carnegie Hall, only three blocks away. New York was large enough for several good men, and the Haskells did all they could to preserve cordial relations with the younger worker. As vice-president of the newly formed Greater New York Conference, Haskell wrote to Mrs. White:

"I had thought . . . that I had not been as cordial as I should have been to Elder Franke and so wrote him . . . I would stand shoulder to shoulder with him. . . . Immediately on the heels of this came your two testimonies that showed my mind was led in the channel of your testimony. . . .

"Now, Sister White, I do not want that you should think that I shall not stand by Brother Franke. I shall invite him over to the house and pray with him and pray for his work. I have no other intention at all. I propose to stand on your testimony not to see bad results but to see good results."[1]

Carnegie Hall was only a few blocks from the Metropolitan Lyceum, where Elder Haskell's interest was centered. Franke was young, vigorous, and eloquent; he conducted a live and well-organized campaign. But his methods of advertising were bizarre, sometimes bordering on the grotesque. Before coming to New York he had conducted an evangelistic series near Chicago. There he had prepared "a two-horse wagon, with a large platform upon it, with a bell fixed in the center, and over that a small tent. Around the whole platform he had banners, upon which were printed, 'Which day do you keep?' and 'Which day is the Sabbath?' et cetera. This was driven through the streets of Kankakee, a boy inside the platform ringing the large bell to attract attention."[2]

When G. A. Irwin, then president of the General Conference, heard about it, he hastened to tell Elder Franke that he did not think such a "method of advertising properly represented the truth, as that was the method resorted to by all sorts of shows, many of which were low down and immoral."

Elder Irwin then read to Franke a statement Sister White had written: "The man who is to come to Chicago must not on any account enter into any controversies with any man. . . . He will seek to be original, and in doing this will get odd notions, and we want nothing of the kind to come in. Our work must move in a dignified, elevated, ennobling manner."[3]

Elder Franke replied that he would drop the wagon idea, but he continued to be, as expressed by Elder Irwin, "a very expensive and extravagant man in his work, so that when they come to ask him to do as other ministers do, he at once rebels and persists in his own way."[4]

Haskell, of course, received only his salary, with no operating or advertising allowance. To him Franke's procedure was inexcusable ostentation and extravagance. Further, he feared that Elder Warren's preaching in Metropolitan Hall could not hold an audience if the full force of interest and attention became focused on the larger, more dramatic evangelistic campaign being conducted by Elder Franke. The latter regarded Haskell's work as divisive. However, as Haskell wrote in June, the meetings in both halls were successful in maintaining a good attendance.

At the end of one year's occupancy of the Metropolitan Hall, Elder Haskell was unable to renew the lease.

Among those who had been attending the meetings in that hall were a number of colored people. These had been visited by the regular workers and also by a young member of their own group, a Sister Williams. Several were ready for baptism. Soon Haskell was able to organize the first colored Seventh-day Adventist church in New York City.

Sabbath, August 16, 1902, was a happy day for these new members. Mrs. Haskell described it in a letter of that date to Sister White:

"Our colored brethren held their first Sabbath meeting today in their own hall. For months we have been praying that God would give us a hall. . . . The Lord heard our prayers and gave us a nice hall in the Miller Building, one of the finest buildings in this part of the city. . . . The new hall is first class, the most aristocratic, black or white, can find no fault with its location. It holds about 150, is up one flight, with elevator or marble stairs as one prefers. . . . Our colored brethren and sisters . . . have gone to work in good earnest. . . . There are about 20 colored people who have taken their stand since we began. We have a young colored woman in our [mission] family beginning to do Bible work and are hoping to find one more to come in and work with her. . . . They hold meetings Tues., Thurs., and Sunday evenings, beside their Sabbath meetings and missionary meeting. Brother [Luther] Warren preached to them this forenoon. I wish you could have heard their social meeting. It did my soul good. Four of them were baptized last Monday. . . . They are an earnest lot of Christians happy in the truth, and have an intelligent knowledge of it."

But the cause of truth was progressing too smoothly to suit the enemy of souls. Working, as he always does, through human agents to hinder the free course of the Holy Spirit, Satan now brought strong temptations to bear upon our two leading evangelists in New York City.

Elder Franke had been blessed with unusual success in his early ministry. In one campaign in Trenton, New Jersey, he had gathered a church of nearly two hundred members. This seemed to turn his head. Self-exaltation was his weakness; he "loved praise and hated criticism," was "impatient of delay or interference." So testified those who knew him best.

Several messages of encouragement, warning, and reproof were sent him through God's appointed messenger. There were 16 letters from Mrs. White to Elder Franke, all written during or near the time he worked in New York.

"You have been presented to me as one who has a message for our cities, not merely for Greater New York, but for many other cities in America." [5]

She urged him to follow Christ; to avoid outward show and display, which entail unnecessary expense and which do not win souls.

"Your danger, my dear brother, is in making the grave mistake of supposing that success depends on drawing a large congregation by outward display. To bring anything of a theatrical nature into the preaching of the word of God is to use common fire instead of the sacred fire of God's kindling. . . . Take up your work with greater humility, and carry it forward by Christlike methods. Let the truth have the field. For Christ's sake do not hinder its progress by your own inventions." [6]

Warning him of the danger in his passionate words and rebellious spirit,[7] she nevertheless assured him of God's concern for his personal welfare—even for his need to rest his overwrought nerves.

"My brother, you must have periods of rest, in which you spend some time in the country. I have been instructed that during the summer you should leave the heat of the city for a cooler atmosphere. Your strained nerves will respond to the grateful restfulness of nature's beautiful scenes." [8]

"Spoil not your influence by overworking, in an effort to accomplish some great thing. When you become worried as the result of overwork, every adverse word appears in large, bold characters before you, and you begin at once to make a raid against those who you think are trying to work against you. Your hasty words are unexpected, because often there is no cause for any such outburst. These things greatly detract from your influence." [9]

"God desires you to unite with your brethren in your work. If you do not do this, Satan will surely ensnare you." [10]

More than once Elder Franke made confession of his wrongs and tried to straighten things up with his brethren. He wrote to Mrs. White that any instruction or counsel she had for him would be thankfully received and fully carried out. This letter brought great joy to her heart and to the hearts of his fellow workers. But again at a conference meeting he spoke insultingly of Elders Haskell, Warren, and others. Again he confessed. There was joyful reconciliation.

"Eld. Haskell came home from South Lancaster Aug. 4th very sick," wrote his wife to Sister White, "and did not leave his bed for over a week. But the Lord has wonderfully blessed him and he is of better courage than I have seen him for a long time. When Elder Franke heard he was sick, he came in so heartily and helped him that Elder Haskell has really fallen in love with him. Eld. Haskell was worrying while sick over things he wanted attended to and Eld. Warren could not do them. Eld. Franke came so lovingly and begged the privilege of running on any business, just took all care of Eld. H., was all an own son could have been, and it did Eld. H. more good than medicine. He had become wholly discouraged about the work here. It seemed as if all his efforts at union had failed to accomplish anything permanent, and he had made up his mind to get out of here as quickly as he well could. I think that was really what brought on his sickness.

"But his very sickness did more than all his former efforts [at reconciliation], and now he is looking forward with pleasure to his fall and winter work with Eld. Franke. They are planning to unite and make a bold front to the enemy. . . . I have not seen Eld. Haskell so happy and in such good spirits for years, and Bro. Franke looks like a new man.

"We had a baptism last Monday; eight were baptized. We have much to praise the Lord for." [11]

This development was short-lived. Complications arose that led Elder Haskell to write three months later:

"A boy was once asked how he got through the woods. It is reported that he said 'he whistled to keep up courage.' I do not think that mere whistling would have always kept up our courage had not the Lord in various ways let shine His smiling face on us in a most remarkable manner from time to time. We have seen His guiding hand in special providences, that has caused our hearts to rejoice in Him, and would then think that we would never be discouraged any more. . . . So our courage is good, and unless we get unusually tired . . . I have no realizing sense that I am about seventy years of age. I have carried a burden for Elder Franke and do now so that quite frequently wife and self awake and rise in the night and pray for him. I think he honestly believes I am jealous of his talents or audience. . . . If I am, I am wholly ignorant of it. . . . This seems so real to him that it is the same old, old story over and over again when we are on committees or in public." [12]

For two years the Haskells had labored in New York under the handicap of criticism and party feeling. Time and again, when about to forsake the field, Haskell would recall messages from Mrs. White such as the following: "Be of good courage. God's providence will certainly open your way and give you precious victories. . . . He was in your going to New York City." [13]

"I know that the Lord designed that Elder Franke should stand in his lot and place, speaking to large congregations. Then when an interest is awakened, many would be benefited by the work that you can do. No one is to seek to close up the way that the Lord has committed to Elder Franke or the work that He has committed to Elder Haskell. . . . Brother Haskell, you cannot do the work necessary to be done to obtain a large audience. God sent Elder Franke to do that which you cannot do. It was His design that you should blend with Elder Franke, and do the part of the work that he cannot do." [14]

Warnings against weaving self into the service of God were also sent to Elder and Mrs. Haskell: "The speaker should never put self into his work; for by drawing the attention of his hearers to himself, he turns their attention from Christ. . . . Let no man weave himself into the work of God." [15]

It was difficult for those two to refrain from defending themselves when slighting remarks about their methods of work came to their ears from Franke, the "great evangelist." Finally, in October, 1902, when the lease on the hall expired, and while, for the moment, relations were friendly, Elder Haskell withdrew to Brooklyn, where he found a desirable location for his Bible Training School. There he had new interests to build up and new workers to train. His helpers increased in number until at one time there were nineteen in the mission family.

Elder Franke, who had brought many people into the church, who could, as one of his converts testified, "present all the Seventh-day Adventist doctrines in a finer and more convincing way than he had ever heard them presented," eventually forgot that he was only the channel of light and blessing, not its source. Before long this once-great evangelist took glory to himself, and finally lost his power, abandoned his mission, and ended by fighting the denomination and the very truths that he himself had once proclaimed with power.

The Haskells remained in Brooklyn about another year, then after visiting various churches and conferences, moved to Nashville, Tennessee.

---

[1] Letter to Ellen G. White, Jan. 4, 1902.
[2] G. A. Irwin letter to Ellen G. White, Nov. 8, 1900.
[3] Letter 96, 1900, to the Haskells.
[4] G. A. Irwin letter to Ellen G. White, Nov. 8, 1900.
[5] Letter 79, 1902.
[6] Letter 51, 1902 (published in part in *Evangelism*, pp. 127, 509).
[7] Letter 21, 1901.
[8] Letter 79, 1902.
[9] Letter 193, 1903.
[10] Letter 19, 1901.
[11] Letter to Ellen G. White, Aug. 16, 1902.
[12] Letter to Ellen G. White, Nov. 2, 1902.
[13] Letter 132, 1901.
[14] Letter 171, 1902.
[15] Letter 49, 1902.

Traveling Teacher

"STEPHEN, YOU ARE a marvel! Not long ago you seemed about ready to retire from the work; now here you are, back in harness and busier than ever!"

"Yes, Hetty, it is amazing how God has renewed my strength."

The Haskells knelt for a moment of prayer and praise and to plead for divine guidance and blessing before going to the early morning Bible class. It was true. The study of the Word and the impartation of its riches to others had given him new life and vitality. Nurses rising at five o'clock and dressing by candlelight; church members walking dark city streets so as to be present at these early morning classes, learning to study the Word of God—seeing such a spirit was what kept him young. As he wrote from Nashville at seventy-two: "If I should fold my hands and sit down and do nothing to further the truth of this last Message I should die in a short time."[1]

About the beginning of 1904 the Haskells had moved to Nashville, Tennessee, and there established a Bible Training School. For a few months during that first year they were assisted by two missionaries, L. J. Burgess and his wife, recently returned from India. They had come home for a short time, hoping to obtain authorization and support for opening a mission among the Hindustani people. But when they presented their request to the Mission Board they were told regretfully that there was no money available for the project.

Mrs. Burgess carried her disappointment to her old friend Stephen Haskell, for she knew he was deeply interested in the people of India. It was Haskell who, several years before, had encouraged Mrs. Burgess—Georgia Burrus—to go alone to India as a self-supporting worker. He had sent her money given him from time to time for mission purposes. These occasional remittances had helped to piece out what little she received from teaching English to a few Hindu

Georgia Burrus Burgess, to whose work in India Haskell contributed.

students while she was learning to speak their language and doing gospel work among the Hindu women in their homes.

At one time a man who conducted a gambling resort became strongly attracted to Elder Haskell. He even asked the privilege of living with the elder for a while. Haskell gave him a cordial invitation to do so, with the stipulation that the man spend an hour every day reading the Bible with him. The gambler cheerfully agreed, and the result was exactly what Haskell had anticipated it would be. His visitor became thoroughly converted.

When this man disposed of his gambling interests, he asked his host how he should use the money obtained from their sale. Elder Haskell, never at a loss for an answer to this type of question, suggested that it be sent to Georgia Burrus in India. From then on, as soon as the man received a payment on the property and equipment he had sold, he promptly gave it to Haskell to be sent to her.

The day she received the first installment of that money she joyfully and thankfully resumed language study, which she had been forced to abandon because she could not pay her teacher. Thereafter the remittances always seemed to arrive just in time to answer some urgent need.

In India she had married Burgess, who at the time was filling the office of secretary-treasurer for the new India mission field. He joined his wife in dedication to the people of India. Their plan was to establish a mission as a center of operations for the Hindustani-speaking people—a work the Mission Board was not in a financial position to support. But could they assume such a responsibility alone, without support from the Mission Board? Yet, how could they give it up?

"Think of it, Elder Haskell! Just think of it!" they mourned, "eighty million people, and no one to tell them of Jesus' soon coming and to teach them how to prepare to meet Him in peace; and we, the only ones among all our workers who understand this people and can speak their language, hindered—just for the lack of a little money!"

Too wise to blame the Mission Board for not undertaking this new venture, Haskell simply said, "Don't be anxious or troubled; the Lord owns the silver and the gold; He is interested in your work because it is *His* work. Come to Nashville and help us for a while. The experience you gain here will be profitable to you when you *do* open your mission in India." The Burgesses accepted the invitation.

While working they often spoke of the things nearest their hearts. One day while Elder Haskell was enumerating the thousands of dollars that the *Bible Training School* journal had contributed toward mission enterprises, Mrs. Burgess' face suddenly brightened and she exclaimed, "Why, Elder Haskell, why can't we earn the money ourselves to start that mission in India? Mr. Burgess and I can sell the *Bible Training School!* If you will print an extra edition for us we will go right out on the streets and get to work." The idea caught fire. "Just the thing! I'm sure we can do it!" her husband agreed.

"I've been thinking," replied Haskell, "of that very same thing since you told me of the Mission Board's decision. I'm sure they will give you the 'go ahead' if you can raise the money." The elder's tone and smile spoke assurance. He wired the South Lancaster press to print an extra edition of twenty thousand of "Help for India" Special.

"But it will take too long for you to sell those thousands of papers by yourselves. We'll get the church folks to help you," he ventured. He suggested that Mrs. Burgess write to her home church in California, and Mr. Burgess to his in Minnesota. Since the Haskells had appointments at meetings, they took the two missionaries with them and helped promote the sale of the papers. Elder Haskell introduced the Burgesses. As the people listened to their recital of India's need for the gospel message their response was spontaneous, and the papers sold readily. The journals were charged against the "Burgess Missionary Fund" at less than cost of production. Printing expenses were partly met by contributions; the printers themselves donated forty dollars in labor.

The Burgesses made their appeal in many Adventist churches. Conferences and tract societies gave full support. Elder Spicer, secretary of the Mission Board, invited *Review* readers to participate. Soon scores of Adventists were out selling the paper. By November 7, just three months from the beginning of the campaign, more than twenty thousand copies had been sold and Mr. and Mrs. Burgess were en route to India with fifteen hundred dollars to their credit and full authorization to open the mission.

Correspondence continued between the Haskells and their missionary friends. For three years the *Bible Training School* contributed largely to the support of the Hindustani mission. One day Elder Haskell received a small journal in the mail, printed in queer, unintelligible characters. An accompanying letter explained that it was a Hindustani edition of the *Bible Training School,* and that it bore the good news of Jesus' soon coming. The little paper was being sold by Indian converts, a thing unheard of before in India.

Elder Haskell rejoiced that this newborn child of his *Bible Training School* journal was being used of God in India. But at home the new mission in Nashville seemed to be accomplishing very little. Helpers were few, expenses high, and the people conservative. In 1904 the city authorities had ordered the publishing house to stop all Sunday work. But instead of bringing misfortune, this state of affairs served to advance the message, for it gave the employees a free day each week to distribute Adventist literature. Also, the public issue aroused interest and discussion on the subject of Sabbath observance. Wrote Haskell: "Our quiet mission seems to be breaking out like a prairie fire."[2]

In 1905 Haskell joined G. I. Butler in conducting evangelistic tent meetings in the city. The Bible subjects there presented were argued throughout the city. A person passing down the street could hear them being discussed on street corners, in the shops, at the courthouse, and in almost every public place. Although attendance at the meetings was disappointingly small, the ministers were told that a large audience on the outside of the tent was listening from front porches and open windows.

The enlarged mission family now numbered fourteen or fifteen. Haskell reported that some were holding Bible studies, some selling the *Watchman* or *Bible Training School,* some canvassing for *Christ's Object Lessons* or other books. All were paying their way, and all were enjoying a Christian experience.

While the Haskells were in Tennessee the Southern Publishing Association printed *The Story of the Seer of Patmos* and brought out as a companion volume a new illustrated edition of *The Story of Daniel the Prophet,* which was advertised as follows: " 'The Story of

Haskell's two books on Daniel and Revelation, respectively.

Daniel the Prophet' by S. N. Haskell is the book of Daniel told in simple, story form. It is the fruit of many years of diligent study. The Scriptures narrating the story are printed in the margin together with 4,048 other Bible References. There are also given over 4,000 questions covering the contents of every chapter of the book. These are not intricate questions, yet will require study. The simple reading of the book will answer every question. It is beautifully illustrated with full-page, half-tone engravings." Further description of the book followed: "It contains 369 pages, is bound in cloth, and sells for $1.00." [3] Later the two books were bound, each in three different styles and sold at $1.00, $1.25, and $1.50, to suit the purses of the various purchasers.

The writer now set his fertile brain to work devising plans by which his books could be made the means of raising money for needy missionary enterprises, as the *Bible Training School* had been doing so valiantly.

In their travels in the South the Haskells frequently ran across companies of new believers struggling to raise money for church buildings. They also found mission schools crippled for lack of a span of mules, a plow, a farm wagon, or school equipment. Whatever the need Haskell would offer to contribute some of his books or journals to help raise money, stipulating that the people get out and sell them and then turn in the full retail price to aid their project. If the need was urgent, Haskell sometimes wrote to friends trying to interest them in helping to pay the costs of publication. One individual or group might pay for the typesetting, another for the illustrating, or perhaps the cost of materials used. By working any one of several different plans Haskell was killing three birds with one stone: hard-pressed mission institutions and enterprises were being aided financially; a help-one-another spirit was encouraged within the church; and the precious saving truth contained in these books was being scattered far and wide.

A transaction between Elder Haskell and Dr. David Paulson during a midwinter convention at Hinsdale illustrates the working of one of Haskell's favorite plans. The doctor was endeavoring to carry out instruction given our medical workers through the Spirit of Prophecy writings that they should open small sanitariums and treatment rooms in various places, thus creating many small centers of light. He was trying to train strong, faithful medical workers who, after training, would go out into different parts of the country to man these centers.

At one such center funds were needed to meet the payment on a church building the brethren were purchasing. Haskell offered the little church company one thousand of his books in the $1.50 binding, the retail value of which would amount to $1,500. At colporteurs' rates the books would cost them $750. Haskell himself offered to donate one half that amount, charging them only $375 for the thousand books. Then if Dr. Paulson's friends and the helpers at the Hinsdale Sanitarium would raise the $375 among themselves, no money would have to be deducted to cover costs, and the whole $1,500 could be turned into the fund for the purchasing and repairing of the church. This and other similar plans were welcomed alike by hard-pressed ministers and conference men, and proved a great blessing.

Everywhere the Haskells went they found crying needs for money. Whereas in former years Haskell had met such needs by appealing to the membership for cash donations, he now offered his books or journals for them to sell. He wrote: "We have consecrated to the Lord every dollar we can get, and He is helping us most wonderfully. No one calls for us to help them but we put them in a position to help themselves." [4]

During the years of its publication the *Bible Training School* was a pilgrim, its editorial department traveling with the Haskells wherever they were called to work. They prepared copy for its monthly issue and mailed it to the South Lancaster Academy printing press, where the paper was published under the direction of an efficient woman manager. A small cottage was purchased, moved onto the school grounds, and fitted up with typewriters, desks, tables, and whatever else was needed to transform it into "the *Bible Training School* office."

All the publishing that Haskell did was carried on entirely in the interests of gospel and missionary work. For many years the *Bible Training School* was listed in the *SDA Yearbook* as a privately sponsored publication. He never used profits for his own personal needs.

The original plantation house on the Madison property.

Mrs. White had suggested the writing of his books; Haskell had found great satisfaction in producing them. She had favored the establishment of the academy printing press. Now it was helping to support the school by furnishing work for needy students, besides training efficient printers for mission lands. She had encouraged Haskell in the distribution of his books; wherever they were received and circulated they brought spiritual blessing and financial aid.

After the Civil War there had been much poverty and suffering in portions of the South. As the work of the church pushed into this part of the land, somewhat later, God sent a call to the remnant church through His special messenger for families to move into those areas and teach the Advent message in a quiet, unobtrusive way. Some purchased small farms from which they could earn a modest living and establish community centers of Christian ministry. A number of them opened schools, either among the colored people or in Appalachia, where boys and girls deprived of educational advantages could earn their tuition by manual labor while receiving a simple but practical Christian education. At Madison, near Nashville, Tennessee, such a school, and later a sanitarium, were established by two leading educators, E. A. Sutherland and Percy T. Magan, Elder Haskell's companion on his 1889-1890 round-the-world trip.

Haskell was especially interested in the Madison institution. He had been a member of the group who in 1904 selected the farm of about 400 acres on which it was established. This purchase had been made against the judgment of some of the wisest heads among them, as the land appeared to be "worn out" and "impoverished." But Mrs. White, also with them at this time, insisted that this was the place the Lord wanted them to have. It was similar to many regions where their students would be working after they had finished their course of study, and they needed to learn how to cope with poor land and other unfavorable conditions; also, Madison was not far from the city of Nashville, a prospective field for evangelistic activity. So these two men, strong in faith, decided to follow the guidance that had ever led them safely in the past.

With a small group of teachers and students from Berrien Springs, Michigan, they started building. From Madison, teachers would establish other schools—smaller schools, but built on the same plan of self-support. The Haskells often visited the little group of hard-working, self-sacrificing workers who were making a beginning at Madison. In 1907 Elder Haskell reported progress made during the three years since the beginning of operations on the old farm. He wrote that they

The new Madison Hospital, built in the 1960's.

had seventy-five acres in corn, sugar cane, oats, and alfalfa; ten acres in garden, and two in small fruits; 600 fruit and nut trees planted, and 350 grapevines. Teachers and students were meeting in a chapel seating about sixty persons. The students themselves had built cottages, and they were now erecting a sanitarium building on the grounds, and they had sent teachers to open schools in other places. He praised God for the prosperity attending the school, and considered it one more proof that following the Spirit of Prophecy counsels brings the special blessing of Heaven.

The Haskells had for a few years divided their time between California and the South in conducting their Bible Training Schools. Now they had a new interest—the betterment of the white population living in the less-favored regions. They also greatly enjoyed working among the colored believers, who showed deep appreciation of every effort made to help them.

In midsummer of 1907 their work took them to Huntsville, Alabama, to the school the denomination had opened in 1896 for the education of colored young people (now Oakwood College).

While they were there, Mrs. Haskell wrote to Mrs. White: "We are here at Huntsville, and I wish you could see the tent full of colored people each day. There are about fifty here in the school working during vacation, and there must be 25 or 30 workers that have come in to attend the convention. They are as bright a set of workers as I ever saw. . . . The girls in the school all dress in uniform. They have a plain gray dress with two white bands of tape around the bottom of the skirt and up the front of the waist. . . . Today as I saw the 24 school girls marching from the tent after meeting, . . . I wish you could have seen them. . . .

"The men's school building is nearly finished. . . . It would have done your heart good to see these colored teachers pledge for papers. . . . Teachers and workers pledged to sell 6,000 copies of a *Bible Training School* Special toward the support of the mission schools. They are planning to close their convention one day this week, and to all go into Huntsville and surrounding territory and sell papers. We wired last week for 1,000. . . . They are planning to take another field day . . . a month later. . . . If we all together can sell 20,000

The original "Old Mansion," on the Oakwood property.

we will clear $1,400 and that will go a long way toward building plain little school houses."[5]

Thus Oakwood became the source of help for other schools also.

During the following winter Elder Haskell was called to the presidency of the California Conference. Immediately upon his release three years later, early in 1911, he and Mrs. Haskell were back in their beloved South, looking after the mission and its interests in and around Nashville and touring the self-supporting schools that were beginning to dot the Southern map.

One such school was situated on Sand Mountain (a long ridge extending into Alabama from near Chattanooga). It was called the Old Paths Industrial School at first, but later was known as the Sand Mountain School. A Brother Tolman had relinquished a well-paying business as draftsman and had invested his entire savings, plus some three thousand dollars bequeathed to him, in this school enterprise. He hoped to make it a blessing in this mountain region by

Peterson Hall (men's dormitory) at Oakwood College, built 1955.

providing children with an opportunity for a Christian education.

Tolman met the Haskells at the railway station with a horse and old farm wagon. After a six-mile climb up the side of a steep mountain, they reached the school. As they clambered down from the high wagon seat and looked out over the valley, Mrs. Haskell, usually the first to speak, exclaimed, "Oh, what an ideal spot for a school!"

Her husband drew a deep breath and gazed at the enchanting mountain scenery. "Yes, indeed," said he, "this is the best possible location for a school—in close contact with nature and with human need. Tolman, you undoubtedly have here the foundation for a successful mission enterprise." They saw the teacher's house, built almost entirely by Tolman himself; also a substantial two-story schoolhouse with an upstairs apartment, occupied at the time by two young men who were helping on the farm.

Haskell preached in the schoolhouse once on Sabbath and twice on Sunday. The mountain people came in with their children and filled the schoolroom to capacity. They were intelligent people, although many of them could neither read nor write.

When they reached home Mrs. Haskell wrote the Tolmans a long letter. Its contents show that both the Haskells were offering advice.

Picture, if you can, these two busy evangelists taking hours of time to discuss the problems of this one little struggling school, then, Mrs. Haskell writing and her husband at his desk prompting her:

"Tell them, Hetty, that first of all they should get out a small leaflet, a sort of 'baby calendar.' Maybe the students at the [South Lancaster] academy press will print it for them without charge. They can scatter this far and wide all around the school. They should be sure to include the word *Academy* in the name of the school; and they should promise that certain industries will be taught that those young people cannot learn elsewhere.

"Poultry raising would be a good industry to begin with because it does not require as large an initial investment as some others. Also they might turn one of the upstairs rooms in the schoolhouse into a shop for cabinetmaking where tables, chairs, and cupboards could be made, then sold. Some of the students could earn their schooling working in the shop. This winter while they are building the barn will be a good time to teach carpentry. When it is finished they might buy a few good Jersey cows and four or five good brood mares. Then each year they can sell calves, heifers, and colts for a good price. And deep plowing will help where land cannot be irrigated."

When the elder's ideas were exhausted, his wife began with a list of her own—sewing for the girls, who should be able to make their own dresses—knitting, laundering, and cooking. The girls could rotate, preparing meals for the family. They would learn to bake good bread, vegetarian roasts, cakes, and all the other tasty dishes that a capable housewife should know how to prepare. At last Hetty sighed and laid down her pen: "It has taken a long time to write that letter, but I thought it was my first duty. We must do all we can to help them, and not allow them to become discouraged."

By this time Haskell was pounding away on his typewriter. "Just writing to one or two friends out West and up North. You see, it will take more than good wishes to get that school under way; they need so many things—wire fencing for their garden, a serviceable wagon and harness, and a good horse. How can a man work a farm with such stock as Tolman has?—one horse that, I'm sure, won't be long in this world, and the other as balky as Satan. I thought surely we would be late this morning when the old girl gave us an hour's pause. At least, it seemed like an hour that we waited for her to lift her feet and go on.

"Then, too," continued Haskell, "Mrs. Tolman should have a light buggy so she can visit among her neighbors. Oh, yes, don't forget to tell them I've requested that one hundred copies of *Seer of Patmos* be sent them, with a receipted bill. I've asked the good people of South Lancaster to prepay the freight."

He also sent along this cheering quotation: "When we have a burden or load to lift, we need not measure our puny strength with the size of the load, for when we take hold to lift, unseen angel hands lift with us."

Soon afterward he wrote that he had received sufficient money from friends to buy the horse and wagon, the harness, and the fencing, and to set the school up in business for the present.

A few weeks later Mrs. Haskell wrote from a workers' institute in Memphis, Tennessee, telling of her joy in finding people so eager to get out and do missionary work as they were there. Fifty or more workers had come together—"the cream of the churches from among the best and most cultured class of the people," she called them, and all Southerners. A big tent had been pitched in the residential section of the city and was filled for the evening preaching services.

One day when Elder Haskell was leading in a field day of home visitation, Mrs. Haskell started out with their stenographer to learn how the colored believers in the city fared. She found their meetinghouse and described it as "a miserable barn of a place," its walls inside partly whitewashed and partly covered with dingy paper. But in it were about fifty or sixty of "as fine looking a lot of intelligent colored people as I ever saw."⁶ She wondered at the atmosphere of decorum and cheerfulness there, and was told that they were working toward erecting a church building. They had one hundred dollars already laid away and the conference had promised to help them. She arranged for her husband to meet with them at the church, and soon he had them all out selling books and journals on his special fund-raising plan. Then he wrote to some of the prosperous California churches, telling of the struggles the colored brethren were having to build a church, and asked them for a few hundred dollars.

"This is joy! This is life!" exclaimed Mrs. Haskell. "Helping God's people wherever we find them—these warmhearted, appreciative people!"

The Haskells never lost their love for the people and the work in the South. One of their joys in later years was to revisit church groups they had helped to raise up there. They rejoiced to see the prosperity attending self-supporting schools and the special blessing of God on the workers. Schools had multiplied. In some places small sanitariums were connected with the schools where workers, in cooperation with local physicians, cared for the sick, and trained nurses.

Elder Haskell usually announced their visits beforehand, and the neighborhood folks thronged the meetings, overflowing the schoolroom. Often services were held outside under the trees. For overnight gatherings, if there was insufficient space indoors to lodge all the guests, they cheerfully slept on blankets spread on the hay in the barn.

At Bon Aqua, a quiet retreat in the hills about forty miles from Nashville, the Haskells visited a rural school operated by the Martin family. The Martins had built their own schoolhouse. Mrs. Martin had taught, free of charge, three generations—grandparents, parents, and children—all they ever knew of the rudiments of book learning. During those years her husband worked the small farm to support the family. Mrs. Martin, a nurse as well as a teacher, was always ready to answer calls by day or night, wherever there was serious illness. She very seldom accepted money for her services. Since her own children were old enough to help she took in some pupils as boarders.

Elder Haskell and his wife often wondered at the willingness of missionary workers such as these to endure privations and wearisome toil, with little remuneration except the gratitude of an appreciative people and the smile of an approving God. They never realized that part of this willingness was a result of their own example of loving ministry which, through the years, had broken down prejudice and opened the way for the timely message of truth to reach the people.

---

[1] S. N. Haskell letter to W. C. White, April 26, 1905.
[2] Letter to Ellen G. White, Aug. 16, 1904.
[3] *The Southern Watchman*, Jan. 26, 1904, p. 63.
[4] Letter to Ellen G. White and W. C. White, June 11, 1907.
[5] Letter of June 15, 1907.
[6] Hetty Haskell letter to Ellen G. White, June 19, 1911.

At Loma Linda

DURING THE FIRST decade of the twentieth century Seventh-day Adventists acquired three valuable properties in southern California. All were equipped with substantial buildings suitable for use as sanitariums. Under divine instruction Mrs. White had urged the purchase of these three properties and the establishment of a medical center at each location. She took a deep interest in them all; but the one known as Loma Linda, or the Hill Beautiful, in a rural community near the city of San Bernardino, captured her special interest and attention.

In her dedicatory address at the opening of that sanitarium she said: "Loma Linda is to be not only a sanitarium, but an educational center. With the possession of this place comes a weighty responsibility of making the work of the institution educational in character. A school is to be established here for the training of gospel medical missionary evangelists. Much is involved in this work, and it is very essential that a right beginning be made."[1]

In harmony with the high ideals of Seventh-day Adventists, and for the purpose of answering calls for medical missionaries from every part of the world where the Advent message was advancing, a unique type of training must be given in this school. Its students were to be taught how to treat the sick without the use of poisonous drugs. Most important, they would be trained to perform double service in medical ministry. While bringing relief to the sick and suffering they were also to direct these suffering ones to lift their eyes to the Saviour, who could heal spiritual as well as physical diseases.

Later, in referring to her talk given at this time, Mrs. White said: "I tried to make it plain that sanitarium physicians and helpers were to cooperate with God in combating diseases not only through the use of the natural remedial agencies He has placed within our reach, but also by encouraging their patients to lay hold on divine strength through obedience to the commandments of God."²

And at this time she wrote: "Our young men and young women are to find in Loma Linda a school where they can receive a medical missionary training, and where they will not be brought under the influence of some who are seeking to undermine the truth. The students are to unite faithfully in the medical work, keeping their physical powers in the most perfect condition possible, and laboring under the instruction of the great Medical Missionary. The healing of the sick, and the ministry of the Word are to go hand in hand."³

In 1905 Mrs. White had appealed to the Haskells to come and join the working force at Loma Linda. She wrote, "We must soon start a nurses' training school at Loma Linda. This place will become an important educational center, and we need the efforts of yourself and your wife to give the right mold to the work."⁴ They responded, as always, to the call, and were soon carrying on a house-to-house evangelistic campaign in Redlands, Riverside, and other neighboring

The original buildings on the Loma Linda property.

Loma Linda University since its unification on one campus, showing the newly completed hospital at upper left.

cities. As young people came to the sanitarium to enroll in the nurse's class or to work as helpers, they were allowed some duty-free time in which to assist in the visitation campaign, to distribute literature, and to sell the book *The Ministry of Healing,* the profits of which were dedicated to medical missionary work.

In the summer of 1906 the calendar issued for the new school listed four courses—"Evangelistic-Medical, Collegiate, Nurses', and Gospel Workers."

The foreword states that the purpose in establishing the College of Evangelists (later renamed the College of Medical Evangelists, since 1962 the School of Medicine of the Loma Linda University) was "to develop and train evangelists. The world needs evangelizing, and the work must be done speedily." The phrase, "To preach the kingdom of God and to heal the sick," was printed at the foot of each page. Included among the instructors were four physicians. And that there might be thorough instruction in Bible doctrines and in field evangelism, Elder and Mrs. Haskell were asked to join the faculty.

In the spring of 1906 Elder Haskell conducted a "medical evangelistic" tent series in the nearby city of San Bernardino. He held only four services a week, relying on house-to-house work as the surest way to establish converts.

For several months prior to this the Haskells had labored exhaustively in connection with an evangelistic campaign in Oakland and were so worn that they felt unable to conduct another Bible Training School without at least two months' rest. But they gathered a few workers around them—Mrs. Haskell wrote that their family numbered ten—and also drew into part-time service the seven students in the nursing class and some members of the sanitarium staff.

Each Sunday night they held a preaching service in the tent. Monday night was cooking class; and "Tuesday night," wrote Mrs. Haskell, "we had our first Health School. Dr. [Julia] White gave a short lecture, and then they [the student nurses] demonstrated the treatments before the audience." Mrs. Haskell told about an opposition crusade that had started up within a block and a half of the tent, where "the 'Goliath of Gath' is still holding forth in the pavilion every night and prancing on the platform and screaming till he can be heard a block away."[5] His invectives were aimed principally at those who taught that Christians are under obligation to keep the commandments of God.

On the Los Angeles campground that August two much-discussed events were the San Francisco earthquake and the founding of the school at Loma Linda. Of the two, Loma Linda received far greater attention. A "Loma Linda Meeting" was held during the camp meeting. Though everyone knew there would be a call for money, there was a large attendance. The fund-raising team was composed of two men: John Burden, promoter and administrator of the school enterprise; and Stephen Haskell, an enthusiast on the subject of medical missions ever since he had seen the suffering in non-Christian lands due to the lack of such ministry.

The meeting opened with a talk by the local conference president in which he repeated the oft-heard warning that there must be strict adherence to the no-debt policy recently adopted by the General Conference. Elder Burden next related some of the special providences that had enabled the promoters of Loma Linda to secure the property, and then to meet each payment as it fell due. He spoke of the importance of the school in training medical missionaries, and of the high destiny it would fulfill as an integral part of God's closing work on earth.

Then he called for thousand-dollar pledges. Two sisters, who had promised beforehand to start the ball rolling, raised their hands. Others pledged. At four thousand there was a pause, and Elder Haskell promised a thousand books if the people would go out and sell them. Valued at from $1.00 to $1.25 each, these books when sold would bring in another thousand or more. Before the meeting was dismissed, twelve thousand dollars had been pledged to the school.

One day the Haskells were surprised by a visit from two young women who were selling the *Bible Training School*. They had enjoyed remarkable success in the Central and Southern States; now they had come to California to help raise money for Loma Linda. They hoped to sell twenty thousand papers throughout the State, enough papers to pay for the seats and necessary apparatus for the schoolrooms. "They are full of zeal," wrote Mrs. Haskell, "and as they go among the churches and tell what they themselves individually have done, they can inspire our people with courage to go out and sell the truth."[6] Frequently, substantial profits were made possible from the sale of *Bible Training School* because the printing of special numbers was often subsidized by individual contributors.

That fall the Haskells spent a few weeks in Oakland and San Francisco, where they had been working before being called to Loma Linda. Before Christmas they were back in southern California. Elder Haskell visited the school at the noon prayer meeting. At its close Elder Burden arose and asked how many would go out and canvass for Elder Haskell's book *Seer of Patmos*. About twenty volunteered. During the week after his arrival they sold between two and three hundred books, working the town systematically. Newspapers gave favorable notice, and the workers were well received wherever they went.

For some time after the Haskells left Loma Linda the question was asked, "Who can be found to lead out in practical field work still being carried on as part of the Loma Linda study program?" About this time, in God's providence, Dr. Lillis Wood Starr moved with her husband and children to Loma Linda. An experienced house-to-house worker, also an able speaker, she agreed to begin a class in the study of Ellen G. White's book *The Ministry of Healing* for the benefit of new converts of Elder Haskell at San Bernardino.

It had been sixteen years since Elder Haskell had first witnessed the misery in various lands that had deeply burdened him with the need of gospel workers trained in the healing arts. He now rejoiced that he could participate in the education and training of these angels of mercy. Percy Magan, who had been with him on the two-year journey, would soon be called to act as dean of the College of Medical Evangelists.

Prayer had gained the accomplishment of great aims—prayer and faith and effort. After a good start in the educational features of the Loma Linda institution, the Haskells with their Bible Training School program soon went back again to the Southern States, but not for long. California needed the elder.

---

[1] *Review and Herald,* June 21, 1906, p. 8.
[2] *Ibid.,* p. 7.
[3] Letter 274, 1906.
[4] Letter 277, 1905.
[5] Letter to Ellen G. White, May 14, 20, 1906.
[6] Letter to Ellen G. White, July 3, 1906.

Leading California

IN FEBRUARY of 1908 Elder Haskell was elected president of the California Conference. The work in the West was rapidly expanding and required a steady leader of wide experience. Since Haskell had served in that capacity in former years he would qualify, and more than meet every requirement. Trembling at the thought of the responsibility laid upon his shoulders, he said in his acceptance speech, "You run a big risk in getting me in as president of this conference. I have to keep my mind on Christ, for if I looked on the billows I should sink as soon as did Peter. But with your prayers and the grace of God, we will try to do the best we can."

He and his wife spent much time in the field visiting churches and companies of believers. Hetty conducted some of the Bible classes and taught methods of personal evangelism and house-to-house visitation; her husband dwelt mostly on Bible fundamentals, such as the three angels' messages of Revelation 14 and the rediscovery of truths lost sight of by the church during the Dark Ages.

During the first year of Haskell's administration the subject of Christian education received much attention from the leaders. They had long regretted the cramped quarters of the college situated in the town of Healdsburg. In June of 1908 the California Conference committee voted to sell the school and re-establish it in a more rural area, with sufficient land to make possible the carrying out of certain instructions that had come to them through the Spirit of Prophecy writings. A tract of land known as Buena Vista was selected nearby, and only a few miles from Sonoma. Arrangements for its purchase were nearly complete when it was discovered that a clear title to the property could not be secured. Rapid action was needed. Healdsburg College had already been closed for a year. It seemed that delay in reopening the school would be disastrous.

Elder Haskell wrote at the time: "We have got our feet on the brink of Jordan, but the Jordan is not divided; the waters are not withheld."[1] However, he was neither impatient nor anxious. "You have said that if we did not get that property it is because God had a better place for us, and I believe it," he said. His brethren were of the same mind, and the search for a suitable location continued. Before long they discovered a suitable property for sale on the summit of Howell Mountain, about a five-mile climb from the St. Helena Sanitarium. Mr. Angwin, the owner of a popular summer resort, was retiring and placing his entire estate on the market. After several attempts at selling, he offered it at a surprisingly low figure. A survey and evaluation of the property revealed that it contained about seventeen hundred acres, with nearly one hundred acres of good farmland, much of it level. There were ten buildings on the estate, including a three-story hotel and six cottages. The hotel dining room accommodated about 150 persons. The large dance hall could, with little renovation, be used as a chapel.

Twenty acres were in fruits of various kinds and thirty acres in alfalfa. During the dry season the farmlands were well watered from three large springs yielding 300,000 gallons of water daily. The water was raised by hydraulic rams and supplied to all the buildings. Barns were piled high with hay and grain; horses and cows occupied the stalls and pens; shops were filled with tools, farm implements, and wagons and carriages.

Forty-five tons of prunes had been gathered that year and more were on the trees. Two thousand quarts of canned fruit stood on shelves lining the cellar walls. A heavy forest covered the surrounding hills and valleys from which timber could be milled for any additional building that might be required in the future. The current buildings were in good repair, waiting only to be readied for occupancy by students and teachers.

The hindrance in securing the Buena Vista property that had caused perplexity was now seen to be a reason for rejoicing. It was obvious that the Howell Mountain property was far superior. Besides, it was situated near the sanitarium where its students could receive instruction in medical missionary service from physicians and nurses.

About a month from the day the papers were signed for the purchase of the property all was in readiness. Pacific Union College, the successor of old Healdsburg College, opened its doors in time for the fall term of school. There had been no time for publishing a school calendar, but about fifty students were present on the opening day.

During the summer months Elder and Mrs. Haskell spent much time at camp meetings, then assisted with workers' institutes, which frequently followed them.

Mrs. Haskell's letters written during the summer of 1908 reveal some rather unusual doings. From the Eureka campground she wrote: "There were no meetings in the camp Wednesday forenoon. About everybody went out canvassing. For most all of them it was their first effort. Old grandmothers and little children went with the others. We had a workers' meeting Wed. evening to report progress, and it would have done your soul good to have heard them. They hardly looked like the same people. . . . There was victory in every testimony. . . .

"Tuesday morning at the close of Elder Haskell's Bible study he offered *Early Writings* for sale, and some of the children wanted them and did not have the money. Sister King [the California Conference Sabbath school secretary] encouraged the children to sell papers and earn money to buy *Early Writings* and *Great Controversy* for their own." [2]

Camp meetings were so much a part of life in those days that Mrs. Haskell wrote little about them. Her description of one she attended in 1910 at Visalia, California, may be of interest here: "The camp meeting opened Thursday night, September 29. . . . Our Sabbath school secretary came to me on Friday morning and said that she did not think she would need more than one tent for children's meetings, as there seemed to be so few children on the ground. I told her to wait till about eleven o'clock, and she would see them coming in.

"Sure enough, about eleven o'clock teams began to come in from the surrounding country. Surreys, carriages, and wagons filled with people began rolling into the camp. And in the afternoon big covered wagons, all covered with dust, having been on the road for two or

Above: Administration build-ing of Pacific Union College. Below: Healdsburg College.

three days, came into the camp. Some of our brethren drove their big cook wagons that they used to cook for the men in the hay fields; so that they had their kitchens nicely fitted up, and had their spring beds, rocking chairs, etc., and were very comfortable. Some of these big wagons contained many children, so there were plenty of children for the children's meetings. . . .

"There was a creek running through the ground with large shade trees along the bank on either side, and a number of our brethren . . . camped there. There must have been about 80 family tents on the ground, and all were occupied; besides these, and those who camped in their wagons, quite a number had rooms in hotels and private houses near the camp. . . .

"This is the eleventh camp meeting we have held since Elder Haskell has been president of the Conference. In the early morning meetings Elder Haskell gave Bible studies on the Spirit of the Lord, and it seemed as if every man, woman, and child on the ground was present at these meetings. On Tuesday afternoon, at the close of the afternoon meeting, a sufficient number from the camp went out to work, and in about one hour the whole town was covered, and the Temperance *Instructor* placed in each home in the town." [3]

In winter, invitations to local meetings, such as this, often appeared in the *Pacific Union Recorder:* "Brethren, come aside from your busy cares for a few days and study God's Word, and the Lord will reward you by blessing your own souls and making you a blessing to others." [4] One such meeting was afterward reported: "The workers' institute, held in the Lodi English church from November 5 to 14, was a profitable season." [5] Mrs. White, her son W. C. White, B. E. Beddoe, J. N. Loughborough, and S. G. White were named as the speakers. Elder and Mrs. Haskell also took leading parts.

A six-weeks' Bible worker and colporteur training course was held at Lodi the autumn of 1910. The elder extended a special invitation through the *Recorder* to those past middle age. For the encouragement of older members he recounted the story of our pioneer missionary to China, Abram La Rue, who took his training for missionary service after he was sixty years old.

Throughout his entire term of conference administration Elder

Haskell heartily supported the development of the medical college at Loma Linda, a work that was close to his heart. From time to time he was on the campus leading in missionary activity. Nursing students were early initiated into the newborn fund-raising campaign, now known as Ingathering, for welfare and missions. For three days formal classes were dismissed and student nurses joined the crusade. In that first effort (1908) they distributed twelve hundred copies of the Thanksgiving special of the *Review* and received a little over four hundred dollars in offerings. The nurses felt that those three days were time well spent. They had invited people to visit the sanitarium. As a result, each Sunday for several weeks thereafter the dining room was crowded with visitors. The mayor of Los Angeles was among the guests. He remarked that "it was such a rest to come to this Christian home, away from the graft of city public life."

One young nurse, inexperienced in this type of work, called at a home where a man was painting. When she presented the paper he very coldly turned her down. As she started to enter the next house he called out that it was useless for her to go there. That was his home; no one would be inside but his wife, and she would not be interested in the paper. The girl first turned away, but something impelled her to go back and knock. As the door opened she saw a woman holding a baby. Suddenly, as she watched, the child went into convulsions. The mother thought her baby was dying.

The nurse noticed a boiler of water heating on the stove. She asked for a washtub and soon had the child in a hot bath. The young mother had called her husband, and together they watched the nurse apparently bring the baby back to life. Overjoyed, they were now ready to hear about the needs of missions and to make a liberal gift.

Elder Haskell called the attention of his fellow workers in the California Conference to a privilege they might enjoy of working in a foreign mission field at home. He was referring to the spiritual needs of the Orientals living in the Bay cities of San Francisco and Oakland. In the *Recorder* he wrote: "It is not enough for us to drop a quarter on the plate for the work in China and Japan, and do nothing for the people from these countries in our own land.... We expect to pay large sums to carry the work in Japan, and it is right we should. Is it not equally as important to carry the message to the Japanese in Oakland? . . . Above all else, we wish that you would pray for the little taper-light that has been kindled for the heathen Japanese within our own borders." [6]

Also in the *Recorder* Mrs. Eliza Swift described a school she was conducting for Japanese students in Oakland, opened May 15, 1908. Thirty students were enrolled. They had Bible studies every Friday evening, the average attendance being from three to five, but increasing to eight or nine.

Among the students were young men of talent and ability, graduates of the Waseda and Imperial colleges of Japan, who came to learn the English language. She opened a Sunday school November 15, and was greatly encouraged as they showed an earnest desire to learn the Bible.

The school was held in a rented cottage, the expenses being met partly by tuition but largely by contribution. She thanked friends who sent Bibles, because the leaves were falling out of the ones they had.

She reported that it was much harder to present the truth to them than to English-speaking people, yet many seeds of truth had been sown, and some had taken root.

A later report bore witness that some seeds did bear fruit; three young men accepted the Adventist truth, and at the 1910 camp meeting held meetings in their own language with good success.

Work had also been done in the past for Koreans in Sacramento, resulting in the conversion of a small company, three of whom attended Healdsburg College. While rejoicing over the work being done, Elder Haskell mourned that there were no schools for the Chinese similar to the one Mrs. Swift was conducting for the Japanese.

But he was able to report on the beginning of work among the Chinese people. At the close of the Oakland institute in the spring of 1910, G. A. Kuhns and his wife began distributing literature in the Sunset District of San Francisco. J. A. Stevens and Brother R. S. Fries joined them. As the result of this work, on December 31, 1910, a church of twenty-two members was organized, called the Park Seventh-day Adventist church.

Haskell also reported that a ship missionary named Peters was distributing thousands of pages of literature among the officers and sailors of ships in San Francisco Bay, and placing bound books in their libraries. These books had been purchased by Seventh-day Adventists attending the camp meetings and donated to him for ship mission work. And so the search for those willing to obey all of God's commandments continued prayerfully, perseveringly, patiently.

The fortieth session of the California Conference was held from February 9 to 19, 1911, in Fresno, California, with 208 delegates. Friday, the second day of the conference, was observed as a day of fasting and prayer. At this session Elder Haskell retired from his position as conference president. Now in his seventy-ninth year, he was weary and felt that the time had come for him to place his heavy administrative responsibilities on younger shoulders. Yet he closed his three years of presidency by presiding at all of its fifteen business sessions and by taking an active part in deliberations.

Those three years had been a period of rapid growth and steady advancement in California. Temperance and religious liberty work were being vigorously promoted. Church schools were multiplying. The St. Helena Sanitarium was staffed with consecrated nurses working wholeheartedly with Christian physicians and chaplains, endeavoring to bring both physical and spiritual healing to their patients.

Twenty-six new churches had been organized in the conference. This advance was not due to abundant ministerial help, but quite largely to the diligence of church members in scattering gospel literature and in holding Bible studies in private homes.

A unanimous expression of appreciation was given the veteran administrator and his wife. The weary warriors took no glory to themselves, but, as they bade farewell to their California brethren, they expressed deep gratitude for the cooperation of their fellow workers and for self-sacrificing, active church members who had so diligently sown the gospel seed.

The Haskells returned to Tennessee.

---
[1] Letter to Ellen G. White, July 26, 1909.
[2] Letter to Ellen G. White, July 28, 1908.
[3] Letter to Ellen G. White, Oct. 13, 1910.
[4] *Pacific Union Recorder,* Dec. 9, 1909, p. 4.
[5] *Ibid.,* Nov. 25, p. 3.
[6] *Ibid.,* July 9, 1908, p. 5.

The Temperance Campaign

"HASTEN ON TO MAINE." Haskell held in his hand a letter from Mrs. White that had come in the morning mail.

"I wonder why—why the need of special haste?" Hetty inquired.

They had already left Nashville, and were at South Lancaster, on their way to Portland, Maine, with the intent of opening a mission in the city. Her husband finished reading the letter. "No reason given— probably because she didn't know the reason. We'll find out when we get there."

In Portland they were more mystified than ever. No special project demanded immediate attention. No preparations had been made for the opening of the mission. Interest seemed to be centered in the coming 1911 camp meeting at Norridgewock, and Haskell's assistance was not particularly needed with that. So not knowing just where to begin or what to do, Elder Haskell began making the acquaintance of some of the businessmen in town; his wife occupied her time visiting from door to door, distributing literature and making friends. They continued to wonder why they had been urged by Mrs. White to hasten to Portland.

But as they mingled with the townsfolk they learned that a fierce battle was being waged between the "wets" and the "drys." Temperance lecturers who had come to Maine from all parts of the country were holding State-wide rallies, working desperately in a last-minute effort to educate the populace in temperance principles, hoping that on election day they would cast their ballot on the right side of the question. The general opinion, as the Haskells heard it expressed, was that the temperance cause would probably lose the battle.

Haskell talked with the leading brethren, presenting to them their responsibility in cooperating with the temperance forces and helping to save their State from the degradation of liquor. For many years

Maine had stood almost alone for the temperance cause. The men listened apathetically, so he thought, then asked, "Why engage in this side issue? Is not the proclamation of the last-day message our great objective? Besides, why waste our strength fighting a losing battle?"

The conference president had been so fully occupied with administrative duties and with preparations for the coming camp meeting that he was scarcely aware of any temperance crisis. He called the committee together and gave Haskell an opportunity to present his plan of action. Haskell had brought a copy of the Temperance Special *Youth's Instructor* of March 7.

Holding the paper out before them he said, "This year's Temperance *Instructor* is, to my thinking, the very best weapon we could use in fighting the liquor demon. No right-minded person could read it without being influenced in favor of temperance. Let us get a copy of this excellent paper into every home in the city; let us scatter it throughout the State. Let every Seventh-day Adventist rise as one man and join in the battle. Whether we win or lose, we shall at least show the world where Seventh-day Adventists stand. There is little time before the election. Even if the *Instructors* are ordered immediately and leave the office promptly, we will still have only four or five weeks in which to cover the State."

His call for immediate action was met with the inevitable question, "Where can we find the money?" Everyone agreed that the elder's plan was excellent—*but!* Before he had time to say more another question was raised, "Who will distribute those thousands and thousands of *Instructors?*"

"We'll work with the Woman's Christian Temperance Union and the other temperance forces," he replied.

"But they have turned down our literature because it is published by Seventh-day Adventists, the people who oppose the Sunday-closing bill," was their answer. The committee members separated without definite action.

Knowing that delay would mean defeat, and still undaunted, Haskell went home and at once ordered an immediate shipment of twelve thousand Temperance *Instructors!* He promised to assume full responsibility for the costs. The papers were sent, with eleven thousand charged to the Maine Conference; one thousand were a contribution from the Review.

Not waiting for the *Instructors* to arrive, Mrs. Haskell donned her white ribbon, the badge of membership, and called on the WCTU president, Mrs. Stevens. She was kindly received, and Mrs. Stevens entered enthusiastically into the plan of distributing the *Instructors*. She also used her influence in securing the use of YWCA rooms for a storage and distributing center for the large pile of twelve thousand copies.

As soon as the papers came all hands took hold with a will, offering the *Instructor* to each family in the city. Adventist workers were called from other States to help organize the campaign. Elder Haskell went in one direction and Mrs. Haskell in another. Elder George B. Starr and his wife found many ministers of large congregations who were glad to use the special issue of the paper. One minister asked for three thousand copies and arranged for the young men of his congregation to distribute them. Others handed them to members at the door as they left the church.

Elder Piper, the conference president, called on the chairman of the Prohibition Committee, who presented the *Instructor* at a mass meeting. As a result ten thousand copies were requested, twice as many as could be spared just then from the rapidly diminishing supply. As the campaign extended from town to town more papers were needed. When an order for twenty-three thousand was sent in, it ran the account at the Review office up to two thousand dollars.

A prompt response hummed over the wire: They would forward the shipment only if Haskell would take personal responsibility for its payment. This was a fearful liability for a poor man to assume, and no one was willing to share the risk with him. Yet if the campaign should lag at this point all would be lost. More than this, he had in his pocket a telegram just received from Mrs. White. It said, "Push the temperance campaign." What should he do? He knew that such directions were stamped with a higher authority than that of Ellen G. White. He wired the office: "Send the papers; I will beg until all are paid for."

His wife remonstrated. "Stephen, you can never pay two thou-

Haskell on his eighty-fifth birthday, 1918.

sand dollars! How do you know whether the people will respond? Remember, Brother Reavis said at the Review and Herald office in Washington that the money is coming in *slowly*. This could mean selling the shelter over your head to pay that amount, and you are too old to be left homeless."

He replied with his usual decision, "I would rather lose every penny I own in the world than fail to do as the Lord directs."

So the campaign continued to intensify. Not even the camp meeting was permitted to interrupt its operations. Wrote Haskell: "I do not think the brethren in Maine have been so stirred before, especially in these late years. They came up to the camp meeting full of courage and hope, for they began to see that they could actually do something."[1] They were discouraged because of past failures, but all they needed was to be set to work and shown how to do it. During the week they distributed fourteen thousand *Instructors* from the campground. Some days there were two or three companies out. The WCTU laid their own literature aside and distributed, in all, over ten thousand *Instructors*. Two temperance rallies were held on the campground with good effect.

As public attention focused increasingly on the misery caused by intoxicating liquor, public sentiment seemed to grow in favor of strict temperance, and the prohibition people frequently heard the hope expressed that their side *might* win.

It was therefore with disappointment that they listened to the final returns of the balloting—the liquor forces had won, with a surplus of *nearly one thousand votes,* in the State-wide election.

But some in close touch with public sentiment suspected an unfair count. A court examination of the ballots was demanded. The second count reversed the returns, giving a surplus of seven hundred in favor of prohibition. It was discovered that town clerks in three towns had made their reports read *"In favor of license,"* when they should have read, *"Not* in favor."

The general public, both enemies and friends, acknowledged that it was the Temperance *Instructor* that had won the victory. Before the end of the month the entire *Instructor* account was settled and the more than fifty-three thousand copies distributed were all paid for. The Haskells now understood why they had been urged to hasten to Portland. Had they delayed even one week, they would have arrived too late to accomplish the desired results.

However, the battle was not ended. A few months later Elder Haskell wrote: "The temperance issue is now at a crisis here in the State. The authorities, especially in Portland, Lewiston, and some of the larger cities, are strong liquor men, and are determined that they will not enforce the laws. They allow open saloons to be kept in the disreputable parts of the city and then claim that there is more liquor sold on the sly than if there were open saloons all over the city, and thus are trying to do what they can to defeat prohibition, and the Governor of the State stands with them. There is a special session of the legislature called for March 20th. One reason, the Governor states, for calling the session is to try and adjust this temperance question."[2] A leading Portland newspaper that had formerly favored temperance now reversed its policy.

When Elder Haskell talked with the editor, the man declared, "We are not dry; we are wet. You have not seen one line in favor of prohibition in our paper since the election, and you will not see any. We are done with it." Only one paper in the city, the *Evening Express*, continued to favor temperance principles.

Haskell laid the matter before his associates: "We must not give up the fight yet," he thundered. "The battle has been too costly and the results too far reaching for us now to abandon our cause to failure. But what shall we do? We must *educate* the people."

He remembered a chapter in Ellen G. White's *Ministry of Healing* entitled "The Liquor Traffic and Prohibition." With Mrs. White's approval, he wrote the Review office requesting that they print fifty thousand copies of that chapter in tract form, direct from the pages of the book. This they gladly did, and donated the entire fifty thousand to the temperance cause, free of charge.

Jennie Bates, Haskell's secretary, sent a sample tract to the leader of every WCTU society in Maine, asking whether they would like to use it in their localities. Requests for tracts ranging from one to ten thousand copies poured in from the various societies. Church members took hold of the work heartily. They spent weekends and holidays distributing tracts at seaside and other pleasure resorts. They visited managers of institutions, factories, and stores, and either passed out the tracts themselves or left them to be distributed by directors and superintendents. The knowledge that these were published by Seventh-day Adventists did much to make friends for the Adventist cause in Maine. Before the appointed date when the temperance question was to come before the legislature, confusion entered the ranks of those promoting the proposed bill, dividing them into contending parties, and the question was not discussed at that time.

In the meantime the Haskells had not forgotten their original purpose in coming to Portland. After a few days' search they found a pleasant apartment on the ground floor of a large house near the Adventist church. Nine days after the first temperance campaign closed, the mission was opened. About seven or eight of the church people were willing to join the mission as helpers and to learn the art of house-to-house evangelism. Most of these were older women not otherwise employed. Among them were one or two nurses. Some had sold books; all were completely inexperienced in city evangelism. Each worker was handed a package of tracts, and after a few brief instructions, was sent out to sell or lend them to the citizens of Portland.

Mrs. Haskell held two classes each day for the staff. The usual Bible-study class came at six o'clock in the morning, followed by an instructional class in methods of home evangelism after breakfast. The workers spent the remainder of the day visiting and distributing literature, and the evenings in study.

New helpers joined the mission family until at one time it numbered twelve. Not all did the same type of work. Some sold books, some did nursing; others distributed literature and conducted Bible studies in homes. One public service was held each Sunday evening. Scores of families were reading journals and tracts lent to them for a week or longer, then gathered up by the workers and passed on to others. Some homes ordinarily closed to religious teachers were now gradually opening to the kindly women who visited and were never too hurried to lend a hand in time of sickness or trouble. Two of the workers were past fifty years of age; one was sixty, and another sixty-five. Elder Haskell maintained that the oldest one of them all was distributing nearly twice as much literature as any of the others.

One of the elderly women, Mrs. Manter, through perseverance was granted permission by the chief of police to set up a literature table in front of a large hotel at a busy streetcar transfer point. Above the table hung a sign printed in several languages. It read, *"Buy Without Money."* Piles of tracts arranged according to subject and language, neatly fastened together with rubber bands, were exhibited on the table. When a passer-by paused to scan one of the papers, Mrs. Manter would separate it from the others and with a gracious smile present it to him.

The mission prospered. Its workers were supporting themselves largely by the sale of the journal *Bible Training School.* Adventist farmers supplied fruits and vegetables in abundance for the mission table; the Pacific Press contributed a club of one hundred *Signs of the Times.* Mrs. White frequently sent small donations that had been given her to be applied wherever she thought best. The conference appointed Elder E. E. Osborne to help as assistant evangelist, and the Melrose Sanitarium sent a doctor and a nurse to help conduct health and cooking classes.

However, in spite of the fact that many were interested in Bible study and deeply stirred, few took a definite stand. Haskell became discouraged and considered closing the mission to seek a more fruitful field of labor elsewhere. But Mrs. White wrote, urging him to continue where he was.

She had hoped to revisit Portland herself. It was her childhood home. There she had first heard the message of Jesus' second coming; in that city she had begun her work. But now she was too busy at her California home, Elmshaven; writing was occupying all her time. She wrote encouragingly to the Haskells that the work they had done there was a good work, well and faithfully accomplished. It would result in much good and Elder Haskell must not regard it as a failure. He accepted her counsel, and though occasionally called away for indefinite periods of time to meet other appointments, he remained in Portland until the middle of 1912.

After moving from there to South Lancaster, Elder Haskell had his attention called to the scarcity of religious literature for the blind. Immediately he turned his attention to securing the publication of good Seventh-day Adventist books in Braille. The first messenger of joy from the Adventist people to those experiencing perpetual darkness was *Steps to Christ*. In 1914 Elder Haskell wrote Mrs. White that the book *Patriarchs and Prophets* had just been published in raised print, and he had ordered a set for her. It filled four large volumes and would be placed in seventy circulating libraries.

The expense of publishing for the blind, amounting to between two and three thousand dollars, was largely met by the sale of the *Bible Training School*. He wrote that Charles Miller, a blind Seventh-day Adventist minister, sold two special editions of the journal of thirty thousand each in the interests of this work.

In 1914 Elder Haskell's *The Cross and Its Shadow* was published. This book was the fruitage of long years of teaching on the subject of the sanctuary. In it he described and explained how the entire system of offerings and ceremonies connected with the worship of ancient Israel illustrated in symbol the ministry of Christ in saving sinners and ridding the earth of sin. Christ Himself was the sacrificial offering, the "Lamb of God, which taketh away the sin of the world." He is also our High Priest and applies His own cleansing blood to the sinner's need. He is now officiating in the sanctuary in heaven, completing His great and glorious work of making an end of sin and obliterating all traces of the curse brought to this world by disobedience.

Mrs. White's secretary, Clarence C. Crisler, was with her when she received her copy of this book, *The Cross and Its Shadow*. In acknowledgment Crisler wrote: "She was much pleased over the thought of your remembering her thus with the first fruits of your long labor of love in preparing the book and in seeing it through the press. . . . Several times when going into her office-room, I have found Sister White with your book in hand. . . . She rejoices also that Brother and Sister Haskell are doing what they can to add to the treasure of good reading-matter, prepared and published in pleasing form, now available for study by our young men and young women. . . .

"So far as I have been able to observe personally, the possession of your books has always given Sister White real pleasure; and this latest one has brought to her comfort and cheer, and is kept within easy reach, close by her own volumes to which she frequently refers." [3]

The next year, 1915, when the Haskells were again in Nashville, they received a telegram from the church in Portland, Maine, containing cheering news, which they immediately relayed to Mrs. White: "Church is free [from a debt they had carried for years], interest and all paid. . . . Sabbath was a glorious day. Church was crowded. We also raised fifteen hundred dollars in pledges for missions. Faith is the victory." [4]

Yet another cheering message reached her that the work in Portland and all through the State of Maine was prospering as she had told them it would. The two faithful workers who had followed her counsel to persevere in spite of discouragements now rejoiced that God had given them faith and patience to obey.

---
[1] Letter to W. T. Knox, Sept. 18, 1911.
[2] Letter to Ellen G. White, Jan. 16, 1912.
[3] Letter to S. N. Haskell, Dec. 24, 1914.
[4] Hetty Haskell letter to Ellen G. White, Jan. 3, 1915.

Workers Together With God

THE AWAITED summons had come; Stephen Haskell was called to Battle Creek to preach Ellen G. White's funeral sermon. On the Sabbath of July 24, 1915, the spacious Tabernacle was crowded to its utmost capacity. The simple black casket had been placed in front of the rostrum amid a bank of flowers; relays of ministers stood as guards of honor while hundreds of friends, fellow workers, and admirers passed by the bier to look for the last time upon the face of one who had been to many of them sister, mother, or counselor, and to many the Lord's messenger. Numerous floral pieces had been contributed. The church at Battle Creek presented a broken wheel; the Review and Herald Publishing Association, a broken column surmounted by a crown; the General Conference and North American Division, a cross and a crown; the Pacific Press Publishing Association, an open Bible of solid white carnations, with the words interwoven in purple flowers, "Behold, I come quickly; and my reward is with me."

The funeral service began at eleven o'clock. A double quartet, partially hidden by a bower of foliage, sang:

"Asleep in Jesus, blessed sleep,
From which none ever wake to weep."

Elder F. M. Wilcox, editor of the *Review*, read promises from the twenty-first and twenty-second chapters of Revelation telling of that day when death shall be no more. Elder M. C. Wilcox, of Mountain View, California, offered prayer, and Prof. Frederick Griggs sang "Rest for the Toiling Hand."

Then Elder A. G. Daniells, president of the General Conference, read the life sketch; and as he told how Ellen G. White had given her life unstintingly in active service to the cause of God, many in the congregation wept.

Haskell preaching at Ellen G. White's funeral, Battle Creek, 1915.

But there was no sadness in the voice that preached the funeral sermon—only the ring of hope, of triumph, as Elder Haskell read: "'And I heard a voice from heaven saying unto me, Write, Blessed are the dead which die in the Lord from henceforth; Yea, saith the Spirit, that they may rest from their labors; and their works do follow them.' ... Although they may have expected to live to see Christ come in the clouds of heaven, yet if they die, no terrible misfortune befalls them. ... She rests from her labors; ... she has met the foe, Death; she has surrendered; but her works live. Being dead, she speaks and will speak as long as souls can be saved. ...

"It was this hope [of the resurrection] that the apostle Paul set before the early disciples. ... 'I would not have you to be ignorant, brethren, concerning them which are asleep, that ye sorrow not, even as others which have no hope. For if we believe that Jesus died and rose again, even so them also which sleep in Jesus will God bring with him.' As Christ was brought from the grave, so will He bring those that sleep in Jesus. 'For this we say unto you by the word of the Lord, that we which are alive and remain unto the coming of the Lord shall not prevent [or go before] them which are asleep. For the Lord himself shall descend from heaven with a shout, with the voice of the archangel, and with the trump of God: and the dead in Christ shall rise first: then we which are alive and remain shall be caught up together with them in the clouds, to meet the Lord in the air: and so shall we ever be with the Lord. Wherefore comfort one another with these words.' 1 Thess. 4:13-18."

The story of the first resurrection morning was then read, and the congregation was reminded that Mary was the first one at the sepulcher, that she ran and told Peter and John, and they came and saw for themselves. It was true; the body was gone from the tomb. They also noticed how carefully the graveclothes were folded, "the napkin, that was about his head, not lying with the linen clothes, but wrapped together in a place by itself." And they believed, for they recognized Christ's very habits manifested there in the tomb. John said, "'That is Jesus. He is risen from the dead.' ...

"Mary's love for the Saviour was so strong that she could not rest at all until she saw Him, until she knew where He was. And when He stood by her side and said, 'Mary,' in that same tone that she had so many times heard before, she was about to fall at His feet and grasp Him and worship Him."

Christ retained His identity, Haskell explained, when He arose from the grave. So it will be with the saints; they will know Christ by His voice, by His habits, by His features. "So it will be with our friends finally. They will come forth like our Saviour; we shall behold them, we shall see them. . . .

"My dear friends, there is a living connection between heaven and this earth, and the promises that the Lord has made to His people will be verified. . . . While we shall not see our sister any more in this world until the resurrection day, may God help us, dear friends, to be among that number that will then see her again in the kingdom of glory."[1]

A long procession of carriages followed the hearse to Oak Hill Cemetery for another brief service at the grave. Around the open grave and the freshly heaped mound, hundreds stood with bowed heads as their thoughts were carried forward to that thrilling scene when, not only in Oak Hill Cemetery, but in ten thousand burying places, graves will open wide in response to the call of the Life-giver, and those who sleep in Jesus will come forth in victory over death and the grave. After a closing song, followed by prayer, the casket of her who had served the cause of God faithfully and lovingly for more than seventy years was tenderly lowered to its resting place beside that of her husband, James White. For thirty-four years he had been sleeping in that peaceful spot, awaiting the day when together they would arise to meet their Lord.

Alone in the evening dusk Elder Haskell, now a white-haired veteran of 82, yielded to the spell of peaceful solemnity that shut him away from the world and transported him back over a trail of nearly fifty years to the day when he first met James and Ellen White. He felt again the warmth of their friendship as he felt it that day when they first welcomed him to their hearts and to their labors. He recalled their words of appreciation of the loyal support he had given the Adventist cause without praise or remuneration.

James White had called the newly ordained minister aside and in his kind, fatherly manner had given him some timely advice. The younger man had wondered just what Elder White meant when he said, "Always look to God, rather than to man, for directions in your work." He had taken those words to mean that he should heed the instructions coming from the throne of God, both through His apostles and prophets of old and through His appointed messenger to the remnant church. He recalled that in those formative years of the church, doubts had been openly expressed regarding the messages Ellen G. White claimed came to her through heavenly vision. He remembered how carefully he had refrained for a time from making any public avowal regarding these "Testimonies," as they were called.

But he had noticed their uplifting, vitalizing influence and he had witnessed the blessings that invariably attended the acceptance of the principles they upheld. He had seen the perfect agreement of their teachings with the truths recorded in Holy Scripture; he had studied the prophetic writings, especially of John the revelator and of Joel, the Old Testament prophet, foretelling a manifestation of the prophetic gift in the latter days through visions and dreams, and he had become fully convinced that the visions of Ellen White are God's voice to the remnant church. Ever afterward, through his more than half a century of service in the Adventist Church, he had stood firmly in their vindication and had prayerfully endeavored to follow their leading. To this heavenly guidance, rather than his own wisdom, he ever attributed his success as a gospel minister.

Elder Haskell greatly prized the letters of counsel and instruction he received from Mrs. White. Just how many she wrote him through the years he did not know. In the White Estate vault in the General Conference building there are copies of nearly three hundred letters from Ellen G. White addressed to one or both of the Haskells. Sister White wrote more letters to them than to any other of her correspondents. How he treasured those letters! He read and reread them. He had them arranged and cataloged; he could find any particular one on a moment's notice. Extracts from them were woven into his sermons, read to individuals in need of counsel and encouragement, and copied into letters.

Words from the pen of Mrs. White were greatly sought after in those early years. Later, when her writings were more fully published in book form, Elder Haskell had less occasion to refer to personal letters. Yet he still continued to carry a small collection of them with him; they were like old friends with whom he was loath to part.

We can picture him, after that funeral, sitting lost in thought. As twilight deepens into night, he rises, draws the blinds and switches on the light. Then he reaches into his satchel and pulls out a thick package of folded typewritten pages. They are worn from much handling, and the lettering is dim with age. He sits down at the writing table, unties the cord binding the pages together and begins slowly to leaf through them, pausing now and then to read a few familiar words. These are letters from Sister White, God's messenger. He handles them reverently. He recalls how, many times when he would be praying for wisdom to meet perplexing situations, there would come to him in the mail, perhaps from halfway round the world, a letter bringing the counsel that he needed at that exact time.

He also remembers times when they had been together, and he would be on the verge of asking advice pertaining to his administrative work, when she would surprise him by answering his question before he even had time to ask it. Then she would proceed to outline the wisest course for him to pursue. How could he doubt that God had spoken? Following this counsel had never failed to bring success. Such are the thoughts that pass through his mind as he continues unfolding and scanning the pages before him, pausing occasionally to read a treasured sentence or paragraph that reminds him of Heaven's special guidance given at a time of crisis.

He is thankful for the kind, motherly interest Mrs. White always took in his personal welfare. How often she counseled him in regard to his health! We can imagine him reading a paragraph from a letter she wrote him back in 1880:

"You must be at the General Conference. Arrange meetings so this may be. The Lord lead and guide you, is my prayer. Only cling to that Hand that is mighty to save and to deliver. Only trust Him and hide in Him, and He will work for you. Take things now lazily. Ride all you can. Write but little that will tax. Save yourself in every way you can. There is work for all who have a mind to work, and your strength will be needed. Come closer and nearer to Jesus, and He will give you peace and rest. . . . Be of good courage and do not be faint in spirit or distrust God for one moment."[2] Perhaps he reads a page copied from a letter received from her during those difficult days when, trying to establish the mission in London, he suffered discouragement because the work moved so slowly. "We must not think of defeat, but of victory. However forbidding may be the circumstances, lay hold on the promises of God. They are for us. We are none of us of ourselves adequate for the work. In our connection with God lies our success. Faith, living, active faith, must be brought into our labors as never before. Faith is the medium of connection between human weakness and divine power."[3]

He is thankful for every word of instruction, every caution and every warning in those letters. How often they prevented him from making mistakes in his administration! He is even thankful for the reproofs. Some of them had been hard to understand. They had brought him to his knees, pleading with God for humility and grace that he might accept them and profit by them, realizing that if his weaknesses had not been pointed out to him, he might never have acknowledged or recognized them as such. He had not thought himself impatient until he read the gentle rebuke:

"We must treat with tenderness those who make it hard work to believe. If they once get hold of that faith that works by love and purifies the soul, what a joy will come into their experience! We must pity them and pray for them. But no tartness of expression must be revealed; not a discouraging word must come from our lips to any soul that lives. We cannot tell what harm may result from a word spoken unadvisedly. 'Love as brethren, be pitiful, be courteous.' . . . If we melt into the love of Christ, if we become as little children, we are more sure of entering heaven."[4]

Some letters reminded him of fierce personal conflicts he had fought with the enemy of souls. For Stephen Haskell, mighty preacher and ardent personal worker, was subject to dark periods of depression and discouragement.

At such times, in search of relief from the weight of despair pressing upon him, he would write to Mrs. White, knowing that from her replies he would gain encouragement and help. During one acute attack of despondency he wrote to her:

"God alone, unless He has opened it up to you, knows the struggles and conflicts I have at times with the powers of darkness. Even at times while I am laboring for others in despair and affliction, I have felt there was a still fiercer struggle going on in my own soul, which I *could* not and *dared* not open to any earthly friend. I have awaked some nights saying, 'Give me victory or give me death.' Then victory would come for a time. Then after days and nights of conflict with temptations of Satan, I would awaken uttering these words, 'In the name of Jesus Christ I will place my will on the side of the will of Christ.' This has brought a victory and a freedom from those particular temptations for weeks and even months. Then at other times I would awaken at night with the powers of darkness pressing upon me so I did not have a ray of hope. After wrestling with God, . . . light would come into my soul.

"Now, Sister White, is there no abiding freedom from these dark conflicts? and seasons? Is it because Satan has such a hold on me he will one day have me anyhow? My soul is full this morning as I write these lines."[5]

Her replies to such letters of distress brought help to him, and they encouraged others to whom he read them. Following are portions of some of her letters:

"You ask me why it is you awake in the night and feel enclosed in darkness? I often feel the same way myself; but these desponding feelings are no evidence that God has forsaken you or me. . . . Gloomy feelings are no evidence that the promises of God are of no effect. You look at your feelings, and because your outlook is not all brightness, you begin to draw more closely the garment of heaviness about your soul. You look within yourself, and think that God has forsaken you. You are to look to Christ. . . . Entering into communion with the Saviour, we enter the region of peace. . . . We must put faith into constant exercise, and trust in God whatever our feelings may be. . . . We are to be of good cheer, knowing that Christ has overcome the world. We will have tribulation in the world, but peace in Jesus Christ. My brother, turn your eyes from within, and look to Jesus who is your only helper." [6]

"Bear in mind, the time will never come when the hellish shadow of Satan will not be cast athwart our pathway to obstruct our faith, and eclipse the light emanating from the presence of Jesus, the Sun of Righteousness. Our faith must not stagger, but cleave through that shadow. We have an experience that is not to be buried in the darkness of doubt. Our faith is not in feeling, but in truth. . . .

"Jesus says, 'Lo, I am with you alway, even unto the end of the world.' He walked once a man on earth, His divinity clothed with humanity, a suffering, tempted man, beset with Satan's devices. . . . Now He is at the right hand of God. . . . He is thinking of those who are subject to temptations in this world. He thinks of us individually, and knows our every necessity. . . . We grieve the heart of Christ when we go mourning over ourselves as though we were our own savior. No; we must commit the keeping of our souls to God as unto a faithful Creator. He ever lives to make intercession for the tried, tempted ones." [7]

She had told him earlier: "Jesus lives; He has risen, He has risen, He is alive forevermore. Do not feel that you carry the load. It is true you wear the yoke, but whom are you yoked up with? No less a personage than your Redeemer. Satan will cast his hellish shadow athwart your pathway; you cannot expect anything else; but he cast the same dark shadow athwart the pathway of Christ. Now all you have to do, is to look beyond the shadow to the brightness of Christ. . . .

"Do not look at the discouragements; think of how precious is Jesus.

"Your memory will be renewed by the Holy Spirit. Can you forget what Jesus has done for you . . . ? You were taken away from yourself; your deepest, sweetest thoughts were upon your precious Saviour, His care, His assurance, His love. How your desires went out to Him!

"All your hopes rested upon Him, all your expectations were associated with Him. Well, He loves you still; He has the balm that can heal every wound and you can repose in Him. . . .

"The Comforter will be to you all that you desire. You will be weighted with the Spirit of God, and the importance of the message, and the work. I know that the Lord is willing to reveal to you wondrous things out of His law. O, let all take knowledge of you, that you have been with Jesus." [8]

He must have remembered the tender sympathy that had bound him and his wife Mary to James and Ellen White. In earlier years when Ellen's feebleness caused her much suffering, Mary had written comforting letters to her. Stephen, too, had always sought to encourage her. He had written glowing forecasts of the time, not far distant, when her writings would be translated into many languages and scattered to the ends of the earth. When in Australia she had lain for months unable even to turn herself in bed because of inflammatory rheumatism, Stephen wrote encouraging her to believe that her present experience of suffering would result in great blessing to the church.

There had also been financial interchanges. Often there would occur an immediate and urgent need of cash for the promotion of a special mission enterprise. For example, in Australia Mrs. White had found a newly organized conference with small membership but large undertakings; it was deeply cramped for means. In that emergency she had appealed to her staunch friend Stephen Haskell; he had sent her one thousand dollars from America to put into the work.

Later on the General Conference was better organized and able to support its foreign work. Haskell needed the thousand for work in the homeland, and Sister White herself returned the money to him.

Perhaps he relived the day when he called at Elmshaven, her California home, to solicit five hundred dollars to aid in erecting a church in the South. The tender solicitude showed in her voice as she responded to his plea, "Elder Haskell, if there's anything I can do to help lost souls find their way to Christ, that's what I want to do." She had sent for her bookkeeper, Miss Peck, and asked, "Sarah, I want you to look carefully over the books of account and see if you can find a way to help, and if you do, *you let Elder Haskell have his five hundred dollars.*" [9]

As he meditated on the funeral that marked the close of a long life of service to the church, and on his own experiences in the work of God, two panoramas must have filled his vision—one of the past, in which Jesus had walked hand in hand with him, guiding him over the rough and difficult pathway of life; the other of a future reunion with loved ones and a glorious companionship with his Redeemer, beginning at the resurrection day and extending through the vast reaches of eternity.

---

[1] *Review and Herald,* Aug. 5, 1915, pp. 9, 10.
[2] Letter 4, 1880.
[3] Letter 24, 1888.
[4] Letter 121, 1898.
[5] Letter to Ellen G. White, April 24, 1893.
[6] Letter 26, 1895.
[7] Letter 40, 1896, printed in *Testimonies to Ministers,* pp. 387-391.
[8] Letter 30a, 1892.
[9] I could not help overhearing this conversation between Mrs. White and the elder, as I happened at the moment to be sweeping the hall just outside her writing room when it took place.

Finishing the Course

THE 1915 Autumn Council of the General Conference Committee was held at Loma Linda, California. During the session Elder Daniells called a meeting of the constituency of the medical college to consider the interests of the school. Early instructions received through the Lord's special messenger to the church stated that many young people were to be trained at Loma Linda as medical missionaries. On one occasion she declared, "Physicians will be trained here." Those who came for instruction were to receive superior training in treating all manner of diseases, both physical and spiritual. Later in response to an inquiry Mrs. White made clear that the school should be prepared to graduate physicians who could pass examinations required by law to enable them to practice as fully qualified physicians.

In harmony with these objectives a charter was obtained in 1909 for "The College of Medical Evangelists." Those close to the new school soon saw that if the Spirit of Prophecy counsels calling for the full medical course to be given in our own new college were to be followed, we must make adequate provision for a strong clinical work that would bring the students into close contact with many people suffering from all types of diseases—the diseases they would meet in actual practice. The answer to this seemed to be a clinical hospital in the city of Los Angeles, but this would be costly. Many thousands of dollars had already been invested in the school; all instructional requirements had been provided except those in the clinical department. Now many more thousands were needed for the hospital building —and this at a time when financial resources of the General Conference were heavily taxed to support new missionary enterprises in many parts of the world.

The men sitting in council that day were serious. Where could money be obtained to erect and equip a hospital building? "If we call on our people for the large amounts of money that are required, will it not discourage them?" they asked. "If sufficient appropriations are budgeted by the General Conference will it not retard our mission program?" Some committee members argued in favor of moving forward without delay at God's bidding, trusting Him to remove these seemingly insurmountable difficulties. Others spoke against becoming further involved until more money was available. "We must adhere to the no-debt ruling of the General Conference," they said. "We must raise the money before we spend it." Mrs. White herself had heartily endorsed that plan.

It was obvious that delay would mean great loss and might result eventually in the complete failure of the school. A sense of the importance of the decision that must be made rested heavily upon every committee member. Strong convictions were expressed on both sides; further attempts to arrive at a definite decision seemed useless.

In this hour of perplexity, when it appeared that an impasse had been reached, a gentle tap was heard on the door. It was opened, and there stood four Adventist sisters. They were Mrs. Haskell; her widowed sister, Mrs. Emma Gray, a self-reliant woman who for four years had managed the home farm and supported her children; Dr. Florence Keller, recently returned from mission service in New Zealand; and Mrs. Josephine Gotzian, widow of a wealthy shoe manufacturer and a liberal contributor to Seventh-day Adventist missions. Courteously they requested admittance and a moment of the committee's time. The women then earnestly presented their plea for the advancement of the medical school and for the erection of the proposed hospital building in Los Angeles as a teaching unit in the clinical division. They further requested that the task of raising the money for erecting and equipping the hospital, estimated at more than sixty thousand dollars, be committed to the women of the denomination.

For a moment there was silence. A hush pervaded the room; all felt the presence of God in their midst. Then without further plea or argument, the four women thanked the committee members for listening to their suggestion and withdrew. This voluntary offer of assistance, so perfectly timed, strengthened the faith of many and inspired fresh courage in all. Elder Daniells, with a few men of strong faith, spent the early part of the night reviewing the instructions Sister White had given regarding the school and praying for further guidance.

The following morning in an address to the conference committee, Elder Daniells declared his conviction that there was only one way to go, and that was forward. Even while admitting fears and apprehensions which he knew were shared by others, he unhesitatingly declared, "We do not say stop! We say, Go on and maintain this school, and make it a success." The voluntary proposal of the four women and the active faith expressed by Daniells, Haskell, Irwin, Evans, Burden, and others gave courage to all; and a motion was carried favoring the expansion of the school.

The conference committee promptly moved into action and authorized the four women to lead the women of the denomination in a campaign to raise the required $61,000. A nationwide drive was inaugurated and placed under the leadership of Mrs. Haskell and Mrs. G. A. Irwin. An article by I. H. Evans in the *Review* of January 13, 1916, explained the need and announced Mrs. Haskell as chairman of the women's committee commissioned to direct the fund-raising campaign.

The State conferences were advised to appoint auxiliary secretaries to take charge of the funds, and Mrs. Haskell was commissioned to correspond with these secretaries. While awaiting news of their appointment she went to work at once, writing to everyone she could think of, arousing interest in the forthcoming campaign.

In the *Review* she addressed the women of the denomination, telling them of their opportunity to raise money to build and equip the Ellen G. White Memorial Hospital. Comparing them to "all the women that were wise hearted" who "did spin with their hands" to provide hangings for the ancient tabernacle, she urged them to do all in their power to furnish the equipment for the medical school.

Articles by leading ministers and by Dr. Magan appeared frequently in the *Review* and in conference papers, setting forth the imperative need of a hospital. Leaflets were broadcast; the churches were stirred into action. Energetic women were chosen as leaders to encourage everyone to help; goals were set, and various methods devised for raising money. Gifts of books from authors and publishers mounted into the scores of thousands—Ellen G. White's *The Ministry of Healing*, Haskell's *Story of Daniel* and *Seer of Patmos*, A. W. Spalding's *Men of the Mountains*—all were sold by enthusiastic promoters of medical missions who turned their profits into the building fund.

An elderly sister came up with an original idea. During the Loma Linda council she had counted several veterans on the grounds, all of them in their seventies and eighties, and five of them past eighty: J. N. Loughborough, G. I. Butler, S. N. Haskell, H. W. Decker, and J. H. Rogers. She assembled them and had photographs taken. The prints sold at fifty cents apiece. Thus these worthies, poor in worldly treasure, were enabled to make a substantial contribution to the hospital fund.

As the Haskells visited camp meetings, institutes, and churches

A picture of veteran ministers (1915) that was sold for the benefit of the White Memorial Hospital. Left to right, rear: J. H. Rogers, J. O. Corliss, H. W. Decker, W. H. Cottrell. Front: S. N. Haskell, J. N. Loughborough, G. I. Butler.

they appealed for contributions to the hospital fund. In California alone they held meetings in twenty-five churches, then journeyed on to other States. All pledges and cash receipts received by them were forwarded to the auxiliary secretaries of the various State conferences.

Sixty-one-thousand dollars, however, was but the beginning. Dormitories, classrooms, and many other buildings would be needed. Dr. Magan, recently called to the medical college as dean, entered the campaign; with his burning interest in the training of medical missionaries and his gift of oratorical persuasion, he was able to swell the building fund. October 14, 1916, was appointed in all the churches for a Loma Linda offering, with the suggestion that it be made a "dollar day."

Two months later the foundation of the Los Angeles division of the hospital was laid. Mrs. Lyda Scott, a year before, had contributed five thousand dollars toward the purchase of land for a building site. The location in Boyle Heights was ideal. As Magan noted, within ten minutes' walking distance from the hospital was a great "foreign field," in which were thousands of poor people—people who needed both medical aid and the gospel. Among these multitudes prospective doctors and nurses would find every variety of ailment and gain experience that would equip them for service in almost any part of the world.

After two years the Los Angeles hospital complex was complete. Elder and Mrs. Haskell were privileged to attend the dedicatory services held at three o'clock on Sunday, April 21, 1918. On that day, marking the opening of the White Memorial Hospital, songs of thanksgiving ascended from many joyful hearts. But it is doubtful that any experienced deeper satisfaction than Stephen and Hetty Haskell at being privileged to share in this, their last major project—the launching of a medical missionary program that would have a worldwide influence.

Throughout his busy life the elder enjoyed social occasions, although he seldom took time to participate in them. He could recall only four or five birthday celebrations. One especially stood out in his memory. He had been enjoying a quiet evening in his library at the old South Lancaster home when he suddenly noticed that the house was rapidly filling with students. Then he remembered it was April 22, 1913; he must be eighty years old that day! The instigator and manager of the surprise party had been Milton Hare, the same person who, as a boy of fifteen, had hauled many loads of bricks for lining the cistern at the Avondale school. Now he was a member of the South Lancaster Academy faculty. There were speeches, gifts, and refreshments. Elder Haskell had been moved nearly to tears by some of the expressions of loving remembrance showered upon him that evening. It is reported that a few salty drops did escape when he saw a large red plush armchair handed in through a window and learned that it was his birthday gift from his devoted wife, Hetty.

Another of Stephen Haskell's special joys had been the horses he had owned. Back in 1902 Hetty had written to Sister White describing one of his favorites. He still remembered how he had enjoyed getting away from New York City to his home in South Lancaster, then hurrying to rattle the barn door to hear that horse whinny. Mrs. Haskell's letter read: "You know how fond Elder Haskell is of a horse, and he has secured one that he thinks is a jewel, and it is a very pretty horse, a dark bay, not quite to my liking because she scares at the trains some, and likes to dance a little bit; but you know he would never enjoy riding behind a horse that doesn't dance once in a while. . . .

"The horse is very intelligent, kind and gentle, and we only had it a day or two until it would whinny every time the barn door rattled. Elder Haskell had made a pet of it so quickly that it knew his step before the first week was out. He takes great delight in driving past the electric cars with the horse to show how much more gentle it is becoming, and I think that in time it will not scare very much, not that I am afraid of it at all now, only if I did not make a little fuss about his driving scary horses, he would be breaking colts half the time, and I think he is too old for that kind of work. He does love a horse that has a good deal of fire to it."[1]

At sixty-nine he would have enjoyed breaking wild colts! Now he was eighty-five, and 1902 was a long time ago.

As the years passed rapidly, Elder Haskell grieved because he felt that he was accomplishing very little. He could do so many things if his strength were only greater. His wife tried to comfort

Haskell at the Alhambra, California, camp meeting, 1921.

him. She said, "Stephen, when you were young you went out and preached your sermons; now you write them out and people distribute them all over the world. Whereas in your younger days you were reaching hundreds, now in your old age your books are reaching thousands, accomplishing a thousandfold more than when you were younger."

And the patriarch was comforted. He could not know that he and Hetty had only a brief period remaining when they could travel together among their beloved church groups, visiting camp meetings and schools. Then in 1919 a severe illness laid Hetty low. After some weeks in the New England Sanitarium she died on October 21, 1919. Since that long-ago day at Lemoore, California, when Hetty, a young teacher, had stood trembling, grasping the back of the chair in front of her, to make a declaration for Christ in the words, "Brethren and sisters, God wants me," she had never swerved in allegiance to Him. That same day she had walked up to one of the ministers, holding something out to him in her two cupped hands. She had said, "Hold fast all I give you," and she had slipped into his hands a gold watch chain, rings, breastpins, and other prized pieces of jewelry. This act symbolized her complete dedication of life to the Master's service. The next May, at the end of the school year, she began her thirty-four years of Christian work.

For the second time Stephen Haskell was alone. Mary had died long years ago and had been laid to rest in California, in a cemetery in Napa. Then God had sent Hetty. For twenty-two years she and Stephen had traveled and worked together. Now she lay on the eastern side of the continent near the old South Lancaster home he and Mary had shared so long ago.

Elder Haskell was eighty-six years old. He could have retired. But a long and busy life had not equipped him to change lifelong habits. In 1919, only three years before his death, he made another contribution to the denomination in the form of a vest-pocket reference book, *Bible Handbook,* listing important Bible texts, paralleled by appropriate quotations from the Spirit of Prophecy writings. It contained 182 pages of references, grouped as Bible study outlines under more than two hundred topical headings.

Above: Paradise Valley Sanitarium many years ago.
Below: The new Paradise Valley Hospital building.

Until "his strength failed and the shadows lengthened" he continued attending institutes and camp meetings in different States, and was actively engaged in the general work.

At the 1922 General Conference in San Francisco Stephen Haskell, along with other pioneers, received special honor. Soon after that meeting, because of increasing weakness, he was obliged to enter the Paradise Valley Sanitarium near San Diego, California. Since to him life and work were synonymous, the one could not long exist without the other. On October 9, 1922, Elder S. N. Haskell died in his ninetieth year.

At one time when asked, "Would you choose to be buried next to Mary in California or by Hetty in the East?" he had replied, "Just place me beside the one I am nearest to when I die." His grave is next to Mary's in Tulocay Cemetery at Napa, California.

Under the title, "A Long Life Spent for God," W. A. Spicer, president of the General Conference, wrote in the *Review and Herald:* "Day after day at the recent General Conference, Elder S. N. Haskell sat with the group of pioneer workers on the platform. We felt that this veteran of many a Conference session and of many a journey in pioneering service, was being sustained in his regular attendance more by his unabated spiritual vigor and the habit of a lifetime of devotion than by his physical forces. And now, nearing his ninetieth milestone, Elder Haskell's life of service is ended, and he awaits the sure triumph of the message and the movement that he loved.

"Elder Haskell was a pioneer in missionary promotion at home and abroad. . . . He found this truth on the road, as a salesman, and until age crept upon him he was ever on the road, carrying the treasure of truth to others. . . .

"It seems inadequate to try to sum up nearly seventy years of service in a short article. . . . His message of faith and trust in God and in the triumph of the work of God will live with us to the end."[2]

F. M. Wilcox, editor of the *Review and Herald,* followed Elder Spicer in tribute: "Brother Haskell was a man loved by all within the circle of his acquaintance, and this circle was by no means a small one. In reality it compassed the whole earth, because Brother

Haskell was known for his work's sake not alone in North America, but in Europe, Asia, Africa, and Australasia. South America is the only great division of our work which he never visited. . . .

"He was a self-made man in the truest sense of that word. Born of poor parentage, with limited school advantages, he heard in early manhood the call of God to a great work—the work of the gospel ministry. . . . Especially did he give himself to the study of the Word. His knowledge of the Bible was extensive and unique. His preaching abounded with practical illustrations and precious principles drawn from its sacred pages. He was mightily used of God through the years in the upbuilding of His work in the earth, rising step by step through perseverance and application until he occupied some of the most responsible positions in the work of the denomination.

"What he accomplished in his life through the blessing of God, other young men similarly situated can accomplish with the same spirit of zeal and determination. The influence of his godly life will roll on until the work is done."[3]

---

[1] Letter to Ellen G. White, Aug. 5, 1902.
[2] *Review and Herald*, Dec. 14, 1922, p. 7.
[3] *Ibid.*

We invite you to view the complete
selection of titles we publish at:
www.TEACHServices.com

scan with your mobile
device to go directly
to our website

Please write or email us your praises, reactions, or thoughts about this or any other book we publish at:

P.O. Box 954
Ringgold, GA 30736

Info@TEACHServices.com

TEACH Services, Inc., titles may be purchased in bulk for educational, business, fund-raising, or sales promotional use. For information, please e-mail:

BulkSales@TEACHServices.com

Finally if you are interested in seeing your own book in print, please contact us at

publishing@TEACHServices.com

We would be happy to review your manuscript for free.

www.ingramcontent.com/pod-product-compliance
Lightning Source LLC
Chambersburg PA
CBHW070547160426
43199CB00014B/2404